NO OFFENSE

Civil Religion and
Protestant Taste

NO OFFENSE

Civil Religion and Protestant Taste

JOHN MURRAY CUDDIHY

A CROSSROAD BOOK

The Seabury Press / New York

1978
The Seabury Press
815 Second Avenue
New York, New York 10017

PRINTED IN THE UNITED STATES OF AMERICA

Library of Congress Cataloging in Publication Data
Cuddihy, John Murray.   No offense.
"A Crossroad book."
Includes bibliographical references and index.
1. Christian sects—United States. 2. Judaism—United States.
3. Acculturation. 4. Americanization. I. Title
BR516.5.C83   291.1'77   77-27556
ISBN 0-8164-0385-6

Dedicated,

in fellowship and in homage, to:

Albert Schweitzer

(b. January 4, 1875; d. September 4, 1965)

who "bore the mark of pain."

Epigraphs

The secret of the Kingdom of God contains the secret of the whole
Christian *Weltanschauung.*   —Albert Schweitzer
*The Mystery of the Kingdom of God**

The reduction, particularly, of the parochial, the exclusive, the
claims of absolute truth seems inevitable in our kind of society. It
is dysfunctional in a mobile and diverse society to have a group of
religions, each of which claims some kind of ultimate superiority;
the elements of Protestantism, Catholicism, and Judaism which
sponsor such claims are disruptive. Claims by Protestants that the
Bible is the final and literal truth, by Catholics that theirs is the
only true church, by Jews that they are the chosen people, can only
exacerbate the divisions of a society . . . In a diverse society in
which absolute religious claims are asserted, three things may happen: the society will be split seriously; or the differences will be reduced; or the traditional religious assertions will lose force, while a
new unifying system of beliefs and actions will be developed. . . .
The constant interaction of people with different national and reli-

---

*Complete sources are listed in the Notes.

gious backgrounds . . . makes tolerance as the minimum degree of accommodation, a vital necessity.   —J. Milton Yinger
Sociology Looks at Religion

. . . the real, inner history [of Christianity] is based on *the delay* of the Parousia, the non-occurrence of it, the abandonment of eschatology, the progress and completion of the "de-eschatologizing" of religion. . . .   —Albert Schweitzer
The Quest of the Historical Jesus

. . . the Independents . . . betrayed the sacred cause by yielding to the heresy of toleration. . . .   —Perry Miller
Errand into the Wilderness

At the level of overt interpersonal relations, adherence to a sense of intrinsic human value is discernible in a wide variety of specific behaviors—perhaps most obviously in "democratic manners." America has always impressed observers from more rigid and hierarchical societies as being marked by an extraordinary informality, directness, and lack of status-consciousness in person-to-person contacts.   —Robin M. Williams, Jr.
American Society

Or read Chapter viii of the First Epistle to the Corinthians which is completely dedicated to tolerance. . . . [There Saint Paul] imposes an obligation on those who are free from prejudice to respect the prejudice of others, and to refrain from eating such meat in order not to scandalize their weaker brethren. Listen to his words: "But take heed lest by any means this liberty of yours become a stumbling block to them that are weak. . . . And through thy knowledge the weak brother perish, for whom Christ died. But when ye so sin against the brethren, and wound their weak conscience, ye sin against Christ. Wherefore, if meat make my brother to offend, I will eat no flesh while the world standeth, lest I make my brother to offend" (I Corinthians viii. 9, 11–13). . . . "To the weak became I as weak, that I might gain the weak: I am made all things to all men, that I might by all means save some" (I Corinthians ix. 20–22).   —Albert Schweitzer
"Paul the Liberator"

When informants fall out anthropologists come into their own.
—E. E. Evans-Pritchard
Witchcraft, Oracles, and Magic among the Azande

Upon its sons and daughters the immigrant Jews branded marks of separateness while inciting dreams of universalism. They taught their children both to conquer the gentile world and to be conquered by it.   —Irving Howe
World of Our Fathers

People of literary inclinations, I believe, have a natural jealousy of sociology because it seems to be in process of taking over from literature one of literature's most characteristic functions, the investigation and criticism of morals and manners. Yet it is but fair to remark that sociology has pre-empted only what literature has voluntarily surrendered.   —Lionel Trilling
A Gathering of Fugitives

Contents

5

6

7

8

CONCLUSION

Preface

————◆◆◆————

I fully realize that in this book I have perpetrated an intellectual misdemeanor, what Harold Bloom would call a wilful "misprision" (misreading) of Robert Bellah's idea of "civil religion" and of the whole "civil religion debate" in America. So be it. Friendly critics will see in it a creative misunderstanding. (Unfriendly critics are, of course, at liberty to join Hilton Kramer's recently founded Society for the Promotion of Misprision Reform.)

I must take—mis-take—civil religion for the religion of civility, because that's the way believers in traditional religions *experience* it, and that's the way it "deconstructs," and that's the way I see it, and that's the way it is

this October 7, 1977.

John Murray Cuddihy

Water Mill, Long Island, N.Y.

Acknowledgments

————◆◄◍►◆————

Many people have helped along the way. There is, as there has
been from the beginning, the hovering figure of Peter Berger,
always encouraging, not always agreeing. I thank him once
more. There are again the people I've conversed with over the
years: Jeff Hart, Joe Sobran—who supplied the title, *No Offense*
—Jeanne Wacker, Rabbi Lloyd Tennenbaum.

My gratitude to my friend Seth Dubin is unbounded. He was
the first person outside the field to appreciate my work, who
thought I had something to say. He likes mavericks, "unbranded
animals," especially lost calves, even when they make off in
directions not precisely his own.

Then there are Hunter College friends and colleagues who
have been kind and encouraging, especially in my own sociology
department, especially in room #901. We've had some fun
times there. Al Pinkney, my chairman, is a godsend; long may
he reign. I will miss departing Divisional Dean, Blanche Blank,
as she leaves to become Vice President of Academic Affairs at
Yeshiva University: her spunk, and commitment to free speech,
her idealism, intelligence and general gaiety.

And then there are books to thank and acknowledge debts to.
In the general cultural canonization of Albert Schweitzer which
occurred some years back, many overlooked hisorseless mind
and the suffering involved in his seeking biblical historical truth.
The late Judith R. Kramer and Seymour Leventman in *Children
of the Gilded Ghetto* (New Haven and London: Yale University

Press, 1961) wrote the finest book on the sociology of American Jewry. Expectably, it got little notice. I wish to acknowledge a large debt to them. Robert Bellah's work in religion as in civil religion, his rediscovery of Durkheim for our time, has been an inspiration to me. He was lucky enough to have been taught in person by Talcott Parsons. My own remoter indebtedness to Parsons, through his books, should be apparent throughout.

None of these people of course—(why do "Acknowledgments" ritually, monotonously, always go on to say?)—is responsible for the opinions opined and the arguments argued in this book. (Are there any readers who would really so hold them accountable? That's hard to believe. Jacques Derrida has probed the oddity of Prefaces, read before the book is read, written after the book is written. Who will do the sociology of "Acknowledgments"?)

Robert Motherwell has, in a sense, been probing "protestant taste" all his painterly life. I want to thank him that a version of his beautiful "figure" of the "Homely Protestant" has found its way onto the dust jacket of this book.

The people at Seabury Press have been most helpful and kind, particularly my chief editor, Justus George Lawlor, who edits, and plays pool, and gives good advice, in Geneva, Illinois.

Lastly, I want gratefully to acknowledge aid and comfort through the years from the members of my family: my brothers H. Lester Cuddihy and Michael B. Cuddihy (poet and editor of the poetry review, *Ironwood,* out in Tucson, Arizona), and Thomas Murray Cuddihy; my sisters Mrs. Mary Jane MacGuire Haley, and Ann Marie Eaton of St. Thomas, V.I.; and my irrepressible children, Heidi, Johnny and Julia who, even when they didn't quite know what I was up to, consented to tiptoe around me occasionally, rather than walk over me; and my wife, Heidi, who, while performing all the chores of a secretary, helped with the ideas and the writing, all the while maintaining the amenity of a home and the amity of a marriage.

NO OFFENSE

Civil Religion and
Protestant Taste

INTRODUCTION:
A NATION
OF BEHAVERS

Defining "civil religion" has become a large and thriving academic cottage industry. First Hobbes, Rousseau, and Durkheim, then, in our own time, Herberg, Bellah, and Parsons have tried to get a fix on the slippery phenomenon known as "civil religion."

I argue in this book that we will never know what "civil religion" is until we stand it on its head, inverting civil religion into the "religion of civility." Like any religion that is alive, civil religion shows its true colors in its practices and rites. Religion is as religion does. Civil religion operationally defined is the religion of civility. It is a myth, then, based on my redefinition, that we can know what civil religion is by doing a credal inventory or by writing a compendium of civil theology. This is the first myth.

There is a second myth: that this elaborate and well-institutionalized civil religion in America exists, as I unpack its meaning, in Robert Bellah's classic definition, "alongside of and rather clearly differentiated from the churches"[1] and that, consequently, the relationship of the churches to civil religion, however defined, has been, Mary Schneider writes, "generally one of peaceful coexistence."[2]

No, despite the word "civil" in its name, it is simply not true that civil religion knows its place and keeps its place, speaks only when spoken to, and runs politely "parallel" to the religions of the churches, coexisting platonically "alongside" their particular creeds. True, civil religion doesn't nail itself noisily to the portals of Protestant, Catholic, and Jewish houses of worship. Nevertheless, under cover of its prim title, civil religion, in its rites and practices, is activist, aggrandizing, subversive, intrusive, incivil. Sometimes it waits outside the churches and waylays with its niceness their members as they file out. Sometimes it enters without knocking into their minds, and penetrates the core beliefs of their theologies, refining and "civilizing" them from within. Sometimes, reaping its benefits serendipitously from social mobility—when entire religious bodies are upwardly mobilized—it refines them behind their backs, so to speak, secretly and gradually substituting its civil and civilized ways for the uncouth truths of an earlier time. "Time makes ancient good uncouth," runs the old James Russell Lowell hymn.[3]

When candidate Jimmy Carter, Southern "born-again" Baptist, campaigned for the presidency in 1976, he ran head-on into civil religion. But the civil religion he collided with was not the civil religion that civil theologians, like Robert Bellah, speak of, a system of national and generalized beliefs supported by most Americans. Carter encountered the civil religion that Americans, more and more, practice, whatever they profess. This complex code of rites instructs us in the ways of being religiously inoffensive, of giving "no offense," of being *religiously* sensitive to religious differences. To be complexly aware of our religious appearances *to others* is to practice the religion of civility. Thus, civil religion is the social choreography of tolerance. It dances out an attitude.

Columnist Meg Greenfield, for example, early in the 1976 presidential campaign, recalling that Jimmy Carter, when asked by a television interviewer whether he planned to address the "uneasiness" of Catholic voters, had replied, "Yes, I do, and [also the uneasiness of] Protestant voters and nonbelievers and Jews," went on to bet that nine out of ten of Carter's Jewish viewers had wondered "what we [Jews] were doing on the wrong side of nonbelievers."[4] Carter, obviously, was so preoccupied in avoiding one religious incivility —his vigilant circumspection had carefully euphemized biblical religion's "unbelievers" into civil religion's "nonbelievers"—that, inadvertently, he had committed another offense! The code of religious etiquette to which civil religion is committed is, indeed, a demanding one.

Miss Greenfield explains Carter's incivil insensitivity as a form of regional and subcultural lag. "I expect that as the campaign wears on," she mused, "Carter will get a load of sensitivity training from his Jewish advisers. He will learn that the word 'Christian,' repeatedly invoked, is regarded by Jews as a close-out, a push-off. He may even be persuaded to use one of those meringue constructions like 'some unseen greater force' or whatever it is."[5] In fact, not so many years ago, as we shall see in chapter three, one of Carter's theologian heroes, the late Reinhold Niebuhr, came "up from Biblical fundamentalism" into the civility of the civil religion by precisely the sensitivity training route Miss Greenfield maps out for Carter.

But even as she wrote, Jimmy Carter was receiving a few tips on the do's and don'ts of "total immersion" in the civil religion from pundit Harriet Van Horne.[6] Carter, the *New York Post* columnist remarked, has, obviously, "risen above the narrow tenets of his church." Nevertheless, his "down-home, born-again Christianity still *offends* many people, and he ought, by now, to see why." Miss Van Horne then proceeds to tell him why: he lacks the premier rite in the civil religion Americans practice (whatever their differences in defining it): he is wanting in religious tact. Hence he gives offense. "In this ecumenical age," she instructs him, "it might be more tactful for Governor Carter to cite the Judeo-Christian ethic rather than attributing all his talk of love and humility to the teachings of Jesus." "What a pity," she later exclaims, "that we cannot find a new spirit of ecumenicalism [sic] in this campaign, a new appreciation of what is properly the *Judeo*-Christian ethic." Finally, this deaconess of civil religion goes to the root of Carter's "offense" against civil religion: his heresy is in his "sectarian divisiveness." "Why," she asks rhetorically, "should any religious sect consider its view of God the only one?" But, whatever his view of God, there was never any question that Jimmy Carter's twice-born smile of Christian sociableness issued from the civility of civil religion, that it at least was undivisive and committed "no offense." Never mind that, to some, this inoffensiveness would itself prove offensive.

Twenty years ago, Philip Rieff, brilliant American-Jewish sociologist, social critic, then husband of Susan Sontag, writing for

Partisan Review from a peak in Waltham, Mass.—viz., Brandeis University—surveyed the American scene and wrote (unwittingly) about the Carter campaign. With the insight that only animus can yield, the dour intellectual noted that "the *pious* smile of sociability, once reserved for women and younger children and ministers, has frozen on the American face." He observed that this smile of "sociability" or, as I shall call it, the civil smile had little or nothing to do with fraternity, with people who "bare their teeth in fraternal greeting." Twenty years ahead of time he was writing of Jimmy Carter and his unremitting chock-full-of-teeth smile that in the 1976 presidential campaign was to please so many Americans while alienating the alienated. Rieff was analyzing with considerable care, but with unconcealed distaste, one of the sacraments of the American civil religion.

This smile, he noted, affecting the cool aplomb of a sociological voyeur, does not crack the American face, "for the American face has been composed around the smile." But Rieff's own metaphors subvert his secular cynicism: they betray his realization that he was in the presence of a fundamentally *religious* phenomenon. The norm of generalized "niceness" that a "civil religion" secularized from Christianity bids us practice in the presence of strangers has roots embedded in a unitarianized Calvinism. What I call the Protestant etiquette is as deeply indebted to the theology of predestination as ever Weber's Protestant ethic was. Everyday behavior has roots in religious creed.

"Sociability," Rieff writes, "like predestination, is an iron creed. The American must smile, or risk challenging the sacramental bond that unites him in one overpoweringly friendly [read: civil] people." This link or "civil nexus" that bonds the members of modern Euro-American civil societies into a solidarity *of the surface* expresses itself in a symbolic expressive form: this ideal typical WASP smile is what Durkheim called a "collective representation."

In its provenance it is a national, protestant, and upper-middle-class smile. A Southern Baptist peanut farmer from Plains, Georgia, as he moves up and out into the mainstream of national politics, seeking a wide, consensus-constituency, converts himself to the generality of this particular smile. The face of New

York's upper-middle-class Irish ex-senator, James Buckley, is by now inseparable from the civil smile (that *certain sourire*). It takes time, it takes constant involvement with strangers—in social, political, or show biz (entertainment) life—to breed this smile. It takes money: "Money's made me nicer," Barbra Streisand confesses. "In that wide, ever-ready smile the material abundance of America may be said," Rieff continues—his anomie betraying him into yet another revealing metaphor—"to be transubstantiated into the personality of the American." This smile is one of the interpersonal rites in the civil religion of Americans.

Max Weber's lifework was to discern, Rieff notes, in the Protestant ethic "an invisible church of individuals." This earlier strenuous athleticism of inner-direction under the spur of scarcity has now in America finally flowered, under the lure of affluence and upward mobility, into the "unremitting sociability" of what I call the Protestant Etiquette. The contemporary American, Rieff concedes, is "a far more civil creature" than his Protestant predecessor. He actually *practices* his civil religion. I call it the religion of civility.*

The civil smile has two features. One is its constancy. Jerome Weidman, an ethnographic precursor of Rieff in the epigraphy of Gentile demeanor, writes: "I had to laugh at these *goyim* and their politeness. . . . They're polite all the time. . . ."[7] The human heart, as Proust noted, may have its intermittences but not the sacred sacramental smile of WASP niceness. (*The Village Voice* was to reproduce triumphantly Sylvia Plachy's photograph, taken at the 1976 Democratic Convention, in which she had, by dint of patient waiting, caught Jimmy Carter "between smiles,"[8] that is, in profane repose.)

A second feature of this smile is its universalism, its unremitting demand for reciprocity: "do as you would be done by." Rieff, fifteen years after his *Partisan Review* piece, returns to the

---

*Philip Rieff, "A Character Wrecked by Success" (a review of William H. Whyte's *The Organization Man*), *Partisan Review*, Spring 1957 (vol. 24, no. 2), pp. 304, 305, 306, 308. It is significant, that this same face, what Rieff here calls the "unremitting sociability" (308) of the typical American WASP goyische face, he had earlier seen as "irremediably blank" and identified by using the Marxist category of "false consciousness" (see Rieff, "Socialism and Sociology," *Partisan Review*, Summer 1956 [vol. 23, no. 3], p. 369).

aggressive universalism and levelling force of this sacramental rite in the civil religion. He writes: "We have long known what 'equality' means in American culture: it means . . . a smile fixed to the face, demanding you return a smile. That famous American smile is a baring of the teeth . . . [it is] in the transgressive mode. . . ."9

Rieff, clearly, is describing middle - class American demeanor in the adversary mode of the disaffiliated intellectual. He is talking about the nearly indefinable subject of the civil nexus, the bond of civil manners that links bourgeois "christian" Americans, and by his animus, as much as by his metaphors, he is telling us how much such manners matter, and how deeply down into the structure of religious sentiment and value their roots go.

This seemingly superficial insistent sociability is the symbolic expression of a certain kind of religious civilization in a certain stage—the denominational era—of its history. Our study will begin with the everyday dimension of civil and civilized interaction, and examine the way in which civil interaction between people "acts back" and alters the very values that gave rise to it. I will explore the process by which, in America, what C. S. Lewis called the "frontier courtesies" work their way back, with relentless logic, into the heartland of the classical theologies—and (as we shall see later) into the classical political ideologies as well. One may view this book as a contribution to the study of what has been called "the heterogeny of purposes," or, the study of unintended and paradoxical consequences. It studies the gossamer threads of civility in America as they bind down the giant Gullivers of religious and political fanaticism.

This book, then, is a study of what happens to European religious and political beliefs when they land on American shores. They are civilized. They are taught how to behave. They are tamed.

Europe is the home of classical religious theology and classical political ideology: Catholicism, Protestantism, Judaism; Socialism, Marxism, Communism. Europe was and, to some extent, still is, the mother of fanaticism. Europe is a continent of believers. America, on the other hand, is "a nation of behavers."*

Immigrants arrive with their sects, shuls, and churches. America then teaches them to be discreet. It does so by means of its unique creation: the denomination, or better, many denominations. This is known as "pluralism." America tames religious sects up into denominations, bringing them into the respectable middle class. America also tames churches down into denominations (the American Catholic church is one of its recent converts and now bears the humble civil demeanor of an American denomination).

The denominational system converts religions to the multi-party system of religious pluralism; the political system converts ideological or third-party politics and movements to the two-party system of political dualism.

Chapter one, on "The Emergence of Denominational Pluralism" is a brief account of the religious history of Western Christianity, culminating in the latest or American "denominational era" of Western history. This era grows out of the dissidence of Protestant dissent. Pluralism is the de facto "established" religion of America. Pluralism has interesting affiliations with civil religion in America, with civic culture, and with what I call the religion of civility. Protestants, Catholics, and Jews collide with this de facto "establishment" on arrival. Pluralism—which is to say, toleration—is what they "encounter."

Chapters two through five consist of three case studies in the encounter of European religions with the fact of religious pluralism in America. Reinhold Niebuhr, Father John Courtney Murray, and Rabbi Arthur Hertzberg—Protestant, Catholic, and Jewish theologians, respectively—are closely followed in their theological struggles to come to terms with the de facto religiously plural "established religion" of America. Their problem is: do our own religious traditions offer us the values in terms of which we can make a positive assent to pluralism? In the course of endeavoring to fashion this posi-

*I allude here to, and coopt for my own purposes, the title of Martin E. Marty's *A Nation of Behavers* (Chicago and London: The University of Chicago Press, 1976). For the innovations of Marty's book see my review of it in *Worldview*, May 1977 (vol. 20, no. 5).

tive assent, these ancient religious bodies begin to turn
themselves into voluntary associations of the denominational
type. Or, at least, they struggle with the problem of trying to
"pass" as a religion of the voluntary and denominational
type, if only for the sake of "protective coloration." As religious groups, they were not "born free." As they convert, in
varying degrees, to the voluntary principle, our studies become case studies in theological anguish. In saying that these
conversions are a taming to American "civil religion," I deliberately give a new and paradoxical meaning to this controversial phrase.

Chapter seven traces this same process in the taming of European political ideologies. Europe with its feudal past and its
ancien régime exported "extremist" politics to our shores. America has managed to tame political, as it tamed religious, fanaticism. As religious or denominational pluralism coopted the classical religious theologies of Europe, so political dualism—the
two-party system—tames ideological politics into civil politics.
The apocalyptic imagination of European socialism and the
rhetoric of "class struggle" are translated, and institutionalized
in America, into party politics and labor-management negotiations. Institutions replace rhetoric. Prose expropriates poetry.
Viewing America, as I do, as a religious civilization, these various changes, as they occur in the consciousness of immigrant
intellectuals, are treated as religious conversions.

Chapter eight is about the power of what I call the Protestant
esthetic. Ultimately, religious and political ideologies are tamed
by good taste. Their cocksureness about their "mission" or the
"coming revolution," their postures of self-regard as "the one
true church" or "the chosen people," in a word, their various
"triumphalisms" are embarrassingly elitist, ostentatious, and
unseemly in America. They are "in bad taste." This chapter—
"Homely Protestant: A Decorum of Imperfection"—is about the
puritan Christian provenance of modernist good taste, and of
how the fear of offending against its canons makes cowards of
us all.

The "Conclusion" indicates the connections between this
ethos of imperfection and civility. The American (puritan) self,
as Sacvan Bercovitch argues, is an uncompleted and "intermedi-

ate" identity[10]: an *Interimsidentität*. This very imperfectness constitutes the "American sublime"; it is rooted in Protestant civilization's core values of postponement and deferral. This, in turn,
of course, stems ultimately from the eschatology of the delayed
Parousia. Jesus came, in silence and humility; we await his second coming in glory, in ostentatiousness.

Chapter 1

---◀◆▶---

THE EMERGENCE OF DENOMINATIONAL PLURALISM: "I HAPPEN TO BE ..."

---◀◆▶---

"Secularization" has, essentially, taken the form of differentiation. . . .
                                                    —*Talcott Parsons*
                              Structure and Process in Modern Society

. . . the enormous changes which have occurred constitute fundamental changes not of values but of the structure of the society in which those values are maintained and implemented.
                                                    —*Talcott Parsons*
                              Structure and Process in Modern Society

Thus in England by the end of the seventeenth century the denominational system, with its recognized patterns of pluralism, was displacing the territorial system, with its expectancy of religious uniformity. In most places on the continent, the territorial system continued.
                                                    —*Robert T. Handy*
                              Religion in the American Experience

. . . Stokely Carmichael writes [Sept. 22]: "It was for example the exploitation of Jewish landlords and merchants which first created black resentment toward Jews—not Judaism."
I suppose the sentence is meant to be reassuring; actually, it is appalling.
    Exploitative landlords who happen to be *Jewish should be condemned as landlords, not Jews. They exploit in their social—not religious—capacity. . . . What Mr. Carmichael himself indulges in—is the* identification *of social oppressors by their religious origin. . . . That Mr. Carmichael . . . should write so unnerving a sentence is unforgivable.*
                                                    —*Irving Howe*
                              letter to The New York Review of Books

*What the Bundists brought to the socialist and union movements in this country was
. . . a Jewish dimension, the persuasion that when garment workers won strikes . . . this
was a victory not merely for workers who* happened to be *Jews but for* Jewish *workers.*
                                                              —Irving Howe
                                                    World of Our Fathers

Once upon a time, in the course of a very pleasant academic
conversation on sociology, religion, etc., I turned to the young
woman on my left and asked, "What is—or was—your religion?
Catholic?" (I had suggested Catholic because of her dark hair
and somewhat Irish look.) She turned toward me and hesitated
before answering and then, looking ever so slightly miffed, said
something about "I was brought up . . ." (I *think* she said "Catholic," but her account was indistinct, somewhat mumbled.) But,
no matter the reply, the point to be made is that my question
was an intrusion; there was—in her restrained response—the
implication that such a question, in such a public place, at such
a congenial time, was somehow prying, impolite, irrelevant, incivil. And, of course, it was. In our era, in our country, religion
—like marriage—is a private affair. It has beat a slow retreat
from the public domain; it has become "invisible." In its withdrawal it has left behind, of course, respectable public echoes of
itself. These echoes or, to change the metaphor, the visual after-
effects in public places of these retreating religions, we know as
the three acceptable varieties of American religion: Protestant,
Catholic, and Jewish.

Definitions are gratuitous; situations are not. How are we to
define this situation, viz., is this a "retreat" of religious institutions and religious symbols in society and consciousness? Is it
loss or is it gain? Is it "secularization" or is it what Talcott
Parsons calls "structural differentiation"? I maintain, with Parsons, that this privatization (or "invisibilization") of religion is
the way traditional religious institutions undergo the modernization process; they experience it as a differentiation process;
and the religious name for this process of modernization (which
other institutions like the family, the academy, the economy,
likewise are undergoing) is "secularization." In this seculariza-
tion-modernization process, at the level of social structure, religion becomes an "aspect," and a largely private aspect, of the

total society. People begin writing books about "the religious factor." Correspondingly, religion becomes an "aspect" of one's social psychological identity and, as an aspect, relevant in certain contexts, irrelevant in others.

From the inside, one feels: "I *am* a Catholic," "I *am* a Jew"; but in a differentiating society, this global, even "oceanic" identity-feeling is broken up; it must not intrude itself embarrassingly, irrelevantly, into secular social occasions. This inner experience of secularization expresses itself in ordinary life in the everyday phrase "I happen to be . . ." a Catholic, a Protestant, a Jew. I will make an effort to unpack the full "secret" latent in that casual but deeply revealing phrase: "I happen to be. . . ." As such, it can be viewed as an exercise in the sociology of everyday life. If successful, I will have made intelligible the experienced social psychological consequences, in consciousness, of the longer macro-sociological process we call modernization. I will also make meaningful the connection between the process of structural differentiation and the kind of fastidiousness this forces on the religious consciousness, and the breakup of the old "fused" religious identities into their component parts. This process distills the religious variable out of its fused state in the older ethnic or regional identities: poor (or rich) Irish Catholic, East European Jew, Midwestern Lutheran Protestant.

In effect, the secularization process upgrades, it spiritualizes, it "refines" out the religious component from the concomitant ethnic, regional, class, and other variables. Like the "cracking" process in petroleum refineries, the "crude oil" of earlier *Gemeinschaft*-type religious identities is broken down—"refined"— into the simpler "hydrocarbons," with religion becoming (if one may push the metaphor) a more "spiritual" gasoline knowing its "proper place" in the differentiated *Gesellschaften* of a modernizing society. Religious identities as such must not be pushy, elbowing themselves into contexts where they do not belong. If they do, they encounter an equivalent of the polite bureaucratic put-down, "You don't belong here; I must refer you to . . . window 73B."

To give another example. In 1964, the then-society editor of *The New York Times*, Charlotte Curtis, wrote a Sunday piece on the Southampton, Long Island, "South Shore Set" in which she noted that the Murray-McDonnell compound was "one of the handsomest properties in the Hamptons" and contained numerous descendants of the Irish-American inventor, Thomas E. Murray. She added: "The McDonnells are like the Kennedys. They are rich Irish Catholics, and there are lots of them."[1] We read later in a book on the *Times,* Gay Talese's *The Kingdom and the Power,* that this paragraph had offended *Times*man Theodore Bernstein who, as editor of the "bullpen," acted as a kind of watchdog or "governess" of proper English usage and decorum on the *Times.* Bernstein reprinted this paragraph in his little inter-office bulletin, *Winners & Sinners,* as an example of impropriety, warning the staff: "Omit racial, religious or national designations unless they have some relevance to the news or are part of the biographical aggregate, as in an obit or a 'Man in the News.' Perhaps it is a tribute to the Irish that 'Irish Catholic' does not seem offensive," he concluded, "but would you write 'rich Russian Jews'?"[2]

Bernstein soon received a note in reply to his rhetorical question from his superior, managing editor Clifton Daniel (husband of Margaret Truman) which Talese includes as follows:

> I agree with you that it is a tribute to the Irish that "Irish Catholic" does not seem offensive, and I also agree that "rich Russian Jew" might be offensive. But it seems to me that . . . we can certainly say that a family is rich, that it is Russian, *and* that it is Jewish, if those things are relevant to the news. In fact, I myself have written about such families and nobody ever questioned the relevance of doing so. *But the trick is not to put these facts together in one bunch* so that they have a cumulative, pejorative aroma. . . .[3]

The rhetorical "trick" here urged by Daniel—polysyndeton—to render religio-ethnic identities "fit to print" in the *Times** parallels how they are made to "behave themselves" before they are fit to appear in modern, civil public places. In the everyday ethnic life of regional or urban America, such identities are defined in an adversary manner: people call each other *spick, mick, kike, nigger, goy, honkie* (with, of course, the mandatory

---

*In a postscript, Daniel added: "Since this note was dictated, we have published an obituary of Sean O'Casey, calling him a poor Irish Protestant."

prefix, *dirty*). These epithets "fuse" a number of variables into one dense pellet of inter-ethnic hostility. As mobility and modernization set in, these subcultural identities (and the epithets thrown at them) are taken hold of by the general culture, and they begin to dissolve. "Irish" and "poor" begin to drop out of Irish Catholic identity; the "mick" becomes a more purely religiously "Catholic" phenomenon. The ideology of a "three religion" America—Protestant, Catholic, Jewish—begins to launder the ethnicity out of Jewish identity, and the regionality out of Protestant fundamentalism. "The trick is," Daniels admonishes his colleague on the *Times*, "not to put these facts *together* in one bunch . . ."—"rich Russian Jew"—but to include them in a parataxic, differentiated manner: "we can certainly say that a family is rich, that it is Russian, *and* that it is Jewish. . . ."[4] Not to do so is somehow to violate the decorum of democratic culture, to descend to a "lower," subcultural level of American life, where experience comes more crudely, where it happens in vulgar "bunches."

The *Times* on its own institutional level, it is clear, is reflecting (and endeavoring to hasten) a societal process already occurring in the institutions of society at large (in business, in the academy, etc.): the modernizing-differentiating process whereby concrete, packaged, "crude" identities are broken down into their component parts, which are then "referred" to their appropriate contexts (public or private, business or leisure, etc.). In most public contexts, to refer to the concrete synthesis which, indeed, we remain "for ourselves" in private *(pour soi)*, is to commit a social fallacy of "misplaced concreteness." Such an impropriety is also a social genetic fallacy, as when we refer, accurately enough, to the *ascribed* origins of someone (e.g. Irish Catholic) in a setting where only his individually *achieved* status (e.g. professor) is relevant and appropriate.

The differentiating and universalizing thrust of the modernization process, then, tends to *dissolve* traditional particularisms. "I believe that there is something peculiar, something 'new under the sun,'" writes Marion J. Levy, Jr., "about the structures of relatively modernized societies. This new factor hinges on the fact that the structures of modernization, once they have reached certain levels of development, constitute a sort of universal social *solvent*"[5] thus becoming "for the first time in social history a sort of general solvent for all other social types."[6] America has been a cruel if liberating agent of this "general solvent" of modernization, applying it to waves of successive immigration (Protestant sectarian, Irish Catholic, East European Jewish). The "differentiation trauma" of these groups is frequently formulated in very abstract culture-system terms (*"separation* of church and state" for Irish Catholics, *separation* of religious and ethnic identities for East European Jews), but our immediate focus is on the social psychological impact of this process, what secularization is *experienced as*, rather than on how it is intellectually formulated.

In the past, when origin (national or ethnic) was fused with affiliation (religion), "Swedish-Lutheran," "East European Jew," "Irish Catholic" were epithets descriptive of a single identity, fused with class, regional, and other variables. "What happens," J. Milton Yinger asks, "when these connections are broken? . . . What happens to the religious aspect of these multiple identities when, as a result of 'Americanization' and of geographic and social mobility, it is no longer bound to the others?"[7] One of the first things that happens is that people begin using the rhetoric of "happen": "I happen to be a Catholic," "I happen to be a Lutheran," "I happen to be a Jew" they begin saying.

"Happen to be" means: we are what we are by choice or chance; choice if the religious identity is congenial and advantageous, chance (fate) if it is a misfortune. "Happen" covers both interpretations. In any case, religious identity is viewed as something that "happens" as a matter of free sociation rather than as fated ascriptive community. With the advent of the usage "happen to be" religious groups have begun their assimilation of the voluntary principle into their religious self-conceptions.

But, some religions are more comfortable saying "happen" than others. Many East European Jews feel very uncomfortable inside when they hear that they just "happen to be Jews."* Irish

---

*Sociologists often do not include, for their purposes, this subjective discomfort when they write, as, for example, Robert K. Merton writes, of the "pre-eminent men and women who *happened to be* Jews."[8]

Catholics, especially of the older generations, feel some discomfort. Calvinists are supposed to make an "ideal-type" good fit with the locution. Indeed, at the core of Calvinist identity is the conviction that they just "happen to be" predestined, in drastic irrelevance to all that they are or might be, do or not do. (To rid themselves of this intolerable uncertainty—we are oversimplifying Weber's story—they reassured themselves by creating capitalism.) To the Jew, his ethnicity is not irrelevant to his religion. It is at its heart, for Judaism is a family affair. The denominationalization of suburban Jewry in America under the rubric "Conservative Judaism," whereby Judaism becomes "a religion like any other religion," forces the social psychology of an *als ob* ("as if") onto members of Conservative Judaism. They know they are more different in the privacy of their own hearts *(pour soi)* than they make themselves out to be for the *goyim (pour autrui)*. Conservative Judaism arose, as Marshall Sklare writes, because the American cultural value system made it clear "that ethnic solidarity would have to be perpetuated chiefly under religious auspices . . ."[9] Though some Conservative Jews, to be sure, really believe in the purely religious definition of Jewry (e.g. some Reform types), others, at the very least, given American traditions, contend that "the designation of the Jewish group as constituting a denomination is a highly convenient fiction which it is wise to cultivate."[10] Both Jews and Catholics struggle, in America, to denominationalize themselves.

A denomination, as Talcott Parsons points out, is neither a church nor a sect (the basic distinction of Weber and Troeltsch) but a third type of religious institution: the denomination "shares with the church type the *differentiation* between religious and secular spheres of interest . . . [yet] shares with the sect type its character as a voluntary association where the individual member is bound only by a responsible personal commitment, not by *any* factor of ascription." Parsons adds, most significantly, that in the American case the denomination is "logically . . . associated with the constitutional separation of church and state."[11]

The denomination is the last phase in the evolution of a differentiating Protestantism. But what is differentiation for Protestantism—an unfolding from within—is secularization for

Judaism and, to some degree, for immigrant Catholicism. That is to say, Jews, Catholics and, to some extent, Lutherans find that the cultural situation in America forces on them, *ab extra*, differentiations (like the separation of church and state, of ethnicity and religion, etc.) that they are unprepared for. These differentiations haven't emerged, as they have in mainline Protestantism, from a quarrel of the churches with themselves (if also with society). They are rather encountered *externally* in the *situation* of religious action and, perforce, are *adapted* to, with varying degrees of expediency.

It is no wonder that, in 1928, Protestants and others united for the defeat of Al Smith, and had a difficult time believing his separation of church and state declaration (written incidentally by the famous Jewish Judge Proskower). There is all the difference in the world between an internal, indigenous legitimation of the separation of church and state—in effect, to declare your religion a denomination—and an external proclamation of a convenient fiction that it is wise and prudent (and expedient) to cultivate.

In the Jewish case, differentiation is secularization precisely because it is experienced as an exigency of the situation, and not as a religious demand of the act of religious commitment. In other words, by *using* the religious identification label as a *means* of perpetuating the terminal value of ethnic solidarity, the ethnic survivalists of Conservative Judaism are in effect foisting a forensic identity on their membership. "All of this," writes Sklare, the sociologist of Conservative Judaism, "results in the strengthening of the religious structure in spite of increasing secularization."[12] This explains, in the Jewish case anyway, the postwar religious revival. (Sklare wrote his book in 1955.) Paradoxically, by stressing the religious identification label as a protective device to maintain the more fundamental—and, to the Jew, more "religious"—community nexus of common ethnicity, Jews, Sklare remarks, "are forced into 'making good' on the stereotype by according some support to religious causes . . . their very desire to project the stereotype means that they have to concede a responsibility for supporting *religious* institutions."[13] In the Jewish case, then, for them—and from the inside —sacralization (i.e., becoming "religious" in the Western *differ-*

entiated sense) is secularization! And, by the same token, what from the standpoint of the Christianizing, differentiating West is secularization (viz., group socials, Jewish "community center" activities, etc.), is for the Jewish group the perpetuation of its *sacred,* primordial, particularistic solidarity.

So much for the social consequences, on American Judaism, of structural differentiation. What of the social psychological consequences of Judaism's projecting itself as a religion (a religious denomination)? This stereotype, as Sklare notes, "reacts back on the Jew himself . . . Gentiles may begin to convey that they consider the Jewish group as just another religious denomination. At this juncture, the Jew may find himself propelled into fulfilling the image projected by the Gentile."[14] The comic ingredient in this self-fulfilling prophecy, whereby Jews become "religious" by courtesy of Gentile convictions, is an obscure if pervasive background ingredient in much Jewish humor. Comedy thus expresses the "distance" between the forensic, external identity and the inner, felt identity. The Jew we are for others, this humor says, is not the Jew we are for ourselves. The humor also expresses the refusal of many Jews to take the religious definition of their situation at face value. To do so would convert a "false position" into an interior *"mauvaise foi,"* resulting in reification and alienation. Thus, in everyday life, though the average American Jew (ideal typically, the Jew of Conservative Judaism) may not believe the stereotype to be wholly valid, he feels—as Sklare writes—"that he must act like the type of 'good Jew' which the Gentile imagines—the Jew who is loyal to his rabbi, interested in his synagogue."[15] And the postwar Jewish religious "revival" follows: while attendance at services may not grow very substantially, "religious institutions will receive increasing financial support and community esteem, particularly if they offer a program which includes *non*-religious activities and is strongly oriented toward ethnic values."[16] This postwar *embourgeoisement* of the Jewish community, whereby it chooses to perpetuate ethnic solidarity under denominational auspices and "to continue group survival under the legitimation of religion,"[17] is at the root of the psychological doubleness or "Marranoism" that even "secular Jewish intellectuals" pressure themselves, to some extent, into practicing.

Thus, in America, Judaism's religio-ethnic identity is "forced" to live a "double life" both in its social structure and socio-psychologically. But this is not the normatively desirable double-life produced by the modernization process under Western Protestant auspices, viz., the "private-public" dichotomy. The East European Jewish community (as also, *mutatis mutandis*, the Catholic community) are forced into a double life on the "secret-open" axis. Though the social structure of private and public, and secret and open, is an isomorphic one, the cultural content of the former is pre-modern as the latter is modern.[18] What this boils down to is that in a modernizing, industrial, protestant society, the "Invisible Religion" that Luckmann speaks of is of two varieties: Protestant denominations are transformed into the invisibility of privacy; Judaism and, to a certain extent, Catholicism are transformed (so long as they remain "faithful") into the invisibility of secrecy.[19] Privacy is a normative structure legitimated by the Protestant value of individualism. Privacy is publicly institutionalized secrecy.

The structure of Conservative Judaism (as the somewhat analogous "ghetto" structure of pre-Vatican II "Irish" Catholicism) is, on Marshall Sklare's account, a denominational façade "behind which" an ethnocentric community maintains ethnic solidarity. Thus, studies of Jewish endogamy in the "gilded ghettos" of suburbia reveal the strength of the intermarriage ban, which is the backbone of socio-religious communalism.[20] As long as these socio-economic communal structures are maintained, wittingly or otherwise, one doesn't "just happen" to be Jewish or Catholic. Thus the individualistic "protestant" voluntarism implicit in the locutions *"I happen to be* Jewish" (or "Catholic"), "I just *happen* to live here," etc. will be used uneasily and/or humorously by Jews and Catholics. Not until such phrases can be uttered unselfconsciously and credibly—to speaker and hearer alike—will genuine Western secularization have set in.

Psychologically, as we have said, only the descendants of ascetic Calvinism feel completely comfortable with these phrases. Only they have grown old with "modernity." Catholics grew up with the West, grew old gracefully (one might say) only until the Reformation and the French and Industrial revolutions. From then on it was Counter Reformation, counterrevolution and counter-modernization and retreat to the "corporate society" ideology of an agrarian and pre-modern value-system. Rome retreated into its seminaries. Jewish Emancipation, analogously, crumbled the "medieval" walls of Ghetto Jewry; Jews were "shocked" by Europe's differentiations, universalism, and role pluralism.[21] They retreated into their own ideologies of delayed modernization: Zionism and Marxism.

It is a high irony of our culture that the current phase of Western civilization—especially in the Anglo-American area of "civic culture" and "civil religion"—which both secularists and religionists agree in calling "post-Christian society" is, for Talcott Parsons—as for me—a genuine, progressive stage in the further institutionalization of Christian values into the social structures and institutions (political, academic, economic, and other) of our society. The gloomy interpretation of "secularization," Parsons would contend, has blinded us to the fact that, by the roundabout route of differentiation, there now exists a more Christian society than ever before in history. Cherished images have been broken, but the values are being installed. Each Protestant advance is marked by a deeper iconoclasm and a more civil countenance, which mask the deepening religiousness of the culture.

Also, one can see here, the paradoxical working out of a kind of "relative deprivation" theorem: the more responsibly Christian—individualistic, universalistic, idealistic, self-critical, concerned—society becomes, the more Christians feel they have failed and become post-Christian and secularized. Their sense of guilty failure is a direct consequence of the hypertrophy of upgraded demands they now make upon themselves and society.[22]

The denominational phase, spearheaded by the core Protestant denominations, puts the "established 'churches' "—Catholic, Lutheran, Jewish—as well as the secularists, under severe strain. The Church of Rome is passing through its Protestant and its denominational phases at the same time; hence there has been much confusion. The English priest, Charles Davis, suffering the Protestant phase, left the Church and wrote a book featuring "conscience." The American priest, James Kavanaugh, experiencing the denominational crisis, left the Church and wrote a book predictably titled *A Modern Priest Looks at His Outdated Church*. Peter L. Berger in *The Noise of Solemn Assemblies* saw the "otherness" of Christian commitment coopted by the syncretism and "civic religion" of the American religious establishment. Rabbi Arthur Hertzberg, as we shall see in chapter five, spearheaded what was essentially a backlash against the not wholly convincing attempt of Judaism to assume the denominational form of "Conservative Judaism."

What is this "denominational phase"? It is the end of the last vestiges of ascriptivity. In the Reformation phase, as in the Medieval phase, one "acceptable church" coincided with a politically organized society. Adherence to that church—*cuius regio, eius religio*—"was the test of the moral quality treated as a minimum for good standing in the society. . . ."[23] The "morally acceptable" religion was "our own." This is no longer true. When the religious organization becomes a *purely* voluntary association, when the last vestiges of ascription disappear, we can no longer "ascribe" moral upstandingness to any given organization, or "ascribe" moral or religious turpitude to apostasy from any given religious organization as such.

As in other phases of the institutionalization of (Protestant) Christianity in Western social structure, this fourth or denominational phase involves both a strictly internal, theological differentiation and a social structural differentiation. In the belief-system, faith as trust finally differentiates from faith as belief. (Robert N. Bellah discussed this at the Summer 1969 Conference on Unbelief at Rome.) "Asking the individual to have faith," Parsons writes, "is essentially to ask him to *trust* in God. But, whatever the situation in the relation of the human to the divine, in *human* relations trust seems to have to rest on mutuality. Essentially," Parsons concludes, "the voluntary principle in denominationalism is extending mutuality of trust so that no *human* agency is permitted to take upon itself the authority to control the conditions under which faith is to be legitimately expected." This is the same principle that was involved, in the Reformation phase, in releasing the individual from sacramental control.[24]

Concurrently with this theological shift to toleration, the elements of trust in the individual are institutionalized in the social structure on the "secular" side as a greater trust in the moral quality of secular conduct. Parsons takes a voting behavior model (rather than, say, an economic model) as a means of illuminating this trust-tolerance shift. Just as there is politically a supraparty consensus, a kind of institutional "medium" in which both the tolerance of the winners for the losers *and* the loyalty of the losing opposition are maintained, so the "good faith" of the denominational "opposition" is maintained and retained, despite shifts of party and denominational allegiance.

Thus, in the three-denominational system of Protestantism, Catholicism, and Judaism, as in the two-party system, two levels of commitment are differentiated paralleling the theological differentiation of faith as creed from faith as trust, viz., party or denominational affiliation from the deeper moral community constituted by trans-denominational and trans-party trust and tolerance. We call this latter "civil religion."

This extension of the principle of mutual trust out into the realm of secular conduct[25] is what can be considered the era of civility. I distinguish the era of the early church as the *agapé* or charity phase of Christianity, where the face-to-face norm of caritative love was dominant. In the medieval synthesis, the functional equivalent is a feudal-type of chivalry, where the agapic component is retained but restricted to the weakness of women. The Protestant phase sees *agapé* institutionalized as courtesy-decency, retaining the structure of *agapé,* extending it beyond the female principle, but tinging it slightly with the class condescension of the bourgeois era ("lady bountiful"). The denominational phase institutionalizes *agapé* as civility. Gone, now, is the warm, caritative affect, but in its place is a wider *extension* of trust (taking the bourgeois-parliamentary form of "respect"). The trust of "respect" is now a civil debt owed to *everyone.* Entitlement to respect and, if not to actual trust, at least to the "show" of trust we call "good faith" becomes universalized and upgraded. The civic culture becomes a community in which trust takes the form of the rites of civility, and in which the "civilities" are the gifts that are exchanged and, in being exchanged, knit the members into the solidarity of a moral community, into a society *(Gesellschaft)* that is also a community *(Gemeinschaft).*

Chapter 2

―◆―

CASE STUDIES: PROTESTANT, CATHOLIC AND JEW

―◆―

As a consequence of the modern theory of religious freedom the churches find themselves in an anomalous position. Inwardly, *to their communicants, they continue to assert that they possess the only complete version of the truth. But* outwardly, *in their civic relation with other churches and with the civil power, they preach and practice toleration. The separation of church and state involves more than a mere logical difficulty for the churchmen. It involves a deep psychological difficulty for the members of the congregation.* As communicants *they are expected to believe without reservation that their church is the only true means of salvation; otherwise the multitude of separate sects would be meaningless. But* as citizens *they are expected to maintain a neutral indifference to the claims of all sects, and to resist encroachments by any one sect upon the religious practices of the others. This is the best compromise which human wisdom has yet devised, but it has one inevitable consequence which the superficial advocates of toleration often overlook. It is difficult to remain warmly convinced that the authority of any one sect is divine, when as a matter of* daily experience *all sects have to be* treated *alike.*

The human soul is not so divided in compartments that a man can be indifferent in one part of his soul and firmly believing in another. The existence of rival sects, the visible demonstration *that none has a monopoly, the habit of neutrality, cannot but dispose men against an unquestioning acceptance of the authority of one sect. So many faiths, so many loyalties, are offered to the modern man that at last none seems to him wholly inevitable and fixed in the order of the universe. The existence of many churches* in one community *weakens the foundations of all of them. And that is why* every church *in the heyday of its power proclaims itself to be* catholic *and intolerant.*

But when there are many churches in the same community, none can make wholly good on the claim that it is catholic. None has that power to discipline the individual which a universal church exercises.
　　　　　　　　　　　　　　　　　　　　　—*Walter Lippmann*
　　　　　　　　　　　　　　　　　　　　　A Preface to Morals

Genuine institutionalization of the constitutional protection of religious freedom cannot be confined to the secular side; it must be accepted as religiously *legitimate as well.*
—*Talcott Parsons*
Sociological Theory and Modern Society

As each of the traditional European religions arrived in America and clambered up out of steerage it confronted an unprecedented pluralistic situation: the existence of the other religions. The sheer non-theoretical fact of these other religions, legitimately co-existing with themselves, created severe theoretical problems for Catholic, Protestant, and Jewish theologians. "Administering a tradition with age-old monopolistic pretensions," Berger and Luckmann wrote, "they have to find ways of theoretically legitimating the demonopolization that has taken place."[1] "Hell," as Sartre said, "is the others."

In the American setting, and under the steady gaze of the American "public philosophy" and its civil religion, these traditional monopolistic pretensions made their own adherents uneasy and embarrassed. The Roman Catholic claim to uniqueness (the one "one true church"); the Jewish claim to uniqueness ("the chosen people"); the Protestant fundamentalist claim to uniqueness ("Jesus only saves")—are variants of a more general claim: the claim to be religiously superior or elite. While the traditionalist spokesmen for these religions, like Protestant evangelist Billy Graham, or Jesuit Father Leonard Feeney, or Rabbi Meir Kahane, "take the option of continuing to voice the old totalitarian claims as if nothing had happened,"[2] few members of their own religions take these claims very seriously, and, of course, even fewer members of the other religions.

The "established" situation of pluralism in America makes these traditional definitions of religious reality sound silly as their large claims echo across the American heartland; the pervasive civil religion of America makes them sound heretical. Civil religion, child of liberal Unitarian Protestantism and secular Enlightenment, is fully at home in modernizing, urban, pluralist society. It reflects and legitimates a process of modernization it assisted in creating. Lacking any formal institutionalization or formulated creed, civil religion is nevertheless inherently subversive of the proud elitist core-claims that traditional Protestantism, Catholicism, and Judaism brought with them from their European past. Whatever the theological experts of traditional religions may do, civil religion and its carrier, the infrastructure of pluralism, change "not only the social position of the traditional [religious] definitions of reality, but also the way in which these are held in the consciousness of individuals."[3]

Civil religion and the pluralistic situation gradually shape the self-understanding of the members of the historic religious communities. Slowly, some would say insidiously, civil religion pressures the traditional believer from without and manipulates him from within, bringing him to the uneasy realization that the beliefs he takes for granted are really marginal and that what he experiences as obvious is really odd. Civil religion manages, in the end, to convince the traditional believer that to make specific allusions in public places to, say, the saving Gospel of Jesus Christ (should he be an evangelical Protestant) or to the chosen-people doctrine (should he be an observant Jew) is to commit a social impropriety that is at the same time a religious heresy. Small wonder, then, as Robert Bellah writes, that "the question, and it is the most delicate issue of all, is how the civil and noncivil religions are to be related."[4] Delicate, indeed, is the manner in which noncivil religions become, in the eyes of civil religion—and, eventually, in their own eyes—incivil religions.

In America, since pluralism is encountered as a social situation, pluralism tends in the end to civilize. In Europe, where pluralism was experienced as an abstract and academic problem, it generated scepticism and the sociology of knowledge. Encountered socially, then, pluralism breeds civility. But not at the start. Early on, the leaders of the incivil or culturally "heretical" religions launched an uncouth public polemic against civil religion. The Catholics called it the "Americanist" heresy, the Protestants "infidelity," the Jews *galut*, "exile." It was—and where it still exists, it remains—a deadly single struggle against a triple enemy: modernization, assimilation, civilization. "Americanization" means to the immigrant religious communities what it has always meant: apostasy, "sell-out," conversion from their immigrant, precivil, uncivil religions to the American civil religion which they *experience as* the religion of civility.

Confronted by the de facto pluralistic situation and the de facto "established religion" that expresses this situation—the humble "one-among-many mien" of denominationally plural civil religion—the historic religions seek for ways and means of coming to terms with it. The early polemical rejections by religious and theological leaders yield, with later generations, to the quest for dignified accommodation and face-saving settlement.

The earlier pluralistic situation, the era of "cold war" and "co-existence" between Protestantism, Catholicism, and Judaism, and between all of them and civil religion, gave way in post–World War II America (1945–1975) to a thirty-year period of religious ecumenism and theological détente. As the rank-and-file of each of the three religions moved up the socio-economic ladder, and acculturated to the norms of civil association in its secular behavior and to the norms of civil religion in its religious behavior, the theologians of these respective religions endeavored to consolidate and legitimate these changes in terms drawn from their own theological traditions.

Rather than generalize on this widespread post-war development across the spectrum of religious difference, I prefer instead to pick one such "reforming" theologian from each of the traditions making up the "tri-faith" religion of America. Each religion went through, and is still undergoing, this internal debate with itself. The *pattern* of the argument is astonishingly similar for each of the three religions, *mutatis mutandis*. The usefulness of the analysis will depend less on the objective merits of each dispute than on its *paradigmatic* character.* In these three case studies, the ideas and principles, tactics and strategies that each of *us* implicitly uses as legitimations, when we change our minds, to show that we have not "really" changed our minds, are here set forth in all their embarrassing detail as each theologian argues that his own particular religion has "always" believed the reformist interpretation he is arguing.

I have chosen the Protestant Reinhold Niebuhr, the Jesuit John Courtney Murray, and the Conservative Jewish rabbi Arthur Hertzberg, because each of them was—and in Hertzberg's

---

*Garry Wills will, I hope, pardon me for vandalizing here two sentences in his *Politics and Catholic Freedom* (Chicago: Regnery, 1964), p. 4 of the Introduction.

case, still is—a theologian with institutional commitments to his respective religion. Each was a teacher, preacher, writer, and representative figure in his religious community, a spokesman, and was so considered by others.* Each was at once a committed loyalist to his tradition and a reforming modernizer of that tradition. Each, finally, was a man of individuality and style, writing with considerable eloquence. In each case their task was the task of all modernizing intellectuals: to register, on behalf of their people and their tradition, the sheer irreversible actuality of that modern religiously pluralistic situation that confronted them in America, and to legitimate that pluralistic situation religiously, if possible. This process meant that each of the three religions would cease to tolerate each other's continued presence on sufferance—provisionally, until the other conveniently disappeared or converted—and instead would accept, with ungrudging inner assent, the existence of the others as of right. Respect, trust, and open acknowledgment of each other's right to exist would, in America, replace the old de facto co-existence, the religious cold war, that had prevailed for centuries in Europe.

But this was easier done than said. Considerable economic, political, and some social interaction had already occurred between rank-and-file Protestants, Catholics, and Jews, but this de facto integration had often far outdistanced the verbal religious justifications the theologians were able to find for it in their classical traditions. The memberships of the traditional religions had, so to speak, presented a fait accompli to their religious leaders. (To be sure, there were discrepancies. If the traditionalist "authoritarian" religion-talk of Irish Catholics, for example, obscured the remarkable extent of their behavioral integration with members of other groups, the anti-traditional and "liberal" religion-talk of many Jews obscured the persistence of de facto behavioral "ethnocentricity.")

These are two of the type of "open-gap" situations that typically invite legitimation from the "priestly" intellectual class. Legitimators close gaps. "Legitimation as a process," Berger and Luckmann write, "is best described as a 'second order' of

*In 1977 Rabbi Hertzberg was in his second term as president of the American Jewish Congress (A.J.C.).

objectification of meaning. Legitimation produces new meanings that serve to integrate the meanings *already attached to* dispa-
rate institutional processes. The function of legitimation," they
conclude, "is to make objectively available and subjectively
plausible the 'first-order' objectifications that have [already]
been institutionalized."[5]

We turn now to the first of our case studies and follow Reinhold Niebuhr as he endeavored to legitimate, by internalizing
theologically, the pluralistic situation he encountered socially
and culturally. His problem is best formulated as follows: how
can Protestant Christian tradition make objectively available and
wholeheartedly plausible to itself, theologically, the socio-cultural and interpersonal acceptance of the Jewish "presence" in
pluralistic America?

Chapter 3

———◆—◉—◆———

PROTESTANT:
THE REINHOLD
NIEBUHR–WILL
HERBERG "TREATY"

———◆—◉—◆———

... in the Christian church ... the individual was released from his ascriptive embeddedness in the Jewish community. . . . Proselytizing on a grand scale became possible without carrying along the whole society immediately. While conversion to Judaism meant accepting full membership in the total Jewish Community, a converted Christian could remain a Roman, a Corinthian, or whatever; his new social participation was confined to the church itself.
—*Talcott Parsons*
Sociological Theory and Modern Society

I.

The Background

In *Life* magazine of July 1, 1957, when Protestant theologian Reinhold Niebuhr objected to Billy Graham and his revivalism, a storm of protest greeted his article. "But the outcry against Niebuhr on Graham was as nothing," writes Niebuhr's biographer June Bingham, "to the outcry against Niebuhr on his statement [the following year] that there is no need for Christians to try to convert the Jews."[1] This statement of Niebuhr, part of a paper read before a joint meeting of the Jewish and Union Theological seminaries, was the culmination not only of a long theological development in Niebuhr's Evangelical and Reformed Christianity, but—even more importantly—the upshot of his social concerns and social aspirations which had led him step by step into a continuing face-to-face encounter with secular Protestants and non-religious Jews. (In America, in the shift of theologians and others to liberalism, social concern and social aspiration are hopelessly, indissolubly, entwined. No mere man can put them asunder.)

Niebuhr began the long journey from tradition into modernity in the rural backwater of Wright City, Missouri. Son of an immigrant, German-speaking Lutheran minister, when he entered the urban and urbane Yale Divinity School he felt himself to be "a raw and timid student," convinced that he could speak "neither English nor German decently," straitened by the genteel poverty of a minister's family.[2] He chose to be ordained in the Evangelical and Reformed Church, an indigenous American denomination, thus beginning his move away from the more compact and European religio-ethnic background of his parental Lutheranism. The raw young ordinand was then sent by the Lutheran Home Mission Board to a teeming urban parish in Detroit. There Niebuhr soon grew to know many "unbelievers," gentile and Jewish, on a face-to-face, first-name basis. He served as chairman of the mayor's commission on race with Fred Butzell, a prominent Jewish attorney, as his vice-chairman. His respect for the growing company of his secular friends deepened as his involvement in community affairs widened.

But already, this early in his career, the fervent Evangelical and Reform believer in Niebuhr had begun to realize that civility and friendliness have their "price." The urbanity of the "secular city" is dearly bought if Christian truth itself must be laundered and manicured so as not to prove socially embarrassing. Throughout his pastorate in Detroit, Niebuhr experienced the differing "pulls" of tact and truth. In 1926, for example, an outspoken friend of his lost his pastorate. Niebuhr was not surprised: "He is courageous but tactless," he wrote; and then—anticipating what we shall call the "dialectic of civility" (which, thirty-two years later, would govern his statement relinquishing a Christian mission to the Jews)—he wrote: "Perhaps loyalty to principle will always *appear as* tactlessness from the perspective of those who don't agree with you. . . ."[3] A refinement of sensitivity, an agonized concern for appearances, with the appearance that loyalty must assume in a pluralistic, religious milieu began to dominate his diary. Private charity began to take the form of public civility.

Over and over he returned to the theme of how hard it is "to speak the truth in love without losing a part of the truth, . . ."[4] The average person, he noted, is characterized "by suavity and circumspection rather than by fortitude. . . . I am a coward myself," he admitted, "and find it tremendously difficult to run counter to general opinion."[5] During his Detroit years (1915–1928) when Niebuhr did allow himself to be rude, he permitted this intransigence only against the socio-economic "prejudices" of his congregation, never against the religious "convictions" of his friends. He was against protecting the "sensitive souls" in his congregation "who might be rudely shocked by a religious message which came in conflict with their interests and prejudices."[6]

Concluding his Detroit pastorate in 1928, he mused that it is "almost impossible to be sane and Christian at the same time, and on the whole I have been more sane than Christian."[7] By "sane," of course, he meant well-behaved and "moderate," a "moderation which I have called Aristotelian, but which an unfriendly critic might call opportunistic."[8] As he left the twenties behind in Detroit and went East to take up his position at Union Theological Seminary, it appears that, if his cynicism had been "tamed," so also had what St. Paul called "the madness of the cross." This dilemma continued to haunt him.

In the New York of the thirties and forties, Niebuhr became a leading figure among socialists and liberals. More and more he came to speak of the "Christian" tradition, of the "Judaeo-Christian" ethic rather than the "Christian" ethic. Gradually, "Hebraic justice" was emphasized as a way of ridding Christian charity of what he took to be its *"noblesse oblige,"* and the "credal" and propositional or truth component in Christianity was muted. By 1944 Niebuhr was telling a Jewish audience that "I have, as a Christian theologian, sought to strengthen the Hebraic-prophetic content of the Christian tradition; . . ."[9] Noting that Niebuhr emphasized increasingly "the conflict between the Jewish and the Greek elements in Christian thought," his Union Theological Seminary colleague Paul Tillich chided him, insisting that Christianity cannot "give a preference to the Jewish in contrast to the Greek encounter with reality" since it "transcends this contrast." He detected in Niebuhr a tendency to absolutize not Christianity but Judaism, and charged him with violating his own principles, since he would never accept the absolute claim of any culture, "not even the Jewish culture over against other cultures."[10]

But the theological "preference" noted by Tillich must be seen against the background of the relentless pressure of social life in New York and the sophisticated circle of Niebuhr's acquaintance.

The fact is that "Reinie" Niebuhr was becoming "civilized." His acquaintance was widening; his commitment to tolerance and the civilities of interpersonal relations was deepening; he was loved, and he wanted to be loved (who doesn't?); the democratic need to *look* inoffensive was becoming more demanding; the tyranny of democratic manners was taking firmer hold; his celebrated hard-line Christianity was becoming adjectival to his ethics and politics, a marginal differentiation making the Niebuhrian brand of liberalism different and "interesting"; he was in great demand; and, last but not least, he was quietly moving up the social ladder.* This son of an immigrant Lutheran minister from Wright City, Missouri, had, on his own admission, come a long way from his provincial Protestant beginnings. Already, by 1916, he had written his first article for a *national* magazine, *The Atlantic Monthly*, and by 1926 had journeyed East to preach at Harvard.[11] Teaching at Union, he met and married Ursula Keppel-Compton—niece of an Anglican bishop—with full Church of England solemnities.[12] There were to be two Niebuhr children, Christopher, who was sent to Groton and Harvard, and Elisabeth, a Chapin and Radcliffe graduate,[13] whose engagement to Charles Proctor Sifton of the law firm of Cadwalader, Wickersham & Taft was duly made known to the readers of *The New York Times* by "The Rev. Dr. and Mrs. Reinhold Niebuhr of Stockbridge and New York . . ." The wedding took place with Nelson Aldrich as best man.[14]

---

*One of the burdens of this book is to show that considerations such as these, in the sacred precincts of theology, are not *infra dignitatem;* on the contrary, they are part of what the sociology of religion is all about.

All of this "co-existed," somehow, with impeccably liberal political behavior. In the 1930s Niebuhr was a member of the Socialist Party;[15] resigning in 1944, he was elected a vice-president of New York's Liberal Party.[16] He wrote for *The Nation*. If Niebuhr locked horns with Bertrand Russell, H. G. Wells, Sidney Hook, John Dewey, and others, he supped with Alex Rose, Arthur Schlesinger, James Loeb, Joseph Lash, James Wechsler, and Felix Frankfurter.[17] Intimacy was working its relentless solvent. Cool, "objective," learned typifications of others, as Jews or otherwise, tend to melt when monitored by the warm self-corrective feed-back of reciprocated intimacy. He was preaching one Sunday in the 1940s in a little chapel near his then-summer home in Heath, Massachusetts, when his friend and neighbor, Supreme Court Justice Felix Frankfurter, remarked: " 'I liked what you said; Reinie, and I speak as a believing unbeliever.' "[18] Niebuhr replied: " 'I am glad you did. For I spoke as an unbelieving believer.' " His biographer adds: "And a thoughtful but nonpractising Jew stated simply, 'Reinie is my rabbi.' "[19]

Sharing more and more of his time with secular, agnostic, and frequently, Jewish intellectuals, Christianity was placed in brackets, the brackets of civility. Unconcern with Christianity was no longer an impediment to social intercourse with Reinhold Niebuhr. His friend Carl Frank (alias Paul Hagen) recalls: " 'I hardly ever think of a time when there was any difference of opinion between us. I had the feeling of complete identity with him even though we have different philosophies. . . . We were polite with each other. . . .' "[20]

But there were a few "intercredal friendships" in which theology was not politely bracketed. Foremost among these was Niebuhr's long and involved friendship with Will Herberg. This interfaith friendship, culminating in a kind of theological "separate peace" between the Christian and Jewish friends in private life, was to serve as the model for Niebuhr's later revolutionary proposal for a "public theological peace" between Protestant Christianity and Jewry.

In the late 1930s, as the God of Marxism was failing him, Herberg had read Niebuhr's *Moral Man and Immoral Society;* this book was to change the course of his life. "Humanly speaking," he wrote, "it converted me, for in some manner I cannot describe, I felt my whole being, and not merely my thinking, shifted to a new center." And the fruits of this "conversion": "I could now speak about God and religion without embarrassment, though as yet without much understanding of what was involved." A telephone call led ultimately to Herberg becoming Niebuhr's friend and theological interlocutor. One day Herberg said: " 'I hope you won't mind, Reinie, but I've decided against becoming a Christian.' " Not only did he not mind, but "Niebuhr beamed."[21] Herberg was converting instead to "biblical faith," becoming, in fact, "the Jewish counterpart of Niebuhr,"[22] and in 1951 he wrote a Niebuhrian version of Judaism, *Judaism and Modern Man.* Ursula Niebuhr "invites him to address her classes at Barnard and teasingly says that he reminds her of St. Paul."[23] A private "Treaty of Westphalia" had been concluded.[24]

If in the 1930s Marxism was, for much of the Jewish intelligentsia, a secular theology, in the 1940s Zionism was gradually to replace the failing god of Marxism. With Nazism rampant in Europe and Jews in concentration, and later, in death camps, Niebuhr soon became an outspoken "Christian Zionist." As early as 1941, in a speech before the national convention of B'nai B'rith, Niebuhr publicly supported a national homeland for the Jews in Palestine, and again in 1942 before the Union of Hebrew Congregations. By 1944 he had, with others, helped to found the American Christian Palestine Committee, and, as its first treasurer, took part in their seminars all over the United States.[25]

Throughout the '40s with the war in Europe raging, issues concerning the nature of ethnic and religious pluralism and the foundation of tolerance became, for Niebuhr, theologically and practically important. In Edinburgh delivering the Gifford Lectures, he struggled to make theological toleration a function not of doubt but of humility. Yet, oscillating, he quoted G. K. Chesterton that "Tolerance is the virtue of people who don't believe anything."[26] Soon he was cautiously admitting that "no toleration is possible without a measure of *provisional* scepticism about the truth we hold," and legitimating his position with a footnote quotation from the Quaker Charles James Fox that " 'the only foundation for toleration is a measure of scepticism. . . .' "[27]

Shortly after, seeming to backtrack, Niebuhr legitimated toleration as a purely moral-religious virtue—not as an expression of cognitive doubt—and wrote that "Our toleration of truths opposed to those which we confess is an expression of the spirit of forgiveness in the realm of culture." But, through the back door, doubt was readmitted in the form of self-doubt: "Like all forgiveness, it is possible only if we are not too sure of our own virtue, . . . toleration of others requires broken confidence in the finality of our own truth."[28] Classical Christology would see in this Niebuhrian analysis a confounding of the moral and the epistemological. Certitude in the truth of one's own faith is beginning to sound like pride; doubt and scepticism about the finality and universality of Revelation is beginning to sound like moral humility. The rhetoric of broken-heartedness has an open field.

The following year Niebuhr was drawn by the logic of his position into conceding openly the role of intellectual doubt in tolerance: he "admitted" that toleration in religion could "probably" not have been achieved in any modern democratic society had there not been a "considerable decay of traditional loyalties"; adding: "Tolerance is the virtue of people who do not believe anything, said Gilbert Chesterton *quite truly.* "[29] But in the end Niebuhr nevertheless rejected both indifference and doubt as rationales for tolerance. Despite its rarity, humility is the true root of tolerance. People can hold ultimate religious convictions, he wrote, "with a sufficient degree of humility to live amicably with those who have contradictory convictions."[30]

This "religious solution" to the problem of religious diversity turned on the old distinction, which Niebuhr reworked for the occasion, between essential religious "faith" and its "actual expressions": each religion is to proclaim its own "highest insights" while yet preserving "an honorable and contrite recognition of the fact that all actual expressions of religious faith are subject to historical contingency and relativity." It is the recognition of such a distinction that "creates a spirit of tolerance . . ." and teaches men to "*moderate* their natural pride and to achieve some *decent* consciousness of the relativity of their own statement of even the most ultimate truth."[31] The Aristotelian "moderation" of the Detroit days thus returns, sporting this

time a biblical pedigree; and a "decency" of consciousness is
said to spring from the relativity of a biblically contrite and
broken heart.

II.

The Bombshell

Clearly, Niebuhr's quest to find the roots of tolerance in biblical Christianity rather than in the scepticism of the Enlightenment was deeply motivated. But the theological implications of
his long meditation on religious tolerance were to remain hidden till 1958, when he read his now famous paper before a joint
meeting of the Jewish and Union [Protestant] Theological seminaries.

Everything was in readiness; nevertheless, it was a bombshell.
It was titled "The Relations of Christians and Jews in Western
Civilization."[32] Let me examine it carefully, commenting as we
go along. Early along in the talk he noted that, despite (or
possibly because of) the fact that Christianity and Judaism have
a common bible and a common historical approach to the Ultimate, the Christian faith "has not had *enough grace* to *extend*
genuine community to the Jew. . . ."[33] The theological language
here already lends itself to a reading in the language of gracious
hospitality. Theological religion and civil religion are partners.
The frustrated zeal of Protestant pietism, he went on to say,
cannot understand "the *stubbornness* of the Jew" in resisting conversion.[34] Niebuhr confessed that the universalism of St. Paul—
"in Christ there is neither Jew nor Greek"—is singularly unhelp-
ful in the problem of the relation of "two religious *communities*
to each other."[35] He claimed it is Judaism's two-fold divergence
from the dominant type—ethnic *and* religious—which is the
Jews' "chief *offense* in the eyes of the majority."[36] The American
Christian majority, he exhorted, must "come to terms with the
stubborn will to live of the Jews as a peculiar people, both
religiously and ethnically." The Jewish problem can only be
solved if the Christians accept this fact and "cease to practice

tolerance *provisionally* in the hope that it will encourage assimilation ethnically and conversion religiously."[37] Niebuhr proposed, in place of provisional tolerance, "genuine tolerance" which the Christian can achieve in "both the moral and the *religious* spheres" only if he *"assumes* the *continued* refusal of the Jew to be assimilated. . . ."[38]

Then, after some words on the shared attitude of both "biblical faiths" to an historic revelation—an "offense both to the Greeks* and to modern culture"[39]—and a discussion of "common grace"[40] and "saving grace,"[41] he shifted from his title-topic—the presumably social relations of "Christians and Jews"†—to the relation of Christianity to Judaism. He began by adopting the definition of this relation proposed by the German Jewish philosopher, Franz Rosenzweig, which, in Niebuhr's words, defines it as "two religions with one center, worshipping the same God, but with Christianity serving the purpose of carrying the prophetic message to the Gentile world."†† Though "in some ways unsatisfactory to Christians," Niebuhr nevertheless adopted this definition as "better than almost all alternative definitions."[42] Certainly, he remarked, it is a better definition than those definitions (Saint Paul's, for example?) "which prompt Christian missionary activity among the Jews."[43]

Niebuhr then went to the heart of the matter: these missionary activities are "wrong," not because they fail, but because the two faiths despite differences are sufficiently alike for the Jew to find God "more easily in terms of his own religious heritage than by subjecting himself to the hazards of guilt feeling" which would

---

*Note here how Niebuhr has Jews and Christians scandalizing Greeks and modern culture, but St. Paul's Christ as scandal to the Jews is discreetly forgotten.

†By the time he gave his address Niebuhr had worked out a whole array of what are, essentially, theological equivalents for the well-known socio-cultural phenomenon of "parallel institutions": there's a revelation for "them," "general" revelation, and one for "us," "biblical" revelation, etc. In fact, Herberg as early as 1951—from the Jewish side—exhibited some exasperation at this trend: "Reinhold Niebuhr, it seems to me, has pushed the possibility of 'general' revelation just about as far as it will go without losing its biblical basis. . . ." *Judaism and Modern Man* (New York: Meridian Books, 1959), p. 255.

††Ibid., p. 108. A student of the development of Niebuhr's proposal should realize that this Rosenzweigian solution to the theological relations of American Jews and Christians had been proposed seven years earlier by Will Herberg in his *Judaism and Modern Man,* 1957, pp. 272–73, and he had compared Rosenzweig's way in Judaism to Niebuhr's as a Christian (p. 246). A year earlier, Herberg had written of Franz Rosenzweig's "Judaism of Personal Existence" for *Commentary* (Dec., 1950).

result from his converting to Christianity. But why does the Jew suffer guilt-feeling in converting to Christianity? Because, wrote Niebuhr—we are now at the very *kerygma* of civil religion, its remorseless dialectic of civility—because Christianity is "a faith which, whatever its excellencies, *must appear to* [*the Jew*] *as** a symbol of an oppressive majority culture."[44] To the Christian these historic Christian "symbols" may be "the bearer of an unconditioned message." But "to those outside the faith they are defaced by historic taints [of anti-Semitism]. Practically nothing," Niebuhr concluded, "can purify the symbol of Christ as the image of God in the imagination of the Jew. . . ."[45]

This argument has a very curious structure. Note, first, how the *Children of Light* distinction[46] between faith and its "expression" reappears; expression has now become—perhaps under the influence of Tillich—"symbol." Note also that Christian faith seems to exist only in its symbols, viz., "as it appears" to the Jew—"conditioned" (tainted)—or as it appears to the believer, i.e., as bearer of the "unconditioned." The "truth-value" of Christianity "in itself" seems to play no role. Note, further, that Christianity appears, to the Jew, as "culture" (an "oppressive majority" culture); and, further, that—given history—it *"must"* so appear to him; Jews are not free vis-à-vis Christianity to see it for what-in-itself it really is.

In this attitude of Niebuhr, it may be asked, is there not a stubborn residue of the same condescension to Jews that he is in the very act of disavowing? For Christians, like Niebuhr, are apparently able to understand not only their own Christianity and its true attitude to Jews, but also how Christianity must "look" to Jews. Christians, in other words, are able to take the role of Jews to Christianity, whereas Jews, for their part, are, by implication, deemed incapable of reciprocating by taking the role of Christians to themselves. Furthermore, Christians are the only ones who understand this whole process inasmuch as they alone understand that the Jewish *lack* of understanding is itself "understandable." Further, Jews are *expected* by Christians to be incapable of finding the Christian position on Jewish con-

---

*Recall his analysis of thirty-two years ago—see page 32—in which he explains the dismissal of a minister friend as due to the fact that his courage and loyalty to principle "will always *appear as* tactlessness from the perspective of those who don't agree with you."

version "understandable." And, finally, only Christians, it would seem, and not Jews, find this Jewish inability to understand in turn understandable.* Note, finally, a curious further implication of Niebuhr's proposal: namely, that even in the (one would have supposed) "privileged" matter of defining one's own religion's relation to another religion, Niebuhr is proposing that that other's "outsider" view of one's own religion—even if erroneous, nay, *because* it is erroneous—become normative for one's own definition of one's own religion.

The mind boggles! Theological courtesy would surely stalemate if a Jewish Alphonse were ever to appear in this situation and reply in kind to the exquisite *politesse* of this Protestant Gaston! It is clear that, with the advent of Niebuhr's rationale for abandoning all effort to convert the Jews, the "vocabulary of scandal"[47] has—for perhaps the first time—entered the sacred precincts of the Christian *kerygma* itself. Small wonder that Niebuhr's friend, Rabbi Hertzberg, detected here "a new theology."[48] Small wonder that Rabbi Stuart E. Rosenberg, describing it as "another way of saying that Jews are equal not only politically but also religiously,"[49] hailed the abandonment of the Christian mission to the Jews as "a major breakthrough" since "for the first time the voice that now speaks up for the equality [not just of Jews but] of Judaism does so *in the name of Christianity.*"[50]

The relative unconcern which Niebuhr demonstrated here for the inner, truth-value that Christianity has had for its believers had not gone unremarked. Irving Kristol had noted of Niebuhr, in another connection, that he "has been enticed by the democratic ethos into representing ideas in their public relations, rather than in their important, private ones."[51]—Enticed also, one should add, by one motif in his own Christianity and by the charity that has institutionalized itself into liberal democratic bourgeois civility, a civility that in turn "acts back upon" its bearers, forbidding them to take their own side in a quarrel.†

---

*Is this philo-Semitism? "To deny the gospel to the Jewish people," Sam Nadler, staff head of Jews for Jesus in New York, declares in an interview, "is the worst form of antisemitism . . . if the gospel is true—you're not being loving in being tolerant." D. Keith Mano, "Jews for Jesus," *National Review*, Sept. 30, 1977 (vol. 29, no. 38), p. 1126.

†Robert Frost once defined a liberal as someone who can't take his own side in a quarrel.

A declaration such as Niebuhr's had been, to be sure, in the Protestant theological wind for some time. Four years earlier, at the World Congress of Churches Convention at Evanston, a resolution calling for the conversion of the Jews was objected to by a number of leading Protestants because, in the words of Seymour Martin Lipset, "it would *embarrass* them in their relationships with their Jewish *friends.*" Lipset viewed this as indicating further growth in the new church of the "civic religion" of brotherhood, and concluded that "the Catholics, of course, are 'un-American' in this sense, since no good American should believe in the superiority of his own religion."[52] The American civil religion turns such a belief into a heresy.

It should be clear by now that Niebuhr's proposal to exclude Jews from Christ's universalistic mandate ("Going, therefore, teach ye *all* nations . . .") was not an impetuous *ad hoc* gesture. Civil religion exercises an unremitting pressure on traditional religions; it forces the traditional theologians into a defensive, apologetic posture. Before he realizes it, the apologist is enticed —to use Irving Kristol's words again—into representing theological ideas in their public rather than in their private relations. And for what particular "public" did Niebuhr represent these ideas? To what group was he referring when he preached and wrote? In a word, what was Niebuhr's "reference group"? It was Christianity's "cultured despisers." "My avocational interest as a kind of circuit rider in the colleges and universities," he wrote in his "Intellectual Autobiography," "has prompted an interest in the defense and justification of the Christian faith in a secular age, particularly among what Schleiermacher called Christianity's 'cultured despisers.' "[53]

One's intended or putative audience enters, often determines and "censors," the inner meaning of one's work. "What will *they* think?" one asks oneself. "How will it *appear* to *them?*" It is a curious fact of American Protestant theological history, but it seems clear that the "them" Niebuhr wrote for, the "them" before whose circumspection the renowned theist was careful to pass muster, was a group Morton G. White—a member—called, tellingly, "atheists for Niebuhr."[54]

Presumably, one cannot hold and interest for long an audience composed of agnostic and atheistic academicians, ADA and

NCCJ members—in a word—Christianity's "cultured despisers," without something happening to Christianity. And what
happens is not essentially different from what happened with
that other end-product of the liberal Protestant epoch, Norman
Vincent Peale: one gets a seemly Christianity "with all the offensive and scandalous edges smoothed off. . . ."[55] Scandal is traded
for scandal: so as not to scandalize the Jews, the Pauline "scandal to the Jews" is abandoned as a scandal to the Jews. Civil
religion with its discipline of appearances has brought Christianity full circle. Why, then, was the Christian mission to the Jews
abandoned by the Protestants? Not because Christ and Paul had
not commanded it (they had); not because it was false to Christianity (it was of its essence); but because of appearances: *it was
in bad taste.* As Marshall Sklare notes, by 1970 the Jewish community was publicly opposing the Christian mission to the Jews "on
the grounds that Reinhold Niebuhr had elaborated a decade
before," namely—in Sklare's words—because of "the unseemliness" of such evangelization.[56]

III.

The Price: The Imagination of Intolerance

Back in 1944, Niebuhr—while the war in Europe raged—had
spoken of the "present embarrassment" of Christians discussing
the religious issue with Jews when Jewish survival was in jeop-
ardy. The "embarrassment" in 1944, as Niebuhr defined it, was
the ancient one: the impossibility, for a Christian, of an "ethnic
church," claiming both particularity and universality. "In the
final analysis," he had concluded, "a nation cannot be a church,
though it must be gratefully recorded that the Jews have come
closer to this impossible task than any other people."[57]

Niebuhr's proposal twelve years later (1958) to end in principle the Christian mission to the Jews, gives inner acceptance, as
a Christian, to that "impossible task." Judaism has been accepted at its own self-estimation. In effect, a major spokesman
for one of the plural religions in America backed off from con-

frontation, controversy, and embarrassment with another of the tri-faith religions by conceding that they each have their "own" God. The civil religion secularized a churchly religion from the inside, so to speak. The civil acceptance of the situation of religious pluralism forced Niebuhr's Evangelical and Reformed Protestantism to return to henotheism.* An external situation worked an inner change; inner secularization overcame the dualism of provisional tolerance; *de facto* or practising henotheism became *de jure* or confessing henotheism.

The gods we encounter in antiquity are, the German-Jewish sociologist, Georg Simmel, tells us in his *Sociology of Religion,* "representatives of the energies of the group. . . . Except for Christianity the gods are, if not exclusively at least in part or in one of their aspects, the transcendental images of the unity of the group and should be understood as the unity of the homogenizing, the socializing, *function.*"[58] In the pluralistic-religions situation in America, the churchly religions reclaim their ancient socializing functions. Civil religion, indeed, looks at the particular churches and, from where it stands, sees this socializing function as their chief function. By "converting," so to speak, to civil religion, Niebuhr saw all the denominational religions—including Judaism—as group and ethnic religions, as henotheisms, coexisting tolerantly in a religious détente.[59]

Classical Christianity had begun by severing the individual from his ethnic group and his family. "The God of Christianity," Simmel wrote, "is the God of the individual. . . . The individual stands before his God in absolute self-reliance. . . . For Antiquity and the ethnic world the picture seems quite different. The god of each closed group is its private god, who cares for it or punishes it; and the gods of other groups are accepted as equally real."[60] With the acceptance by Niebuhr of Judaism as "equally real," an era of religious embarrassment came to an end. Historical and "incivil" religion yielded to civil religion.

Some years later, in a Perry Miller *Festschrift,* Niebuhr con-

---

*Henotheism: a stage in religious development antedating radical monotheism, in which one believes in one supreme god for one's own particular region, race or nation, without denying the existence of other gods for other regions, races, or nations. The tolerant message of henotheism is: to each his own. The history of Israel, Niebuhr's brother, Helmut Richard Niebuhr, writes, "is marked by an almost continuous struggle between social henotheism and radical monotheism. . . ." H. Richard Niebuhr, *Radical Monotheism and Western Culture* (New York: Harper & Bros., 1960), p. 57.

gratulated the historian for a parallel achievement in liquidating an embarrassment in American secular history. Prior to Miller's Calvinist historiography, our Puritan secular "fathers," Niebuhr wrote, "embarrassed us, because their theocracy seemed an inauspicious forerunner of our vaunted democratic civilization."[61] After Miller's work, they "ceased to embarrass our democratic hearts."[62] After Niebuhr's work—"Reinhold Niebuhr and Our Embarrassment"—neither Christian nor Jew need ever again be awkward in each other's theological company.

What, then, is the upshot of what Niebuhr has done? What would a "cost-benefit" analysis show? Is this an exercise in expiatory masochism or a genuine act of public contrition? Is it shame or is it guilt? If guilt, is it "real" or "neurotic" guilt? Is it a plea for tolerance or a "sellout"? Is it Christian charity or the "higher" *noblesse oblige?* In a word, has Niebuhr removed, as Elmer Wentz charged, "the offense of the cross" from Christianity?[63]

In the brutal logic of ideas, tolerance and particularism go (belong) together like a horse and carriage. The tolerance of Brahmans, Simmel notes, is "the supplementation of their particularism." In fact, "the all-exclusive relation of a particular god to a specific circle of believers *requires* the religious adherents to admit that there are other gods besides their own—the gods of other groups. Believers in a specific god are allowed no other gods besides him," Simmel concludes, "not because they do not exist, rather . . . because they *do* exist (otherwise there would be no reason for alarm), although they are, to be sure, not the right ones for this particular group."[64]

The logic that expects intolerance from universalistic monotheism is but the other side of the tolerance that goes with particularism and henotheism. By granting an "edict of toleration," Niebuhr transformed his Reformed Christianity into a variant of civil religion. But, as Simmel saw so clearly, "Christianity does not concede tolerance. To it tolerance would be as logically contradictory as intolerance is to the particularistic religions."[65] In Roman and Greek religion, the gods were fused with the social group; in ancient Judaism, as Philip Rieff notes, "an identity of culture and society" existed in undifferentiated solidarity.[66] Christianity's advent, Simmel contends,

tremendously revolutionized this solidarity of the God with the social unity as an always particularistic trait by rejecting all other gods
besides the one it confessed, not only in its own behalf but indeed
in behalf of all the world. The God of Christianity is the God not
only of those who believe in Him, but the God of the universe. This
God not only lacks the exclusiveness and jealousy of a personally
owned god; the Christian religion indeed is committed to bringing
its God to every soul, for He is anyhow the God of this soul. Conversion to Christianity only affirms an already established fact.[67]

To renounce in principle the theological necessity for Jewry's
"conversion to Christianity," as Niebuhr did in 1958, is, clearly,
to renounce a crucial element in the Christian creed. Niebuhr
wished to be Christian and tolerant at the same time (not tolerant only in the personal sense, but in the structurally religious
sense which carried him inexorably toward henotheism). Furthermore, he grounded tolerance in the Gospel; he legitimated
tolerance biblically. He was tolerant in the name of Christianity.
Chesterton would no doubt charge him with sentimentality.
"The sentimentalist . . . is the man," Chesterton wrote, "who
wants to eat his cake and have it. He has no sense of honor about
ideas; he will not see that one must pay for an idea as for
anything else. He will have them all at once in one wild intellectual harem, no matter how much they quarrel and contradict
each other."[68]

What did Niebuhr pay for the idea of tolerance? What is the
price-tag of conversion to civil religion? Jesus said: "He who is
not for me is against me." Only one sociologist of religion has
seen this fanatical—or, at least, fanaticizable—saying for the
momentous lordly word that it is. "The saying, 'He who is not
for me, is against me,' " Georg Simmel writes, "is one of the
greatest turning points of world history in the sociology of religion. Someone believing in Wotan or Vitzliputzli is not necessarily 'against' Zeus or Baal: each god is the concern only of his
believers. . . . The God of the Christians was the first to extend
His sphere of influence from those who believed in Him to those
who did not. Of all the vital powers He was the first to break
through the exclusiveness of the social group. . . ."[69]

To religions rooted in the particularism of tribal, national,
and ethnic groups, such a concept of such a God, with such a

universalistic claim and such an omnipotence, and consequently, with such an absolute intolerance, is unthinkable, is, literally, unimaginable. It is simply, as Simmel concludes, "beyond the reach of these groups' imagination." Niebuhr paid for civil religion, then—since one must pay for an idea as for anything else—by surrendering the imagination of intolerance. The poetry of this literalism is simply beyond the reach of civil religion and its quotidian rites, the rites of civility. But it is not beyond the reach of the Anglo-Irish poet, W. B. Yeats:

> Odour of blood when Christ was slain
> Made all Platonic tolerance vain
> And vain all Doric discipline.*

*William Butler Yeats, "Two Songs from a Play," from *The Tower*, in eds., Peter Allt and Russell K. Alspach, *The Variorum Edition of the Poems of W. B. Yeats* (New York: Macmillan, 1957), p. 438.

Chapter 4

------◆◀◆▶◆------

CATHOLIC: A TALE
OF TWO JESUITS

------◆◀◆▶◆------

*Now that there are, and can be, no longer any exclusive national religions, we should
tolerate all creeds which show tolerance to others, so long as their dogmas contain nothing
at variance with the duties of the citizen. But anyone who dares to say "Outside the Church
there can be no salvation," should be banished from the State, unless the State be the Church
and the Prince the Pontiff. Such a dogma is good only where the government is theocratic.
In any other it is pernicious.*　　　　　　　　　　　　　　　*—Jean-Jacques Rousseau*
　　　　　　　　　　　　　　　　　　　　　　　　　The Social Contract

Leonard Feeney, S.J.

Father Leonard Feeney and the Boston Heresy Case was a kind
of "Last Hurrah" of unreconstructed, ultramontane, Tridentine
Catholicism in the United States. The controversy that sur-
rounded the Jesuit priest and poet and his interpretation of
Catholicism's ancient formula—"Outside the Church there is no
salvation" *(extra ecclesiam nulla salus)*—was a kind of dress re-
hearsal for the Catholic church-state controversies of the fifties,
and Vatican Council II of the sixties, which were to center
around another ancient formula: *extra ecclesiam nullum ius* which,
freely translated, means "error has no rights." If Feeney's heresy was a heresy from the Right, construing the former formula
strictly and literally—yes, there is no, repeat: no, salvation outside the Church—making his position "holier than the Pope's,"
the leader of the 1950s church-state controversy—another Irish
Catholic Jesuit, named John Courtney Murray—led an "opening
to the Left" in church-state theory.

During the forties Catholics were achieving greater middle
class status as World War II ended and, under the G. I. Bill, were

flocking to the elite secular universities. Seminaries and fashionable Catholic prep schools like Portsmouth Priory (now Portsmouth Abbey) were sending their graduates on to Harvard, Yale, and Princeton; a mood of relaxation and liberalism—and attendant apostasy—was in the air. There had been founded in 1940, in Harvard Square, a center for Harvard-Radcliffe students called Saint Benedict Center. Its relation to Harvard was comparable to what on college campuses the Newman Club had been, or what Hillel was for Jewish students. Beginning in 1941, Father Leonard Feeney, popular essayist and poet, began addressing the students every Thursday night.[1]

Father Feeney was soon making many converts among non-Catholic, wealthy, often patrician students. (Concurrently, in New York, Monsignor Fulton J. Sheen was giving instructions to young Henry Ford II in preparation for his forthcoming marriage to Anne McDonnell, a member of the well-known Murray clan.) Increasingly, Feeney attacked Harvard, the agnosticism and atheism of its professors, and the Catholic and ex-Catholic members of its student body. His famous "Thursday nights" became a kind of oral *God and Man at Harvard.* His brilliance and aggressive proselytizing had soon made Father Feeney a large number of disciples and not a few enemies. By September 1946 St. Benedict Center had started its own magazine called *From the Housetops,* in scriptural allusion to the admonition that followers of Christ should not whisper but should "shout" their faith "from the housetops." Increasingly, the message shouted was that there is "no salvation outside the Catholic Church."

Father Feeney's *From the Housetops* was founded not primarily to win Protestant converts but to attack Catholic liberals. It was to be a weapon in an intra-Catholic quarrel. Like its lineal post-Vatican II descendant of twenty years later, L. Brent Bozell's *Triumph* magazine, it was created to proclaim an unembarrassed and militant Catholicism and to stem the "leakage" from the Church that was becoming increasingly evident. The particular circumstances surrounding the founding of *From the Housetops* are revealing. Two undergraduate Harvard Catholic GIs had told the Center people, Catherine Clarke relates, that they had just been talking to " 'a fellow who's left the Church. He and four others. Five of them. And they all come from that Catholic preparatory school in Portsmouth, Rhode Island' "[2] [the Portsmouth Priory—now Abbey—School]. This disclosure was a kind of "aha" experience for the Feeney circle. It "made our duty clear. Someone had to tell the truth before it was too late."[3] But, more important even than the truth—for wasn't Catholic truth being told, more or less?—was the *manner* of its telling. "The full, unequivocal, uncompromised message of Jesus Christ," Mrs. Clarke recalls,

> had to be thundered in the world again. It could not merely be told. It had to be shouted, bellowed, because the world was deaf, asleep, already half-dead. *Polite* talking would not wake it, nor would vague reference, large gesture, platitudinous utterance. "Never give offense" seemed to be the Catholic policy of the day. We knew that it was impossible to tell the truth, and not to give offense. Christ had given offense to the Pharisees of His day. . . .

From the Housetops, Mrs. Clarke concludes, would "borrow from the saints and doctors their thunder. . . ."[4] A "God with Thunder" was soon to be shouted in Harvard Square. And most of the shouting would be about politeness and civility.

And with good reason, since, as we have seen, the logic of modernization generates civility. All the traditionalist religions, Protestant, Catholic, and Jewish, share a generic "fundamentalism" that collides with the differentiating thrust of the modernization process. The cutting edge of modernization is differentiation, professionalization, specialization, the division of labor, the separation of private feeling from public expression, of church from state, of science from philosophy and philosophy from theology. Every form of anti-modernism is a version, then, of de-differentiation, of what French Catholics once called "integralism," or wholeness. Resentment of modernity will always come to a head in resentment of civility because the regime of bourgeois civility, a regime which keeps everything in its place and has a place for everything, is the social guarantor of the achieved differentiations of modernity. Civility, as the social institutionalization of modernity's separations—of church from state, sacred from secular, private from public—becomes a symbol of all the losses that modernity has entailed. It reminds us of our grief; it becomes our grievance.*

It is my thesis that, beneath all the civility and differentiated, refined restraints of even the modernizing theologians we study —Niebuhr, Murray, and Hertzberg—there lies an unreconstructed, not to say fanatical, "true believer." Scratch a Niebuhr and you'll find a Billy Graham; scratch a Murray and find a Feeney; scratch a Hertzberg and find a Kahane. These latter act out without restraint, without civility, an aspect of the lost "integralism" the others have repressed in their forced march into the civil disciplines of modernity. Something in the most refined liberal Catholic resonated to Father Feeney's wild campaign. Something in the most reformed liberal Jew resonates to the "low road" taken by Rabbi Meir Kahane's Jewish Defense League (J.D.L.).

I think, in this matter of civility and its professional decorums, of the late great Catholic philosopher, Jacques Maritain, a convert from Protestantism, who, in his first book, after three hundred pages of the most careful analysis of the philosophy of Henri Bergson, asked whether it is allowed to a professional philosopher, in his search for objective data, to investigate the possibility that God may have revealed himself to man. And he wrote movingly in 1913 a "from the housetops" of his own. I quote at length:

> Truly, philosophers play a strange game. They know very well that one thing alone counts, and that all their medley of subtle discussions relates to one single question: why are we born on this earth? And they also know that they will never be able to answer it. Nevertheless they continue sedately to amuse themselves. Do they not see that people come to them from all points of the compass, not with a desire to partake of their subtlety but because they hope to receive from them one word of life? If they have such words why do they not *cry them from the housetops*, asking their disciples to give, if necessary, their very blood for them? If they have no such words why do they allow people to believe that they will receive from them something which they cannot give? For mercy's sake, if ever God has spoken, if in some place in the world, were it on the gibbet of one

---

*See Peter Marris's brilliant study of the modernization process as grief-work in *Loss and Change* (New York: Pantheon Books, 1974).

crucified, He has sealed His truth, tell us; that is what you must teach. Or are you indeed masters in Israel only to be ignorant of these things?"*

It is as though the great passionate classical theological commitments are repressed by modernization and are forced to lead a double life, and occasionally erupt uncontrollably as a passionate *cri de coeur* in the decorous, professional precincts of philosophy and history. The late Sir Lewis Namier, the Anglo-Jewish historian, for example, in the midst of a long and disciplined account of the social foundations of the English gentry in the age of the American Revolution, suddenly breaks off and writes the heart-breaking plea:

Only one nation has survived for two thousand years, though an orphan—my own people, the Jews. But then in the God-given Law we have enshrined the authority of a State, and in the God-promised Land the idea of a Mother-Country; through the centuries from Mount Sinai we have faced Arets Israel, our land. Take away either, and we cease to be a nation; let both live again, and we shall be ourselves once more.†

Is this any different, fundamentally, from the story historian Judd Teller recounts about A. M. ("Abe") Rosenthal, who ranks, as executive editor, just under publisher A. O. ("Punch") Sulzberger on *The New York Times*? Rosenthal back in 1948 was a member of the *Times*'s U.N. staff, and through many months of the Palestine debate preceding the vote to establish Israel as a state he had been "pokerfaced and noncommittal." "But when

---

*Jacques Maritain, *Bergsonian Philosophy and Thomism*, 2nd. ed., translated by Mabelle L. Andison and J. Gordon Andison (New York: Philosophical Library, 1955; originally published in 1913), pp. 297, 298 (emphasis mine). In the Preface to the second French edition (1929) Maritain regretted the "insistence" of the tone of his book and notes that since being right is such an undeserved privilege, "it should always make one feel apologetic—a form of politeness we owe to truth. Christ, when he taught, proclaimed aloud the divine truth; that truth should be *shouted from the housetops*. Human truths require in the telling a voice more modestly pitched. If the decisiveness of the affirmation should correspond to the certitude of the proof, the modulation should be proportioned to the difficulties of the search." *Ibid.*, pp. 12, 13 (emphasis mine). Maritain is struggling here with the inevitable conflict of faith and charity, truth and love, certainty and civility. The encounter is a spiritual ordeal.

†Sir Lewis Namier, *England in the Age of the American Revolution* (London: Macmillan & Co., Ltd., 1930), p. 18.

the news of Truman's recognition came through, followed by a General Assembly roll call which approved, *post-factum,* Israel's statehood," Teller writes, Rosenthal "flopped into a wheelchair that had been standing nearby and raced down the corridors shouting 'Yipee'!"* Modern professionalism imposes a modulated "even-handedness" on the passionate premodern religious commitments of the human heart. Most "true believers" in Protestantism, Catholicism, and Judaism settle their accounts with the regime of civil religion by various accommodating strategies. Father Feeney chose not to live this kind of double life.

Father Feeney and his band of disciples and converts, by insisting on the ancient formula *extra ecclesiam nulla salus,* and giving it a rigorist, intransigent interpretation, were soon in trouble. Harvard College complained to Archbishop Cushing. Catholic Boston College resisted the Feeney interpretation; students and priests took sides. The problem was both theological and sociological.

Theologically it was the ancient Catholic triumphalist claim: the one hope *(unica spes),* the only-begotten son *(unigenitum),* and the one true Church *(unam sanctam catholicam et apostolicam ecclesiam).* Theologically, also, there was the ancient insistence on *universalistic* charity, giving rise to the problem of the *massa damnata:* what of those who haven't heard the message of salvation? who lived before its proclamation (time), or outside its ambience (geographically)? How many are saved? How many lost? Is God "cruel," Calvinistic, and predestinarian? Or "loving," "tolerant," and Universalist Unitarian?

A "sociology of knowledge" reading of the *extra ecclesiam nulla salus* maxim, however, brings us closer to our story of Father Feeney and his endeavor to reconstruct not only Catholic ecclesiology but Catholic social reality in order to check further Catholic apostasy. "Father Feeney used to say," Mrs. Clarke recalls, "that the tragedy of conversions to the Faith was that after the catechumen had finished instruction and had received the sacraments, he had no Catholic culture into which to return

---

*Judd L. Teller, *Strangers and Natives: The Evolution of the American Jew from 1921 to the Present* (New York: Delacorte Press, 1968), p. 216.

with his Faith. He was obliged to go back into our secularized society, where it was impossible to tell a Catholic from a non-Catholic. There used to be a time when this was not so, when becoming a Catholic meant a conversion in a total sense." Thus, when a research physicist at Harvard was converted by Father Feeney, he resigned his Harvard position and took a teaching post at Catholic Boston College in order that he would be teaching "in the same building with the Blessed Sacrament, [where] there would be a crucifix above his desk, [where] he would have priests for his colleagues."[5] But, instead of finding there the supportive Catholic community he sought, he was dismissed for advocating the "extremist" doctrine that there is no salvation outside the Church.

It is significant that as the crisis between Saint Benedict Center and the Boston Archdiocese deepened, the Center people and their historian, Mrs. Clarke, saw the problem, increasingly, as one of the Boston Irish "minding their manners" as they performed before their status audience, Boston's WASP Brahmins. Noting the "formality and restraint" of Boston Irish Catholicism, its weird and difficult regime, Mrs. Clarke remarked: "Irish theology and Plymouth Rock manners . . ."[6]

It was the growth of these well-bred, tolerant manners, the phenomenon of Irish Catholic "Liberal Catholicism," that Father Feeney and his Center conceived of themselves as trying to stem. *Commonweal* magazine was the weekly voice of this liberal Catholicism. A "Commonweal Catholic," in Feeney's circle, was a Catholic who was fastidiously discreet about his Catholicism. He was "passing." A liberal Catholic, Mrs. Clarke writes, is one who always knows "how God should behave. God's behavior is invariably made to conform with the Liberal's own fine feelings . . . [he knows] how an incarnate God should talk and behave . . . [he] does not like the statement 'No Salvation Outside the Church' [not because the statement is false but] because 'it isn't nice.' "[7]

Several of Father Feeney's Harvard disciples broke with Lowell House and its elite classicist housemaster, John H. Finley, Jr. Soon Feeney forbade the twenty-four Jesuits studying at Harvard from coming to the Center because they disedified their Harvard-Radcliffe classmates and undid the work of the Center.[8]

Temple Morgan, one of Feeney's patrician converts, a few months from graduation and planning to become a Jesuit priest, ostentatiously resigned from Harvard. One of the Deans of Harvard College, Morgan's cousin, visited Father Feeney. Morgan's family was outraged, and Archbishop Cushing was approached. The Boston hierarchy "came in for unusual attention at this time, in the form of dinner invitations from people who had heretofore held them at arm's length." Jesuits, the sons of St. Ignatius Loyola, were also lionized. "This was a strange alliance," remarked Mrs. Clarke, revising the famous quatrain to read:

> And this is good old Boston
> The home of the bean and the cod,
> Where the *Loyolas* speak only to Cabots,*
> And the Cabots speak only to God.[9]

Meanwhile, writings in *From the Housetops* were escalating their case against liberal Catholicism which had "blunted" the sharp weapons of Christ, wrapping the "virile" doctrines of the church in a "conspiracy of silence," so completely covering the "no salvation outside the Church" doctrine "with reservations and vicious distinctions as to ruin its meaning and destroy the effect of its challenge." Catholic truth is made a sad story "for which we need apologize." "Sentimental theology" tells Christ's "stern" story in a "subdued and hesitant voice."[10] The Boston Catholic establishment was both enraged and ashamed that Father Feeney "should be talking so plainly." Plans were soon afoot to close St. Benedict Center not because it was not telling Catholic truth, "but because it was not telling the truth in quiet and measured words. . . . The Center was shouting from the housetops, and this was offending people." Sister Madeleva, President of St. Mary's at Notre Dame, visited the Center; she "told us, in her lady-like manner, that nobody goes to hell."[11]

Finally, the axe fell. On August 25, 1948, the Jesuit Provincial

---

*The third line of this quatrain is the origin, of course, of Mrs. Clarke's title, *The Loyolas and the Cabots: The Story of the Boston Heresy Case*. In the Foreword she calls attention to the importance of the "strange connection" contained in this title which, as she conceives it, is the essence of her story of the Boston heresy case.

ordered Father Feeney to leave Cambridge and go to Holy
Cross College in Worcester. Insisting that obedience to the
order would misleadingly give a doctrinal dispute the appearance of a disciplinary matter, Father Feeney refused. "Father
Feeney was asked to leave the diocese because the truth he was
teaching was embarrassing to too many people," wrote Mrs.
Clarke, including "social Catholics with Harvard connections.
. . . The Church in Boston was saying 'Hush, hush! Father
Feeney. This isn't the time to preach the doctrine of No Salvation Outside the Church. . . .' " Boston College then dismissed
its three "Feeney" teachers for teaching ideas *"leading to bigotry
and intolerance."* Appeals were taken to the General of the Society
of Jesus in Rome, and finally, to the Pope, but to no avail. The
doctrine of "tolerance," Mrs. Clarke concluded, "amounts now
to a species of tyranny."[12] Denouncing Feeney had become a
"loyalty oath" for liberal Catholics.

Modern civility, lineal descendant of Victorian respectability,
holds us accountable for our appearances. Any member of the
historic religious communities, Protestant, Catholic, or Jewish,
who violates the rites of sensitivity institutionalized in civil religion—be he unwilling or unable to practice them—does so at his
peril. Father Feeney defended himself before the American As-
sistant to the General of the Jesuits, Father Vincent McCormick,
S.J., who had been his teacher, long ago, at Woodstock College,
Maryland, and concluded a litany of his own defects by admitting that " 'I am not overtactful in taking into account what
non-Catholics will think when I talk.' "[13]

"I am not overtactful." Was Feeney bragging or complaining
or confessing here? This "defect" of tactlessness amounts, in
the end, as we saw in the case of Niebuhr, to a lack of "sensitivity" as to how one's own religious convictions will *appear* to
others who do not share them. In the end, Feeney was silenced
by Church authorities. Soon, the Center was closed, and placed
off limits to Harvard-Radcliffe Catholic students. Only the core,
the school, remained open in April, 1949.

Father Robert C. Hartnett, S.J., the editor of the Jesuit weekly,
America, wrote an article on the "no salvation" question, taking
issue with Father Feeney. In a generous but misguided note to
his fellow Jesuits, Hartnett wrote that he hoped he has written

"inoffensively"![14] Father Feeney was offended precisely by the inoffensiveness, by the modulation the *extra ecclesiam* maxim underwent in Father Hartnett's hands. Feeney attacked Hartnett's euphemistic reinterpretation:

> All the "Christianity" of the dogma seems to come from Father Hartnett's kindly presentation of it, for the sake of well-meaning Americans. The "bigotry" and "intolerance" of the doctrine is made to come from the way it was originally devised and phrased by the Church . . . the Liberal Catholic clergy, . . . particularly the Liberal Jesuits, are phrasing the teachings of the Church differently for American ears than they were once phrased for European ears by the saints and doctors of the Church.

Their "softly-phrased evasions," Father Feeney continued, are what is called "the 'charitable' presentation of doctrine, or the adaptation of it to the modern mind. What this dishonesty really does," he concluded, "is to kill off the chastity of truth. . . ."[15]

Here Father Feeney was, of course, correct. Charity in the form of civility was softening and eroding the old intransigent truths. Ancient, uncouth truth was being polished up and manicured. A rhetoric of modulation was staging a take-over. Now Feeney was a poet as well as a theologian. He knew that *how* something is said is at least as important as *what* is said. In the nervous reinterpretations of the Hartnetts of the Church, adverbs and adjectives were no longer modifying verbs and nouns; they were devouring them. (Jewish thinkers, as we shall see, perform a similar rhetorical massage on their equivalently embarrassing "chosen people" doctrine.) Feeney's keen nostrils detected the civilized workings of civil religion.

There was an ethnic dimension to this Boston heresy case, too. Feeney, lest we forget, was Irish. Deep in the passionate recesses of Feeney's ancestral consciousness an ancient equation reigned: for Catholic Irish to euphemize the *no salvation outside the Church* formula was to kowtow to the Anglo-Irish Ascendancy. As in the collisions of other immigrant subcultures with the civil culture, to modulate is to betray. Immigrants and immigrant intellectuals *live* metaphors. ("Cossack!," novelist Herbert Gold muttered as we walked away after enduring a cop's frisking in Morningside Park years ago.)

Besides an ethnic, there was also a national dimension to the Boston Heresy Case. Feeney felt that the authority structure of the European Church was wilting in America. It no longer gave *commands*. Civil religion in America inflates enormously the occasions for "piacular ritual," as Durkheim called it, or "remedial interchange" as Erving Goffman calls it. Any untoward appearances must quickly be accounted for or apologized for. Any intrusion into the sacred precincts of the self, any *command*—even those backed by political or ecclesiastical authority—must be softened into a request. In May of 1949, Archbishop Cushing called Father Feeney, asking him if he "would like to" come to the Chancery to hear a letter from the Holy See concerning his doctrinal errors. Feeney knew that this civil American *interrogative*—would he like to come?—remedies the European Catholic *imperative* Cushing had received: Father Feeney had been condemned by the Supreme Sacred Congregation of the Holy Office—"the Inquisition"—and *commanded* to cease and desist in the promulgation of doctrinal error. Feeney, never for a moment uncertain of the structural elements—modernity and its civility—at work in the tragedy that had befallen him, replied to Cushing with the query: "Why such a *polite invitation*, Your Excellency? . . . why don't you give me an *order* to come and listen to it?"[16]

As Erving Goffman observes, "the value of transforming a virtual violation into a request is recognized so broadly *in our society* that a whole style is available whereby . . . all compellings are clothed, howsoever lightly, as requests."[17] This liberal American "style" that steers clear even of the appearances of old-fashioned authority is not all mere cynical manipulation, as some of its critics contend. It is also non-utilitarian, an expressive interpersonal rite in the civil religion's cult of the sacred individual.

Feeney, in any case, refused Archbishop—later Cardinal—Cushing's "polite invitation," and so had to wait to read the condemnation of his doctrine by the Holy See when it was duly promulgated in *The Pilot*, official organ of the Archdiocese of Boston, on September 3rd, 1949. Shortly after, on the afternoon of October 28, he received from Rome, in Latin, a notification even more grievous to him personally than that of September

3rd. Without reading it, he gathered his remnant, the seventy
students who had remained with him, and announced: "My dear
boys and girls, I have been dismissed from the Jesuit Order."[18]

Before going on to our other Jesuit, John Courtney Murray,
and to the church-state controversy of the 1950s and 1960s—
ostensibly about another Latin maxim, *extra ecclesiam nullam ius*—
let us examine the full range of the "Boston heresy case" of the
1940s. It amplifies in several directions.

In the post-war era Catholics were already quite "at home" in
the secular world. Their actual behavior, their actual "assimilation," had outrun its legitimations. Father Hartnett's "soft-
spoken" reconstruction of the Catholic "chosenness" teaching
merely legitimated in theory what, in practice, had already been
institutionalized in innumerable ways (interfaith meetings,
"mixed marriages," suburban social intercourse). Upper-class,
prep-school Catholics, as we have seen, sensed the barrier to
social acceptance in the general uncouthness of Feeney's intransigent stand and were predictably "shocked." Robert F.
Kennedy, who had attended Portsmouth Priory School, had
heard, Hugh Sidey recalls, while attending Harvard, "a cleric
declare that all non-Catholics were going to hell. 'He was in-
censed,' Sidey reports, 'and even though he was a guest he
disagreed openly with the man . . . [and] stoutly insisted that no
Catholic had a right to teach this.' As it happened, the cleric was
later excommunicated for this teaching."[19]

We can, for example, view Feeney's attacks on Harvard liberalism and the increasingly urbane liberal culture of Catholicism,
as the theological forerunner, in the 1940s, of what were to
become in the 1950s Senator McCarthy's *political* attacks on the
"pin-striped Harvard pinkoes" infesting the State Department.
(These same gentlemen, by the way, would return in the 1960s
as the deplored "Arabists," this time as guests of the Jewish
imagination.) What Robert Kennedy had repudiated in Feeney-
ism, he later swallowed as McCarthyism. For urban Irish Catholics and East European Jews alike, a lingering fundamentalist
mind-set,loosed from its religious moorings and lacking the option of nativism open to Protestants, easily secularized itself into
a fanatical and ideological politics. In large part, writes Jack

Newfield, "it was [Robert] Kennedy's cultural conditioning as a Boston [Irish] Catholic that made it so easy for him to make a mistake of the magnitude of working for—and admiring—Joe McCarthy. For Kennedy to drift into the atavistic subculture of McCarthyism was as logical as for a Jew at [New York] City College in the 1930s to become a Marxist."[20]

An accompanying irony was that the Feeney heresy, with its "Good Soldier Schweik" look of being "holier than the Pope," caught the Boston Catholic authorities completely off guard. *Pas d'ennemi à droit,* "no enemies on the right," was one truism they felt they could count on. Father O'Donnell, dean of the Graduate School, Boston College, remarked to one of his about-to-be-dismissed ultra ultramontane teachers, who pleaded "academic freedom" to teach the *extra ecclesiam* doctrine: " 'It is very strange that the first time the question of academic liberty arises here *we* should be to the 'left' against an extremely 'right' position!' "[21]

There was a certain strangeness, too, in the miscasting of Archbishop Cushing as an obsequious prelate seeking accommodation with the Boston Brahmins. This prelate with the Irish common touch, whose gravelly-voiced unctionless words would rasp across America a decade later as he delivered the Invocation at President Kennedy's inauguration, hardly fit the role. A populist man of the plain cloth, he later summed up his point of view on the Feeney case: " 'We are told there is no salvation outside the church—nonsense!,' the prelate said. 'Nobody can tell me that Christ died on Calvary for any select group.' "[22]

In the end, ironically, Father Feeney needed Protestants to make his case. "There is not an informed Protestant living," he said, "who, in his heart, does not look upon Father Hartnett's interpretation of the dogma No Salvation Outside the Church, as anything but sheer casuistry and subterfuge."[23] John Sutherland Bonnell, the Presbyterian minister, vigorously concurred and defended the Feeney interpretation as the orthodox Catholic one.[24] Harvard, too, ended up defending Feeney's position as the orthodox one, and emissaries brought words of encouragement.[25] The reaction of the Protestant Nativist, Paul Blanshard, who had received considerable notoriety in the forties and fifties as an anti-Catholic publicist, was to add a note of comedy. He was furious at the Pope's excommunication of Father Feeney. Instead of rejoicing at these signs of a growing Catholic liberalism, a development, presumably, his indefatigable circuit-riding had played some not inconsiderable role in bringing about, he refused to believe what was occurring before his eyes. (It would take Vatican II to instruct him.) He simply reset his sights and mocked "the liberal make-believe adopted by Archbishop Cushing."[26] As for the Pope who excommunicated Father Feeney, Blanshard wrote: "For the sake of appearances the Vatican nominally stood by its archbishop and his synthetic liberalism in the Feeney case. Then, when Archbishop Cushing was due to receive a red hat [be made a Cardinal] at a Papal consistory, he was conspicuously passed over."[27]

Some of the Jewish reactions to the Feeney heresy embody the same ambivalence as Blanshard's. Princeton philosopher and "religionist" Walter Kaufmann is an example. (Princeton was later to have its own Feeney brouhaha in the person of Father Hugh Halton.) Kaufmann wrote a curious poem called "Father Feeney." The final stanza reads:

> Now even Feeney ought to know,
> if he is right then he is wrong,
> for he himself does not belong:
> where does he think that he will go?[28]

To the translator of Rabbi Leo Baeck's *Judaism and Christianity* —"one of the most important polemics ever launched against Christianity," as Kaufmann describes it in his "Leo Baeck: A Biographical Introduction"[29]—the silencing of Father Feeney and his militant and, in the American sense, intolerant Christianity was a pleasing event. But, as with Blanshard, it was a mixed pleasure. Professor Kaufmann was also discomfitted by the Catholic Church's excommunication of Feeney and its public disavowal of the strict construction of the *extra ecclesiam* doctrine. For was this not an omen that Catholic orthodoxy was updating itself *(aggiornamento)*, becoming more modern, liberal, and relevant? And were not its chances for survival and success enhanced by such renewal? The Protestant theologian William Hamilton has analyzed what he calls "the Walter Kaufmann syndrome," in which there is an attempt to fixate a religion at some point in its past, making that past normative, because such a religionist likes his "theological foes to be as orthodox as possible so they can be rejected as irrelevant."[30] Hence the curiously mixed tone of Kaufmann's poem on Feeney: there is the element of *schadenfreude* in the paradox that the very Pontiff whose fealty Feeney had so proudly proclaimed has excommunicated him. But this news was disturbing: would Rome soon be joining Reformed Protestantism and Reform Judaism—Rabbi Baeck's Judaism—in leaving the old time religion behind?

There is inconsistency, comedy, and there is tragedy in a man so sophisticated as Feeney trapped in a "fundamentalist" posture. One part of his self going against another part. He saw the Church's position as a sell-out to the genteel tradition of Boston. He missed—or did he?—the inexorable workings of civility as different groups confront each other in a pluralistic society. Sociologist Robert K. Merton asks, "How does it happen that some select the Joneses to keep up with, others the Cabots, or the Cassidys, and finally that some don't try to keep up at all?"[31] The liberalizing Catholic Loyolas had not *selected* the Cabots to keep up with. They were simply living out the value-system of the culture. To them Father Feeney *had* to appear gauche and bigoted. What to him was *fides vere intrepida* was to them the claim to religious superiority, fanaticism, and vulgar group narcissism. To Feeney their urbane stance was a pusillanimous betrayal of the faith. Civil religion heard Feeney to be saying: "Holier than thou." Feeney heard back from them: "Urbaner than thou."

Father Leonard Feeney was the son of a solidly middle-class Massachusetts family. His father was an insurance executive. Two brothers were priests (one a Jesuit). Father Feeney was, before the Boston heresy case, perhaps the best known American Jesuit poet. Paradoxical as it may seem, poets make the best fanatics (most fanatics don't *look* very poetical, I concede). He refused to yield his affection for what critic John Crowe Ransom called "substances." In defending concrete "substances" which he loves, the poet often becomes abstract—i.e., fanatical—about everything else, excepting the thing he loves. For Feeney any move by the Church toward a universalist view, viz., that, ultimately, everyone is saved—either by their "invincible ignorance" or by their more modern "sincerity"—was, fundamentally, unpoetical, unimaginative.

———◆◀●▶◆———

John Courtney Murray, S.J.

A prescient friend said thirty years ago, "God help the Church of England if the Church of Rome ever learns good manners."
                                                 —*Martin Jarrett-Kerr, C.SS.R.*
                                                           "E pur si muove"

An honest ballot and social decorum among Catholics will do more for God's glory and the salvation of souls than midnight flagellations or Compostellan pilgrimages.
                                                 —*Archbishop Ireland, 1891*

I.

"What we abhor is feigning."

After this "Last Hurrah" in Boston, we turn to a very different kind of Jesuit, John Courtney Murray, whose church-state work legitimates the integration and participation of Catholics in the pluralistic society of late twentieth century America. If modernization, as has been said, is the "moral center of our time," Father Murray has lived intensely at that center, in this oldest of new nations, leading the Catholic community into the "take-off" of full participation in its national, political, and industrial life. In his great legitimation dispute, he waged a two-front war: against the Feeneys—in this case, Father Joseph C. Fenton and Father Francis J. Connell—and against the Protestants and secularists. Father Fenton was the conservative editor of *The American Ecclesiastical Review;* Father Connell was dean of the School of Sacred

Theology of the Catholic University of America. They proved to be formidable adversaries.

Catholics, Murray argued, though *living* a twentieth century American life, were saddled with a thirteenth century or unitary *conception* of that life. In the medieval conception, he wrote in 1949, "the spiritual was part of the very definition of the temporal. The dogmatic maxim, *extra ecclesiam nulla salus*, had as a reflection the political maxim, *extra ecclesiam nullum ius* [error has no rights]. Not only were *imperium* and *sacerdotium* coextensive, but they were united as two integral parts of one society, one family, one body, and distinct only as functions within that one body."[32] As Murray saw the problem, Catholics were *living* the American dualistic separation of church and state, often exuberantly; but, when they *theorized,* they fell back upon the medieval, unitary concept of the union of church and state. This latter, *theoretical* predicament, forced them to *say* that they were giving only an expediential, half-hearted, provisional assent to the American system of plural religions, no "establishment," and separation of church and state.

This contradiction between Catholic practice and Catholic theory exposed Catholics to charges of hypocrisy, "lip-service," double-life, dual loyalty, double-think. They, it was said, did not "really" believe in the American system. Throughout the 1940s and 1950s, this was *the* controversial "Catholic issue." A Paul Blanshard traveled the low road, a Talcott Parsons the high, but the substance of the campaign was the same: Catholics were being accused—as, concurrently, in Washington, a certain Wisconsin Irish Catholic was accusing certain Protestants and others—of being "un-American." The charge against Catholics was unfair, and it hurt, but it was not altogether beside the mark. Stereotypes are seldom altogether groundless. Father John Courtney Murray set himself the task (it became a vocation) of replying in depth to this attack on the loyalty, if not of Catholics, of Catholicism. In the process he wholly revamped Catholic church-state theory and when, on December 12, 1960, *Time* magazine put him on its cover, a Catholic had just become the President-elect. Murray's thinking had prepared and legitimated this religio-cultural event, and the "Declaration on Religious Liberty" of Vatican Council II, a few years later, was to ratify it.

How was an absolutist religion like Catholicism to live in a pluralistic American milieu? On *either* the "soft" *or* the "hard" reading of the *extra ecclesiam nulla salus* formula, Catholicism still proudly claimed to be the one, true Church founded by Jesus Christ. We have seen how Reinhold Niebuhr internalized the theological implications of pluralism—vis-à-vis the Jewish community—by domesticating Protestantism into a humble henotheism. We have seen how Father Feeney recognized but refused the "natural implications" of pluralism. He rejected scepticism and "indifferentism." He underwent the ordeal of pluralism; it forced him into intransigence and "triumphalism." Rousseau, in *The Social Contract,* had spelled out the terms of the problem: ". . . we should tolerate all creeds which show tolerance to others, . . ." he wrote, "But anyone who dares to say 'Outside the Church there can be no salvation,' should be banished from the state. . . . Such a dogma is good only where the government is theocratic. In any other," he concludes, "it is pernicious."[33]

The parameters of Murray's problem were thus clearly set: to come to terms somehow with the de facto condition of religious pluralism, to accept, with theoretical sincerity—inwardness—the Constitutional settlement safeguarding religious liberty and guaranteeing separation of church and state, and to legitimate all this in terms of Catholic tradition, and without intellectual apostasy or even the appearance of "trimming." A tall order indeed and one requiring intelligence, conceptual elegance, and the intellectual poise a two-front war exacts. Let us note how he went about his task, beginning in the early 1940s.

In perhaps his earliest paper on the general subject of pluralism, "Christian Co-operation,"[34] Father Murray faced up to the obstacle to such cooperation that the axiom "There is no salvation outside the Church" appears to be. He chided the paraphrase of French thomist Jacques Maritain—"there is no salvation 'outside the Truth' "—for leaving unsaid "the fact that for us the Truth has assumed a corporate form, in Christ and in His Body, the Church."[35] Here we see Murray nailing down one term of the problem, and on this he never changed: the Catholic Church is the true Church, it is corporate, visible, historical, and scandalously particular. Then going to the other side, to the pluralistic others "outside" this one, true Church and, following a suggestion of the French Jesuit, Henri de Lubac, Murray found it better that "the *seeming* rudeness" of the negative phrase—*"no* salvation outside the Church"—be "tempered" by giving it a *positive* meaning, viz., " 'It is by the Church alone that salvation has come to humanity, and by the Church alone it comes to the individual.' "[36] Such a positive formula, he believed, would be more intelligible "in these days of 'ecumenism.' "[37]

This, then, is the other pole of the dilemma: the problem is not so much of "rudeness" as of *"seeming* rude" to others in a religiously free and pluralistic society. (Appearances have, this early in the argument, put in an appearance. The norm of civility makes taking appearances into account a structural element in any solution to the problem of religious pluralism. It is civility, in the first place, that transforms the *fact* of pluralism into the *problem* of pluralism.) As Reinhold Niebuhr struggled with appearances, with how Christianity *"must* appear" to Jews, so John Courtney Murray would struggle with how Catholicism "must appear" to Protestants. He would endeavor to disembarrass the Church of the appearance of incivility that accrues to it in the Anglo-American environment of the "civic culture" (Almond and Verba) and its "civil religion" (Robert Bellah).[38] The agenda he set himself called for two skills: "exact theological intelligence" and "great practical tact." Murray's dream was of a merger: to "doctrinal exactness" there was to be joined "a greatly *courteous* charity, which excludes any tendency to ally orthodoxy with undue suspicion, complacency, or rudeness."[39] This agenda spelled out from the beginning Murray's double commitment: to the religion of Catholicism and to the religion of civility, the civil religion.

In the same issue of *Theological Studies* there was a lead article on "Some Questions as to Interdenominational Co-operation" by Father John LaFarge, S.J., commissioned by the editor, Father Murray. It was to serve as a curtain-raiser on a series of articles on the whole question of "civic amity," the attribution of "good faith" to non-Catholic and non-believer, and the relation of "inter-religious amity" to "civic amity."[40] Over these questions there hovered a single problem-complex: the fact of the American pluralistic situation and the way this situation

expressed and justified itself in American civil religion. In this
pluralistic context, traditional Catholicism could not but appear
to be subversive of the American polity—"unAmerican"—and
deviant from the American civil religion—"heretical." We shall
follow closely how, in the 1940s, Father Murray set the stage for
his breakthrough of the 1950s: he answered the charge of heresy
with a *Catholic* legitimation of pluralism.

First, Father Murray chose, in Father LaFarge, a man of
unusual and paradoxical qualifications: a convert out of the very
Protestant and very patrician LaFarge clan, who had worked for
years among blacks, who had retained throughout his life his
listing in the New York *Social Register,* and who was personally
unassuming, plain, and frank. He had no "side." He was trusted
by Protestants. This extraordinary man, a LaFarge, a Jesuit, a
"socialite," an early civil rights "activist," entitled his autobiography: *The Manner Is Ordinary*[41] (the Jesuit Ignatian Rule promoted this kind of democratic civility of manner; i.e., no "manner" at all). Then, in the December issue of *Theological Studies,*
T. Lincoln Bouscaren, S.J., wrote on "Co-operation with Non-
Catholics: Canonical Legislation," and distinguished co-operation with non-Catholics in public discussions from co-operation
with non-Catholics in religious services (called *communicatio in
divinis*). The editor noted that the series of articles signalized the
existence of "a distinctly new and unmistakably urgent" problem in our contemporary "religious *and social life.* Discussion of
it," he concluded, "is at once imperative and delicate by reason
of the complex theological values involved."[42] And, I should
add, by reason of the social exigencies involved.

In the March 1943 issue, Father Murray himself took up the
subject of "Co-operation: Some Further Views." He found Max
Pribilla's arguments for "the legitimacy of practical co-operation" with non-Catholics,[43] based on the formula "to compart-
mentalize is not to lie" (*abstrahentium non est mendacium*), to be
"legitimate enough."[44] Nevertheless, even this legitimation was
jeopardized by the fact that for the Protestants, such *"co-operatio
in caritate* was very likely to imply a certain *communicatio in fide.* "[45]
Catholics, then, would *appear* to Protestants and others to be
doing what they are not, in fact, doing. How does one control,
not so much one's actions, or the theory legitimating those

actions, as the unintended appearances of social actions? This is the matter of appearances again (Catholic moral theology deals with it under the ancient rubric "scandal"). For the same action will "look" different to someone operating on a different theory. It was, then, "the real divergence in the *theory* of co-operation, as between Catholic and Protestant"[46] that was the biggest obstacle to the *practice* of such co-operation.

Yet, when the proposal of cooperation on the temporal plane with Protestants is made, Catholics "cannot antecedently demand" that Protestants accept the Catholic theory of church unity. "I say 'cannot,'" Murray wrote, "on the principle of respect for the actual state of one's neighbor's conscience."[47] One should note how Father Murray has introduced the unexamined concept and attitude, "respect," and has elevated it to the status of a "principle." We merely note here the difference between the sheer fact of "those plural others" and *respect for* the fact of those others. The sheer fact of others has consequences for those who co-exist with them; but it is the normative component, the "principle of respect," the attitude of civility, that lifts these consequences from the plane of external situational circumstances to the level of being meaningful to, and internal to, the value-system of the agent confronting them. The former is pluralism as a fact of life in the "foreign policy" of a given religion; in the latter case, it affects the "domestic policy" of a given religion also. The religion's idea of itself, its very theological identity, undergoes change with the internalization of the idea of respect.

To return to Murray: if one "cannot" demand theological agreement of Protestants as a pre-condition of cooperation (today we would say "dialogue"), because of the "principle of respect" for the actual even if erring state of one's neighbor's conscience, what, then, is to be done? "We shall . . . set forth our doctrine of the unity of the Church with complete clarity, courage, and courtesy. This," he concluded, "is our first charity, to be charitably performed, on the principle (was it Francis de Sales'?), that, *'la vérité qui n'est pas charitable, vient d'une charité qui n'est pas véritable.'* . . ."[48] We see here a modulation introduced into the ancient rivalry of Christian truth (which is fidelity) and Christian charity. With Salesian help, *both* charity and truth were becoming adjectival and adverbial; they were being civilized into adverbs of each other. There, for the moment, the matter stood.

But the 1943 article is notable for introducing one further structural element in the problematic of pluralism. For a church which claims to be "the one, true Church," hell—as Sartre wrote in *Huis Clos*—is the plural "others." *They* are an ordeal. The attitude to "the others," their rejection or, if they are to be accepted, the kind and degree of acceptance, is absolutely crucial. Murray noted, in passing, that with these Protestant enterprises on behalf of civic amity, one is never quite sure whether they regard the existence of divergent religions as "an established *fact* in the present . . . or whether they regard this religious pluralism . . . as a *good*-in-itself, a social enrichment, etc. (which is quite stupid, and unacceptable . . .)."[49] Clearly, Murray was not yet about to abandon the distinction of values from facts. Plural religions are a fact of our situation; but they ought not to exist, since truth is one. With his Catholic intellectualist and "high" thomist concept of religious truth, Murray saw truth and the Church as one, and experienced pluralism cognitively, viz., as falsehood contradicting Truth. To accept pluralism implies that one religion is as good as another. This is the traditional Catholic polemical stance against "indifferentism" (adiaphorism).

But a raw nerve had been touched. Murray cannot dismiss the question (perhaps it *isn't* a peripheral question; perhaps, in fact, it is the key): how does one *religiously* legitimate religious pluralism? And so he dropped down to a footnote for freedom to muse: "It would, of course, be extremely interesting to pursue the question as to the sense in which we can say, *'felix culpa!'* with regard to our religious divisions, on the principle that God's permissive will has a good for its object in permitting evil."[50] (For Murray's "interesting" we must read "tempting.") Is pluralism merely given, or is it, perhaps, God-given? Is there a religious legitimation of religious pluralism, or is such *religious* legitimation itself, in the end, nothing but Protestant denominationalism? These preoccupations, seldom central to Murray's ostensible argument, haunted it at every turn. They were a further inescapable element in the problematic of pluralism.

In *Theological Studies* for June 1943, Wilfrid Parsons, S.J., treating of "Intercredal Co-operation in the Papal Documents," introduced the tactic of accusing Catholics of a "curious crypto-Calvinism which thinks that God gives His grace only to Catholics. We have no right to push our dogmatic exclusiveness into the field of human relations."[51]

Not until September 1944 do we hear from Father Murray again. In "Towards a Theology for the Layman: The Pedagogical Problem" he faced a problem bequeathed him, in effect, by Catholic modernization. The old, subcultural "plausibility structures"[52] were crumbling. Catholic ethnic *urban* enclaves—especially the Irish, but also the German, the Italian, the Polish—where, indeed, the medieval "unitary" theory reigned, where church and "state" (i.e., socio-ethnic infrastructure) were one—were dissolving. A new *suburban* layman was emerging, shedding his ethnic and regional particularism, manicured and ready for his "great ascent" into the middle class. The old, authoritarian, obediential, *external* relation to the spiritual authority and sanctions of the Church was abating. Father Murray sought to equip this new layman with a Catholic formation strong enough to be "plunged into the modern secularized milieu and confidently left to the *inner* resources of a mature faith that is able to *stand by itself,* supported by the strength of its own deeply experienced reality,"[53] and not, presumably, by the now-crumbling scaffolding of primordial, community, kinship, and ethnic loyalties. And the purpose of this layman's theology? To provide equipment against shame, so that, *in partibus infidelium*—"plunged into the modern secularized milieu"—he will not be shamed into apostasy, embarrassed into throwing out the baby, his faith, with the bathwater, its ethnic and class "vessels"; in a word, so that he would be able to say with Saint Paul, wrote Father Murray, " 'I am not ashamed of the Gospel; for it is the power of God unto salvation for all who believe . . . (Romans 1:16).' "[54] Murray's church-state theory also was designed to legitimate Catholic participation in the neutral-secular structures of the national civic culture. (It would prove to be in providentially "pre-established harmony" with the legitimation needs of a young Irish Catholic layman named John F. Kennedy, who would have cause to demonstrate to the ministerial body of Houston a Catholicism decisively disembarrassed of "external" ties to prelates and such—a Catholicism very "inward" indeed.)[55]

Christian charity almost from the beginning imposed the obligation of a curious double-life on its faithful: "love the sinner, hate the sin," was one of its early formulas. "Go, sin no more," Jesus says to Mary Magdalen. Catholicism codified a version of this "doubleness" in reference to credal matters with such unprepossessing phrases as "dogmatic intolerance" but "personal tolerance," or "credal intolerance" but "civic tolerance." This is the old and human conflict, which everyone has in some version or another, between kindness and candor. Father Murray passed much of the early forties wrestling with this problem, as we have seen. Finally, in June 1945, in "Freedom of Religion. I. The Ethical Problem," with Catholicism under attack from many quarters for its intransigence, Father Murray burst out, insisting passionately that Catholics love God and His truth

> with a loyalty that forbids compromise of the truth, even at the promptings of what might *seem to be* a love of man; were it otherwise, our love of both God and man would be a *caritas ficta*. And we love man and his conscience with a loyalty that forbids injury to conscience, even at the promptings of what might *seem to be* a love of truth;

were it otherwise, our love both of God and man would again be a *caritas ficta*. "In either case," he concluded, "what we abhor is *feigning*."[56] "We will not feign for the sake of appearances!" was what Murray was saying. Here is open acknowledgment of how deeply—as in the case of Niebuhr—the civil "argument from appearances" penetrated the old theological argument from religious realities. Civil religion was knocking at the door. Murray refused to open it.

There is no contradiction, Father Murray insisted, between Truth and Charity. This double-loyalty is not double because the loyalties are compatible. But the problem is that there is no really good double formula for expressing this theological position ("dogmatic intolerance," for example, was intolerable to American ears). Yet, as he almost conceded "between the lines," this very series of *Theological Studies* articles had failed to get the problem off the ground. "Perhaps," concluded Father Murray, returning to an earlier position, "St. Francis de Sales came as close as anybody to a good double formula, when he spoke of *la vérité charitable* and *la charité véritable.* "[57] But what was needed, as Murray himself well knew, was not a new formula—double or single—but new theory, new theoretical legitimation. This theoretical breakthrough was to occur, not *pro domo* in the scholarly intramural pages of the Jesuit *Theological Studies,* but a year and a half later, in the heat of passionate and brilliant public polemic. And it was to occur in the form of an "inspired" double formula: "articles of peace" *versus* "articles of faith."

II.

"A dangerous patience of polite logic"

This breakthrough came in the series of six polemical articles in *America* magazine (1946–1948) which Thomas Love has called "An Interim After Failure."[58] In this series Murray left the attempt at explicit theory-construction behind and engaged in a dispute with Dr. Morrison of *The Christian Century* over the interpretation of certain Supreme Court decisions, and with the assumptions of a highly vocal pressure group entitled "Protestants and Others United for the Separation of Church and State." This latter polemic, "Separation of Church and State,"[59] is most telling and fruitful. Certain Protestants, he observed, assume that the First Amendment "no establishment" clause is a "theological document—a sort of dogmatic decree that lays down a rule of faith . . . [and which] implicitly 'establishes,' as the obligatory belief of the American people, the doctrine that all churches are simply voluntary societies, of equally human origin and of equal value in the sight of God. . . ."

On this assumption, Murray argued, the First Ammendment "canonizes Liberal Protestant ecclesiology . . . [and convicts] Catholics of supporting the First Amendment only 'in practice' (on grounds of 'expediency') and not 'in principle' (on grounds of conviction). . . . It makes the First Amendment," concluded Murray, stumbling on the first half of what was destined to become the "inspired" double formula of all his subsequent work, "do the very thing that Congress is forbidden by the First

Amendment to do, namely, to play the theologian and promul-gate articles of faith." The Constitution, he insisted, is not a theological but a political document, defining the concept of the state, not of a church, proposing—as he would later complete his formula—articles of peace, not articles of faith. If the reli-gious pluralism in American society is the factual basis of the First Amendment, the ethical dualism in man—between civic person and religious person, citizen and believer—is *"the* princi-ple of the First Amendment."[60] Even though the citizen and the believer are concretely one—*civis et Christianus idem*—they are analytically distinct. If the believer needs the true God and the one true Church, the citizen requires the pluralism of the public peace.

The *America* articles (1946–48) must be read for their bril-liance of style and tone. One thinks, in reading them, of G. K. Chesterton writing on the strength of Newman's style (in the *Apologia*): as "a sort of stifled passion, a dangerous patience of polite logic,"[61] or of W. B. Yeats on philosopher A. N. White-head as having "something aristocratic about his mind," con-trasting "his packed logic, his difficult scornful lucidity" with the "plebian loquacity" of Bertrand Russell.[62]

But all this effort of Murray cut very little ice with Protestant theorists. Paul Blanshard, of course, continued his crusade. Reinhold Niebuhr remained unconvinced. And Talcott Parsons, soon after, came very close to blowing his academic cool when, with detectable insistency, he wrote that the Roman Catholic Church "does not believe and never has believed in principle in religious toleration in the specific American sense; it accepts it, because being in a minority status it has no alternative." What does one do with Catholicism, Parsons, in effect, was asking, the specter of Father Feeney still haunting Harvard Square. There is no easy solution, he contended, to the problem of the " 'struc-tural strain' of considerable proportions" which the rise of Ca-tholicism has introduced into America. But of one thing, he concluded, displaying "insensitivity" (as we say today) to Cath-olics and their problems, there can be no doubt: "simple toler-ant 'good will' and avoidance of prejudice are not enough."[63]

Thus, in September 1950, in the *American Ecclesiastical Review*, Murray opened his attack on the unitary church-state theory, which bids Catholics "tolerate" the American system *faute de mieux*. The "better" system more ideally suited to Catholicism, the conservative thesis runs, is the "confessional state" where Catholic church and state are united.[64] Soon the Redemptorist, Father Francis J. Connell, of the Catholic University of America, was calling Murray's thesis of a lay (not laicist) state (not society) which is theologically neutral, and which neither "confesses" Christ's church nor grants it preferential status, a "very definite and radical departure."[65] Father Connell, noting that some defenders of this new theory—he means Murray—believe that it affords "a means of smoothing the way" toward a better understanding of the Church on the part of non-Catholics, suggested that such assurance is wasted effort. "Fair-minded" people already know that Catholicism constitutes no menace to American freedom; and bigots won't listen anyway.

Father Murray's reply, "For the Freedom and Transcendence of the Church," scored Father Connell's "logicism" and "conceptualism"* and—I am omitting most of the arguments at issue —spoke of "a ferocious bit of logic, ending in political nonsense —in a denial of the essence of Western constitutionalism, the doctrine of consent. . . ." "The logic is impeccable, the conclusion is absurd," Father murray noted; he praised, in a footnote, Father Connell's "genius for the peripheral." In his discussion of the church-state problem, Murray reminded him, "there is such a thing as ordered discussion." Clearly, Father Murray was indignant. Connell had hinted that Murray was overconcerned about appearances, about respectability. Remarking that he had not undertaken to defend any of his own theories, because he cannot see that they have been touched, Murray added: "But one remark is necessary. Father Connell credits me with the intention of trying to 'smooth the way toward a better understanding of the Catholic Church on the part of non-Catholics in America' by a process of compromising Catholic principles, or concealing them, or understating them. The suggestion is mistaken and injurious. I reject it."[66]

---

*These ideas derive, I believe, from the Irish-Canadian Jesuit, Bernard J. F. Lonergan, S.J., who was concurrently writing for *Theological Studies* the articles which would culminate in his monumental work, *Insight*.

This was a sore point with Murray. In June 1951, the editor
of the *American Ecclesiastical Review,* Msgr. Joseph Fenton, in
"The Status of a Controversy," had attacked Murray's thesis
that the proposition that the state has an objective duty to accept
and to profess the Catholic religion, was not a principle, but
merely a contingent application of a principle (viz., the primacy
of the spiritual). Msgr. Fenton maintained that the objective
obligation remains, in principle, even when state and citizenry
are subjectively unaware of it; and then he had proceeded to link
the current *nullum ius* controversy with the earlier *nulla salus:* "In
exactly the same way, the necessity of the church for salvation
is in no way modified or negated by the fact that there are
individuals who remain unaware of that necessity through no
fault of their own."[67] In the same article, editor Fenton had
taken occasion to speculate that "it would appear that much of
Father Murray's anxiety to overthrow the teaching of the manuals [of public ecclesiastical law] on this question is due to his
belief that the usual theses on this subject in some way injure the
Church's *reputation.* "[68] The fact that Catholic teachings and dogmas are perverted, twisted, and misstated by anti-Catholics for
their own ends is no reason, the Monsignor instructed the Jesuit,
why the truths themselves should be "abandoned or soft-ped-
aled. . . ."[69]

Going straight for the jugular, Msgr. Fenton remarked that
Father Murray seemed to be under the impression that "Catholic books *de iure ecclesiastico publico* are in some way *distasteful* to
his fellow-citizens,"[70] and he then took it upon himself to remind Murray that "Neither the Church nor the *faithful* teachers
of the Church try to understress any section of Catholic doctrine, simply because it happens to be *unfashionable* or happens
to be abused by the anti-Catholic agitators at the time."[71] (The
cruel accuracies and exquisitely inaccurate cruelties of in-group
in-fighting are endless and fastidious, and may be lost on outsid-
ers—except for the dismal sociologist, whose business it is to
take in everybody's dirty wash.)

Predictably, then, Murray attacked the "specious simplicity"
and "seeming orthodoxy" of the "curialist premises" of this
"crypto-monarchist,"[72] this "man of the Right."[73] Continental
Liberalism is dead; totalitarian Communism is the enemy, a

threat to all that "both the Church and the [American] liberal tradition stand for." *This* unsolved problem and not currying favor with non-Catholics had been his concern, Murray insisted. And this problem does not turn "on the purely factual distinction between a 'Catholic majority' and a 'Catholic minority'; it turns on a whole theory of society, the state, the government, the body politic and the people."[74] Father Murray was rejecting, in other words, as a *theoretical* solution, an ad hoc, provisional tolerance of religious pluralism and religious freedom that stems from the sheer fact of Catholicism's minority status. He insisted on a *de jure* solution, unindentured to historical contingency and accommodational ad hockery. Accused, by implication, of opportunism, Murray retorts the charge, finding the willingness of the "curialists" to live *in hypothesi* while thinking *in thesi** a scandalous kind of "double-think," betraying a complacency in "cognitive dissonance" astounding in *soi-disant* theorists whose intellectual integrity should demand that theory and practice be made consonant. ". . . I consider myself to be dealing with a speculative problem," he wrote; "my speculative problem is very real, as real as the political context from which it takes its rise. There are those who do not see it; nonetheless, it remains as visible as it is real."[75]

In fact, Father Murray continued, moving to the heart of Father Connell's suggestion of obsequiousness, "curiously enough, among those who see [the theoretical problem] are some of those fair-minded non-Catholics whom Father Connell with illusory confidence expects to find quite satisfied with the thesis-hypothesis disjunction. They see quite clearly the fact to which Father Connell is seemingly blind—that the hypothesis, as understood in this disjunction, is not the *American* hypothesis."[76]

What, then, we may ask, was *un-American* about it? Does it not lie precisely in the fact that the traditional Catholic position involved withholding, by its rationale of expediency, "inner" assent to the First Amendment? And would not giving such

---

*In *thesis* or theory, the Church rejects the American "neutral" state as less than ideal; but, on the *hypothesis* that it works rather well and that it seems here to stay and that it is impossible, in fact, for any minority religion to change it, the American system is thus to be accepted in practice, albeit with theoretical misgivings.

"interior obedience"—to use traditional Catholic language—to the First Amendment be, precisely, a "religious" act in the sense excoriated in Father Murray's *America* essay of six years earlier?[77] Returning to the matter of the "fair-minded" non-Catholic critics of Catholic church-state theory, Father Murray suggested that Father Connell "underestimates their capacity for reason and logic, while putting too great a strain on their fair-mindedness."[78]

These non-Catholic and often secular intellectual critics, with whom Father Murray here made common cause against Father Connell, basing themselves presumably on "reason and logic," simply "do not consider the current attitude of the American Catholic Right, which condemns the First Amendment in principle and praises it in practice, to be either intellectually or morally *respectable.*" Father Murray, significantly, was quick to add, "What these men think is indeed quite secondary to the prime problem—the truth of the matter," but despite this ritual purification, the word "respectable" still glows for us like neon on that dusty page forty-eight of the January 1952 number of the *American Ecclesiastical Review.*[79]

Respectable. This Victorian concept reintroduces the matter of appearances; "civility" is its lineal, more egalitarian, descendent; "respectability" belongs to a "nice" family of words which can supply the intervening variables linking, for the sociology of knowledge and religion, the history of ideas and legitimation problems with the everyday world and with what "passes" for knowledge. Ideas, like people, like attitudes and actions and movements (like, e.g., psychoanalysis) are intellectually or culturally respectable, in doubtful or good taste, decent or indecent, etc.

Respectability. I take it that Father Murray, a fastidious Latinist, used the word with conceptual and linguistic propriety. He meant what he said, he said what he meant. He had been accused, inferentially, by Fathers Fenton and Connell, of being (to use Catholic diction) a "respecter of persons," that is, one whose behavior, whose theological behavior, toward people is influenced by their social status and prestige. For a colonized people such as the Irish, even soft-pedaling the Faith, let alone apostasy, was invariably construed as social climbing, as an act of ingratiation with the Anglo-Protestant Ascendancy. And perhaps it was. An act of interior disloyalty—sometimes even if feigned—can inaugurate many things, from apostasy to adultery and many other kinds of cultural success. James Joyce, for example, began his great ascent into literary modernity with his letter of November 1902 to "Dear Lady Gregory," declaring his need "to achieve myself—little or great as I may be—for I know that there is no heresy or no philosophy which is so abhorrent to the church as a human being, and accordingly I am going to Paris . . . I am going alone and friendless . . . I am writing to you to know can you help me in any way. . . ."[80] What Kevin Sullivan in *Joyce Among the Jesuits* calls this "appeal to the ascendancy's prejudice against the Roman Catholicism of the mere Irish" is grist for the mill of Dubliners with their theory of Joyce's apostasy by snobbery: "His theological difficulties were really social," Montgomery writes flatly, "he felt it was not the thing to be a Catholic."[81]

Connell and Fenton insinuated an analogous charge against Father Murray. Murray's reply is to concede that these "others" do, indeed, operate in his life as a reference group, not in their social but in their intellectual and moral capacities: he respects their respect for moral and intellectual respectability. Murray walked the razor's edge here. These distinctions were too fine for Fenton and Connell (as were analogous ones for Father Feeney). It was enough for them that Murray could not avoid the *appearance* of seeking respectability for Catholics and Catholicism. They detected, and rightly detected, in Murray's dissatisfaction with *home-grown* Catholic church-state theory, his awareness that the Church had lost its monopoly on truth, that today —in Berger and Luckmann's words—"the sociologically crucial legitimations are to be found *outside* the area of institutionally specialized religion. . . ."[82] Murray's enterprise, in other words, was manifestly a response to the secularization-pluralism of modern American society. That a Msgr. Fenton should find the European laicist separation of church and state "neither legitimate nor expedient" was acceptable enough, but that the best he could say for the American separation—citing Pope Leo XIII —was that "this situation is allowable and expedient" was, to Father Murray, unacceptable.

It became Murray's mandate to quest for legitimation *in partibus infidelium.* (What he was to find was, in its turn, to be legitimated—as we shall see—under the "sacred canopy" of Catholicism.) This great "legitimation struggle" took place in the course of a series of articles written during the 1950s, which appeared, finally, divested of scholarly apparatus, in book form in 1960 under the title *We Hold These Truths: Catholic Reflections on the American Proposition.* [83]

In these essays, Murray carries his argument boldly to the outside general American public, leaving behind him the intramural Irish Catholic insinuations of Fathers Connell and Fenton. But before we also leave them behind it would be well if we faced up openly to the between-the-lines implication of their polemic against Father Murray. They imply as, earlier, we have seen Father Leonard Feeney imply about his "liberal Catholic" adversaries, that these innovative moves in Catholic church-state theory are the result of Catholic upward social mobility. They charge Murray with ingratiating himself with high status WASPs. They wonder to themselves why *Time* magazine should be so eager to have Murray on its cover. They suggest, as we have seen, that he is a "respecter of persons"; they hint that Murray is—put crudely—a theological and social climber.

In noting earlier that Reinhold Niebuhr's theological liberalism seemed to ride in uncanny pre-established tandem with his social ascent, I noted—in a footnote on p. 34—that it was one of the intentions of this book "to show that considerations such as these, in the sacred precincts of theology, are not *infra dignitatem;* on the contrary, they are part of what the sociology of religion is all about." Religion may have its ritually delicate objects; not so the sociologist of religion. He, like the sociologist in general, is the man who, in Peter Berger's words, "must listen to gossip despite himself, who is tempted to look through keyholes, to read other people's mail, to open closed cabinets ... [he] will occupy himself with matters that others regard as too sacred or as too distasteful for dispassionate investigation." [84]

There was, then, I am convinced, a class element in these often rancorous exchanges between Murray and the Irish clergy —as there often is in the disagreements of Irish with Irish. And, of course, Fenton and Connell were right: this tall, elegant, and brilliant Jesuit priest, John "Courtly" Murray, *did* indeed hob-nob with the Henry Luces and the Robert Hutchinses; he did travel—and they knew it—in the "right" social circles of the wealthy Irish Catholic "Our Crowd," the group whose story is told by Stephen Birmingham in *Real Lace: America's Irish Rich.* Although he was not at all what the French would call a *"salon priest"*—his monumental rectitude alone would have forbidden it—and although he was not a blood relative, it was nevertheless not unimportant to Father Murray's "social security" and hence to the poise of his mind, that he was long a close friend and adviser, a kind of "chaplain," if you will, to the well-known Murray clan in its heyday in Southampton and New York.

Father Murray was frequently a houseguest, and would cele-brate Mass in the Murray private chapels in New York and Southampton. He was a consultant to Thomas E. Murray, Jr., during his term as member of the U. S. Atomic Energy Commis-sion. Close readers, for example, of the independently argued decision of Commissioner Murray in the matter of the security clearance of the famous physicist, J. Robert Oppenheimer, will note the Thomist armature of much of the argument, with its *in foro interno* and *in foro externo.* [85]

It was a sociological oddity of this "Murray clan" to have concluded a kind of Westphalian "separate peace" with the patrician and Protestant WASP society surrounding it. It had managed, for a time anyway, to have mingled socially in *con-vivium* and commensalism with this particular society without going on to either *connubium* (intermarriage) or apostasy. (This was something of a feat for, by the sociologically iron logic of assimilation, who says A must say B, etc.) The social "settle-ment" of this subculture, I suggest, prefigured for Murray what was possible for the larger, rank and file Catholic community in post-Vatican II America. It became a model in the back of his mind for the possibility of a truly civil intercourse with a Protes-tant culture without the predicted demeaning accommodation of Catholic truth to social opportunity. This was the solid social ground on which Murray stood; it valorized his argument even though it did not validate it.

I take now the recent appearance of another book on this

milieu—John Corry's *Golden Clan: The Murrays, the McDonnells and the Irish American Aristocracy* (Houghton, Mifflin, 1977)—as occasion to make an idiosyncratic "confessional" settling of my accounts with both this background—my own "roots," as it happens—and with its import for the thematic core of this book: viz., as a demonstration of how the genius of American pluralism and its attendant civil religion "convert" *religious* scandal into *social* offense. This excursus on clan Murray, will, I hope, climb till it reaches high "structuralist" ground, where it will end; then the story returns in section IV to the other Murray, the namesake priest, John Courtney Murray, S.J.

III.

Excursus: Praying Well Is the Best Revenge

The rich Irish Catholics would be a bore if they were merely and only rich. "Money of itself," Lionel Trilling once noted, "no longer can engage the imagination."[86] What makes John Corry's *Golden Clan: The Murrays, the McDonnells and the Irish American Aristocracy* absorbingly different from the story of the rich of most other minorities is a curious social fact: their wealth, and the social recognition achieved through their wealth, made them, on the whole, more rather than less religious. Unlike, say, the German Jewish rich of "our crowd" whose piety (with the notable exception of Jacob Schiff) abated as their wealth increased—Cynthia Ozick calls this the "Law of Diminishing Concerns"[87]—the money of Corry's "golden clan" served to shore up its religiousness. The Murrays were rich, Irish, attractive, and intensely Catholic. And John Corry, an American of Protestant Irish extraction and a columnist for *The New York Times,* tells their story featuring, accurately, the "high" yet literal Catholicism that was so much a part of the innocence and glamour of their era.

But, good as it is, *Golden Clan* is flawed by three types of error. There is, first of all, the social historian's inevitable quota of smallish but nagging inaccuracies. For example (to pick one

close to home) my father died on July 4th, 1953, "choking on
a chicken bone that caught in his throat."[88] Wrong; he choked
on a piece of steak. (Would any really solid gold clansman be
caught dead choking on a chicken?) Then there are more conse-
quential inaccuracies, such as those that sacrifice (unintention-
ally) a person's character to the exigencies of a story line. For
example, he portrays Marie Murray as "shadowed" by envy of
her cousin, Anne McDonnell, over an event—the announce-
ment of Anne's engagement to Henry Ford II—that hadn't even
happened yet.[89]

Finally, Corry's book suffers from larger errors of historical
perspective. Obsessed, like everyone else these days, with "un-
meltable ethnicity," Corry errs in reading back into the "golden
clan" an Irish self-consciousness it never had. The first job of
historians—they have others—is to understand the past as the
past understood itself. In America, in the identities of the various ethnic minority groups, the ethnic component soon recedes,
the religious component gradually dominates. German Lutherans become more Lutheran, less German; Eastern European
Jews become more Jewish, less Eastern European; Irish Catholics become less Irish, more Catholic. (The late Will Herberg, the
sociologist of religion, was the first to discover and formulate
this American theorem: "where ethnicity was, there shall religion be.")

The "golden clan," the Irish Catholic "our crowd" of Corry's
book, was no exception to this rule. In my paternal grandfather,
publisher R. J. Cuddihy, for example, there was hardly any *conscious* Irish self-identification (he never denied it; he just never
went out of his way to assert it).* My maternal grandfather,
Thomas E. Murray, was so little interested in Ireland, yet so
intensely Catholic, that his two trips to Europe were pilgrimages
(literally) to the two Catholic shrines in *France,* Lisieux and
Lourdes. He went, paid his religious respects, turned around
and came home. American-born (Albany, 1860), he gave no
thought to any nostalgic return to the "old sod" of Ireland. But

---

*When he and George N. Shuster edited a book together, it was not about ethnicity
but about religion. Cf. Robert J. Cuddihy and George N. Shuster, *Pope Piux XI and
American Public Opinion* (New York: Funk & Wagnalls, 1939).

if Corry over-Irishizes the clan, he is absolutely right to place Catholicism at its center.

Corry's story begins with the founding great-grandfather, State Senator Daniel Bradley of Brooklyn. He was a stately, incorruptible man who, with his stovepipe hat, blackthorn stick, and collar turned around backwards, looked at once Lincoln-esque and priestly. When the anti-Tammany campaign of the crusading Protestant clergyman, the Rev. Dr. Charles Parkhurst, led to the formation in 1894 of the famous Lexow Committee which investigated corruption in the New York City Police Department, "Honest Dan" Bradley was appointed a member as a "reform" Democrat. In the committee's last act, Bradley moved that the chairman's chair—"with its thirteen nails"—be sent to Dr. Parkhurst.

In the first Nuptial Mass ever held in Brooklyn, Bradley's daughter married the Albany engineer and inventor, Thomas E. Murray—"the Patriarch" of the clan—who was soon to "consolidate" the scattered gasworks of New York into the Consolidated Gas (later Edison) Company. Corry sketches a charming picture of the Albany of this era, with its Dutch burghers, and the growing respectability of the children of thousands of the uncouth Irish—"canal Irish"—who had recently dug a famous canal all the way from Lake Erie to Albany (1817–1825).

Murray, who commuted from Albany to New York every day, had worked out an arrangement with an engineer on the New York Central: "Rounding a curve at 140th Street, the train would slow down, and Murray would jump off."[90] By the turn of the century, his inventions having already amassed him a fortune*—at his death in 1929 Grandpa Murray held 1,100 patents, second only to Edison—he moved his family (there were now eight children and many servants) to a huge house at 783 St. Mark's Avenue in Brooklyn.

A devout Catholic, "the Patriarch" could be seen going to Mass and Holy Communion at 7 A.M. every day of his life. He brought his family up in the strictest piety and propriety. His only known vice was "Velvets," a yellow salt-water taffy of the period (he was later to die of diabetes). A man of enormous drive, he triangulated all his energies between his family, the

*Now, alas! gone.

electrical industry, and the Catholic Church. Although knighted twice by the Holy See in the pontificate of Pope Pius XI, his Catholicism was not a public performance, but an inward matter of private devotion and prayer.

He neither drank nor smoked. But he had a lively memory of the Penal Laws the English had used to colonize Ireland, and so the day Congress passed the sumptuary legislation Americans know as "Prohibition," and the "symbolic crusade" of the temperance Protestants became the law of the land,* Corry writes, Murray "sent Raymond, his dignified white-haired butler, out for a bottle of bourbon . . . as a matter of principle, he would keep liquor in the house from that moment until he died."[91] (Until then, the only liquor in the house had been a bottle kept in Grandma Murray's medicine cabinet. Whenever the children needed castor oil, she mixed in a little whisky, to implant an aversion to the "Irish curse." The inoculation took.)

"The precise moment when the Irish Catholics passed truly into society is unclear," Corry writes, "but it is almost certain that the place where it happened was Southampton."[92] It was there, in 1926, that Grandpa Murray bought a great shingled summer "cottage" called Wickapogue. One by one his children and their children—eventually there were forty-eight Murray grandchildren—bought or built places in, around, and near what came to be known as the "Murray compound." On these 160 beachfront acres, which included a lake, in the heart of a patrician WASP summer colony, Thomas E. Murray built two pools (the smaller one for his grandchildren), a polo field, stables, and—granted this rare privilege by the Pope—his own private chapel with the Blessed Sacrament reserved.

It is hard to know what the Southampton Old Guard thought about this inundation, this world within their world. This polyphiloprogenitive Golden Clan raised hackles, partly because of its sheer size. Patrician Newell Tilton, in a demographic dither, proposed, only half-facetiously, renaming the resort "Murray Bay."† My cousin Rosamund Murray made off with every Good Hands cup in sight. Others of us won junior tennis trophies at

---

*Cf. Joseph R. Gusfield, *Symbolic Crusade: Status Politics and the American Temperance Movement* (Urbana: University of Illinois Press, 1963).

†See Stephen Birmingham, *Real Lace: America's Irish Rich* (New York: Popular Library, 1973), chap. 4: "Murray Bay."

the Meadow Club. The clan got its listings in the *Social Register*. It taxed the resort's facilities and fascinated its gossip columnists. Corry tells the story of Auntie Anna McDonnell, mother of fourteen, taking nine of them to Hildreth's to buy shoes. "One by one they filed in and were fitted, and when Mrs. McDonnell was presented with the bill she examined it in her careful way and then protested to the clerk that it wasn't enough. 'Oh, madam,' he said, 'we always give reductions to institutions.' "[93]

But, of course, the "Irishtocracy" were intruders, and there was naturally a conflict of morals, manners, and theologies. Thus, it is in these middle chapters that Corry's prose shifts from the social historian's chronicle to the implicative style of a novelist. Even if he fails finally to comprehend the thoroughgoingness of the Catholicism of the golden clan, Corry's social notation of Murrays-in-upper-WASP-Southampton is frequently brilliant. Contrasting them with the Episcopalians of Southampton who attended the fashionable St. Andrews Dune Church, Corry remarks: "Neither group knew it about the other, but at bottom they were all Puritans, and in any contest between Puritans, the ones who believe they are closest to God will always win. This meant the Episcopalians hadn't a chance."[94] Praying well is the best revenge.

When Grandpa Murray died in 1929, my uncle Thomas E. Murray, Jr.—later appointed by President Truman to David Lilienthal's "seat" on the Atomic Energy Commission—inherited "cottage" and chapel. Sunday morning Mass there was almost feudal. As "the clan" assembled from the surrounding countryside, the doors of the simple paneled chapel would be opened out into the living room to accommodate the overflow of latecomers, houseguests, and servants. These knelt on the rug. Inside were blue velvet-covered prie-dieux. Then Fathers Stephen MacNamee of Georgetown, or John Courtney Murray of Woodstock, or James Keller of Maryknoll, or Martin C. D'Arcy of Campion Hall, Oxford—or whichever priest happened to be the weekend houseguest—would intone the ancient *Introibo* and Mass would begin. Catholicism was all in all—and not "only on Sundays." "With the utmost regularity every afternoon Anna McDonnell and Marie Murray would retreat to the private chapel. . . . While their peers at Southampton had tea, or sat about at the Beach Club, [they] would stay in the chapel for a holy hour, sixty minutes of prayers, readings, or other devotions, communing with their God. . . ."[95]

The generation of the grandchildren mingled with everybody but, like their parents, married largely into the circle of the Catholic rich. "In an odd way," Corry notes, "the most flamboyant thing the Murrays and McDonnells ever did in Southampton was to withdraw from it and set up something like a community of their own."[96] When Henry Ford II courted Anne McDonnell, it was taken for granted that he would receive instructions from Msgr. Fulton J. Sheen and become a Catholic, which he did. The enormous McDonnell-Ford wedding of summer 1940 is one of the highlights of the book.

When, later, another Murray grandchild, the glamorous Jeanne Lourdes Murray, married "up" socially, becoming the wife of patrician Alfred Gwynne Vanderbilt, Jr., in the eyes of the clan she had done something "truly unpardonable"[97] not because he was a multi-millionaire, or a socialite, or un-Irish, or "even" Protestant—the Church can authorize a "mixed" marriage—but because he had been divorced and therefore, in Catholic terms, there was, literally, no marriage, and Jeanne had excommunicated herself. For over a hundred years in America, no member of this "golden" Murray clan had ever left the Church. On December 12, 1945, Jeanne and Alfred eloped, she knowing her mother and family could not and would not attend a secular wedding ceremony. Flying to Philadelphia in a small plane, "Jeanne Murray had been possessed by a single thought. 'We will crash,' she told herself. 'I am marrying out of the church, and so we will crash.' "[98]

They survived; and Corry depicts "scenes from a marriage" in a marvelous chapter called "Aristocrats at Last." Wintering in Beverly Hills because Vanderbilt's horses were racing at Santa Anita, Jeanne continued to go to Mass on Sundays, though unable to receive Communion. The parish priest, in a sermon on fallen women, "especially those who had been suborned by famous names,"[99] singled Jeanne out by name publicly from the pulpit. Jeanne, Corry notes, returned to the same church for all the Sundays she remained in Beverly Hills.

The following summer, 1947, the Vanderbilts having returned to Southampton, there occurred an incident which Corry
reveals but whose full import lies, alas, just beyond his grasp.
Walking along the beach at the compound one day, Jeanne and
Alfred saw Auntie Anna and Uncle James McDonnell. They were
staring at the ocean and did not see the Vanderbilts until they
were almost beside them. "The McDonnells looked, and then
with great deliberation," Corry relates, "they turned their backs
and stared once more at the ocean. They would not recognize
their niece and her husband, although their oldest daughter
would. This was Catherine, who was standing a little apart from
her parents. Haltingly, and with an embarrassed smile, she said:
'Hello, Jeanne.' It was a kindness," Corry concludes, "that
Jeanne remembered for years."[100]

Everything comes to a head here in this minute tragedy of
manners as if American religious history itself had contrived it:
the devoutly Catholic aunt and uncle, faithful to the end to
religious propriety—"Catholic legalism"—shun the excommunicated niece and her blueblood husband; to avoid the scandal
of the appearance of religious impropriety—the approval of an
uncanonical marriage—the McDonnells are forced to risk the
appearance of social impropriety, namely, of having their religious "shunning" construed as a social "cut." The act of "turning their backs" is inherently ambiguous: at once religious
fidelity and social incivility. Two orders of "scandal" and
"offense" collide. For neither party is there "one best action."
There is no way of *not* giving offense or scandal, either religious
or social. Giving "no offense" is an unavailable option; taking
offense is inevitable.

Into this ordeal, ending the stalemate and embarrassment,
comes the "Hello, Jeanne" of her cousin "Cackie." By choosing
to perform this rite of the religion of civility (civil religion),
Catherine, in effect, takes sides, signaling the "conversion" of
the next Murray generation and, by synechdoche, of the post-
Vatican II American Catholic cohort, to the wider communion
of civility. It is a measure of how "natural" the artifice and
complexity of civility have managed to become in this, the pluralistic era of our Anglo-American protestant civilization, that
Corry takes this deceptively simple verbal symbol—this "show
of respect": "Hello, Jeanne"—romantically, at face value, as the

voice of the heart, and misclassifies it as a "kindness." On the contrary, it is a categorial act: it constitutes, in fact, the unkindest cut; it marks a new religious boundary; it deconstructs an old identity; it performs an apostasy; it cures, at long last, a subcultural anomaly.

IV.

An End of Ideology, a Beginning of Civility

In 1960, in *We Hold These Truths: Catholic Reflections on the American Proposition,*[101] John Courtney Murray's debates of the '50s assume finished form. "For Catholic liberals, . . ." Garry Wills writes, "as for their secular counterparts, the Fifties was a time of nice distinctions, neat divisions, of a critical liberalism and liberal criticism." In a three-front debate with Protestants, militant secularists, and traditionalist Catholic theologians, Murray had been forced to "make intricate distinctions—not only separating church from state, but state from society, and society from individual conscience. . . . He broke single acts of decision down into *neutral* expertise, *political* conscience, and *religious* informing of conscience. He neatly packaged sacred and secular, private and public in their proper wrappings."[102]

Despite their intellectual intricacy, these writings of Murray were to become the public Catholic legitimation of the bid John F. Kennedy was even then making to become the first American Catholic President. Candidate Kennedy made his way down to Houston on September 12, 1960, and in his now famous "Remarks" proceeded to offer, to the Baptists of the Greater Houston Ministerial Conference assembled there, "a separation of church and state wide beyond the wildest dreams of their theological avarice"—as I wrote in another connection.[103] The words of the speech had been penned by John Cogley and Theodore Sorensen, but the ideas had been created by Father Murray. "Before the speech was delivered," Wills informs us, "Sorensen read it over the telephone to Father Murray, its doctrinal father, for a final blessing."[104]

The central thrust of Murray's *We Hold These Truths* is to eliminate a personal *and* theoretical "embarrassment" for Catholics. "It is customary," he began, "to put to Catholics what is supposed to be an embarrassing question: Do you really *believe in* the first two provisions ["no establishment" and "free exercise"] of the First Amendment?"[105] Murray's retort was: these articles are not dogmas requiring religiously motivated assent. They are not articles of faith, but articles of peace enabling a people of plural beliefs to live together in civic amity and public peace. They are legal not credal; pragmatic not dogmatic. Murray thus evicted from the First Amendment the theologies— Protestant, secularist, and other—that had been brazenly thrust into it. He demythologized the Constitution. Like others in the '50s, he called for an "end of ideology" and its replacement by "civility." "The American Catholic is on good ground," he wrote, "when he refuses to make an ideological idol out of religious freedom and separation of church and state, when he refuses to 'believe' in them as articles of faith."[106] On this interpretation, on Murray's constitutional hermeneutic, then, the supposedly "embarrassing" question addressed to Catholics— Do you really believe in the first two provisions of the First Amendment?—was "invalid as well as impertinent; for the manner of its position inverts the order of values. It must, of course, be turned around to read, whether American democracy is compatible with Catholicism."[107] The answer, on Murray's interpretation, is "yes."

The answer is "yes" providing, of course, that the American consensus which constitutes the underlying unity of our democratic pluralism—*E Pluribus Unum*—is a version of ancient Natural Law doctrine. The *unum* which conditions, and is conditioned by, our American religious pluralism, makes possible the civilized co-existence of men with divergent if not contradictory "ultimate concerns." These plural ultimates are unshared and private; what is shared, what constitutes the public consensus is the "public philosophy" of natural law. Thus interpreted, the "American Proposition," the "truths we hold," is the framework of our civility. As Walter Lippmann had done five years earlier in his *Essays in the Public Philosophy*,[108] natural law doctrine was employed to legitimate civility. If Lippmann's book concluded with "The Defense of Civility," Murray's book opens proclaiming it: "The Civilization of the Pluralist Society."

Abandoning the question of whether the free society is really free, Murray turned to the immediate question of whether American society is properly civil. He contrasted the "cool and dry" climate of the City, in which civic amity thrives, with the "passionate fanaticism of the Jacobin." The state of civility "supposes" a consensus that is constitutional, whose focus is the idea of law. If the consensus is real, public argument is possible: disagreement—"not an easy thing to reach"—is possible.[109]

This public consensus of civility was equated by Murray with Western constitutionalism.[110] We "hold these truths" of civility in the first place because they are our essential patrimony, a heritage from history, "through whose dark and bloody pages there runs like a silver thread the tradition of civility." Subsequently, "we hold these truths" because they are true, and keep them alive not by privileged inheritance but by "high argument."[111]

But the barbarian is ever at the gates of the city, perhaps in a Brooks Brothers suit, perhaps in academic gown beneath which lurks "a child of the wilderness, untutored in the high tradition of civility." He may be a member of what Murray called the "generation of the third eye"* whose "impotent nihilism" is even "now [1960] presently appearing on our university campuses." This generation, he believed, psychologizes excessively, and is too narcissistically self-aware to commit its mind and will to objective truth and the good. Essentially, the barbarian is a reductionist, and his constructions put an end to "the possibility of a vital consensus and to civility itself."[112] However many people may practice civility, it is "only the few who understand the disciplines of civility, and are able to sustain them in being and thus hold in check the forces of barbarism that are always threatening to force the gates of the City" by devising both gross and subtle ways of "massacring ancient civilities."[113]

If "civility dies with the death of dialogue," the question, whether pluralist American society, which calls itself free, is genuinely civil, reduces to the question, is there genuine dialogue between the plural religious communities? Or is what

---

*In *Generation of the Third Eye,* ed. with an Introduction by Daniel Callahan (New York: Sheed and Ward, 1965), twenty-two Catholic leaders under forty years of age examined themselves and their Church and proudly if wryly dubbed themselves with Father Murray's phrase.

passes for dialogue merely a series of monologues conducted in solipsistic vocabularies?

At this point it becomes necessary to take note of Father Murray's distinction between urbanity (or politeness) and civility. (An unfriendly observer, of Murray as of Niebuhr, might note that every legitimation of "the civility tradition" takes place —quite correctly, in fact—amid denunciations of "the genteel tradition.") Barbarism can be abroad, "whatever the surface impressions of urbanity," Murray wrote. Among Americans, he noted, "civility—or civic unity or civic amity, as you will—is a thing of the surface." The factual reality of our religiously pluralist society has received its structure, he continued, through religious wars, and these wars are still going on "beneath a fragile surface of more or less forced urbanity. What [Eric] Voeglin calls the 'genteel picture' will not stand the test of confrontation with fact," the fact of latent war.[114]

The distinction urged here is of the utmost importance. It never became completely explicit. It has to do with the fact that, with the advent of civility (what we shall later examine as "the religion of civility"), everything becomes surface. As in decorum, as in art, the appearance *is* the reality. There is no "reality" of power or malice "behind" the forms of civility, "using" them for "ulterior" purposes.

Father Murray was deeply engaged with this issue. Thus, he complained of ecumenical pseudo-dialogue: "We are not really a group of men singly engaged in the search for truth, relying solely on the means of persuasion, entering into dignified communication with each other. . . ." Rather, "the variant ideas and allegiances among us are entrenched as social powers; they occupy ground; they have developed interests; and they possess the means to fight for them. The real issues of truth that arise," Murray concluded, "are complicated by secondary issues of power and prestige. . . ."[115] There is nothing, in other words, "behind" civility: neither interest, influence, power, or prestige. Civility, like the "civil association" of Michael Oakeshott's monumental study, *On Human Conduct* (Oxford: Clarendon Press, 1975), is a thing of the surface; but, with this difference: civility would wish to be *all* surface. Civility takes ideas and people "at face" because its belief, its faith, is in the "good faith" of the face of the surface. It refuses the "depths," it declines to *interpret* motives; the argument *ad hominem* is revolting to it.

In the "structure of war" beneath the surface of our gentility
—not our civility—Murray continues, "the forces at work are not
simply intellectual; they are also passionate. There is not simply
an exchange of arguments but of verbal blows. You do not have
to probe deeply beneath the surface of civic amity," Murray
argued, "to uncover the structure of passion and war."[116] A
society with a "beneath" to be "uncovered," Murray was saying,
is not a genuinely civil society. Courtney Murray is here touching on a "touchy" subject: the residual, enduring, neo-nativist
mistrust of Catholicism: a high, well-bred, academic anti-Catholicism, what the poet Peter Viereck once noted when he
dubbed anti-Catholicism "the anti-Semitism of the intellectuals."

This distrust of Catholics as Catholics is manifold. Jews, Protestants, and secularists share it. Murray, smarting from twenty
years of public questioning of his Catholic *bona fides* by Pfeffer,
Blanshard, the secularist sectarians, and others, wrote:

> There is the ancient resentment of the Jew, who has for centuries
> been dependent for his existence on the good will, often not forth-
> coming, of a Christian community. Now in America, where he has
> acquired social power, his distrust of the Christian community leads
> him to align himself with the secularizing forces whose dominance,
> he thinks, will afford him a security he has never known. Again, there
> is the profound distrust between Catholic and Protestant. Their
> respective conceptions of Christianity are only analogous; that is,
> they are partly the same and totally different. The result is *odium
> theologicum,* a sentiment that not only enhances religious differences
> in the realm of truth but also creates personal estrangements in the
> order of charity.
>
> More than that, Catholic and Protestant distrust each other's
> political intentions. There is the memory of historic clashes in the
> temporal order; the Irishman does not forget Cromwell any more
> readily than the Calvinist forgets Louis XIV. Neither Protestant nor
> Catholic is yet satisfied that the two of them can exist freely and
> peacefully in the same kind of City. The Catholic regards Protestant-
> ism not only as a heresy in the order of religion but also as a
> corrosive solvent in the order of civilization, whose intentions lead
> to chaos. The Protestant regards Catholicism not only as idolatry in
> the order of religion but as an instrument of tyranny in the order
> of civilization, whose intentions lead to clericalism. Thus an *odium
> civile* accrues to the *odium theologicum.* . . .[117]

The chief sign of incivility is mistrust. Civility remains under-institutionalized as long as intentions are relevant to arguments, as long as the forms of rational discourse are "situational" and not "internal" to the other participants in the dialogue. Distrust rejects appearances and thus violates civility.

The result of this incivility is neo-nativism in all its manifold forms, Murray wrote, "ugly and refined, popular and academic, fanatic and liberal" with its ancient charge: "You are among us but you are not of us." The Catholic, "if he happens to set store, *pro forma,* on meriting the blessed adjective 'sophisticated,' will *politely* reply that this is Jacobinism, *nouveau style,* . . ." or, if a Catholic War Veteran, he is more likely "to say *rudely,* 'Them's fighten' words.' And with this exchange of civilities, if they are such, the 'argument' is usually over." Finally, Murray concluded, the secularist also *mistrusts intentions* rather than meeting arguments. "He too is at war. . . . Historically his first chosen enemy was the Catholic Church, and it still must be the Enemy of his choice. . . . What alarms him is religion as a Thing, visible, corporate, organized . . . with an armature of power to make its thought and judgment publicly prevail." Under this threat, the secularist—like the Jew and the Protestant—rallies to the defense of the City: "He too is at war."[118]

Thus, the religiously pluralist society, Murray, distinguishing gentility from civility, insisted, "honestly viewed under abdication of all false gentility," is not a genuinely civil society.[119] One must first strip away gentility before civility can prosper. In an earlier time, another American Catholic—an apostate and Spaniard—George Santayana, had attacked the "genteel tradition" in, curiously, much the same terms, making much the same point, informing Boston, and using its own decorous prose to do so, that Jesus Christ was neither Unitarian nor transcendentalist.[120]

In all this, we see an extraordinary reversal performed. What Murray had done was to turn the charge of "dual loyalty" and duplicity against the accusers of Catholicism. Instead of Catholics *affecting* an unreserved participation in the American consensus, here construed as the tradition of civility, while secretly planning its downfall when Catholics attain a majority—conspiring a demographic takeover—we have the spectacle of Protestants "and others" *affecting* to dialogue unreservedly with Cath-

olics on the First Amendment—they "are never rude"[121]—all
the while so construing its meaning (theologically, ideologically)
as to make Catholic agreement tantamount to conversion. They
first thrust Protestantism into the Constitution and then would
stuff it down Catholic throats as Americanism . . . let us call it
a kind of "forced conversion." The very principles of civility are
being used, expediently, to impose a kind of loyalty test on
Catholics.

It was a question, for Murray, of civility *versus* ideology (in this
case, theology). By demythologizing the First Amendment, by
emptying it of its Protestant residues, and interpreting it as an
article of peace, of civility, not as an article of faith, he could
reassure fair-minded critics of the Church that Catholic participation in the American consensus has been "full and free, unreserved and unembarrassed. . . ."[122] By the same token, he
could turn to his Catholic "constituents" and reassure them that
their assent to the First Amendment was not an act of faith
entailing "indifferentism," but a strictly limited moral, legal, and
political act, assenting to an article of peace necessary to the
unity and order of the temporal life of the City, an article of
peace continuous, in fact, with the Western, Roman, and scho-
lastic tradition of civility.

This act of legitimation of the American system by John
Courtney Murray did many things for American Catholics. It
signaled a double "end of ideology": it de-Romanized and de-
Europeanized Catholic church-state theory by persuading it to
drop its "ideal" demand for a "confessional" union of church
and state; it did this by construing the legal-governmental system as theologically neutral. If the "Protestant" interpretation
of "America" and its Constitution is false—i.e., if America is not
Protestant—there's no longer any need to insist it be Catholic.

Catholics were thus invited to participate fully in secular
America. Simultaneously, Protestant misgivings were allayed.
This legitimation by Murray was both an invitation, looking to
the future, and a codification of present Catholic acculturation:
the "boss" politics of *the cities* was yielding, even as he wrote—
with the advent of John F. Kennedy—to the civil, and more
national, politics of *the City*. Catholics were becoming more civilized and more middle-class. They were behaving better. So
well, in fact, that we have the spectacle of one of their number

—John Courtney Murray—indicting the WASP establishment for intellectual misdemeanor and for violating in practice the high traditions of civility it presumably professed.

V.

"Hinc illae lacrimae"

The modernization process—the "moral center of our time" —creates double-loyalties and, psychologically, duplicity. In new nations as in old, it enters a wedge between traditional, primordial ties—to use Edward Shils's phrase—and emergent national and civic ones. The intellectual elite "ride" this modernization process, guiding it, legitimating it, mediating between old and new. John Courtney Murray was situated in the eye of this storm, trying to steady it. Jewry loses its elite to secularism, leaving the Jewish community leaderless, a prey to the scavengers of the modernization process. Protestant theologians often do not legitimately "represent" any identifiable community; a Niebuhr's theological transactions with, say, the Jewish community (as above) are thus *ad hoc*, not the act of a community, and thus "unrepresentative." Murray, on the other hand, was uniquely placed, in space and time, to mediate American Catholicism's transition to modernity. When he acted (despite his being under "ban" for a time) he acted, self-awarely, as a representative man; he was a *shtadlan*: a density of overdetermined meaning thickened and solemnized his every word.

Three other Jesuits played analogous modernizing roles: in philosophy, the Irish-Canadian Bernard J.F. Lonergan, whose *Insight: A Study of Human Understanding*[123] is magisterial; in theology, the German Karl Rahner; and in science, the French Jesuit, Teilhard de Chardin. Each, *mutatis mutandis*, struggled with his own functional equivalent of Murray's problem: the all-relativizing, secularizing consequences of pluralism and the strategies— political or dialectical—of stemming these consequences by reducing a mob of contradictions to the unity of a "civil multitude."

In Europe, until their Emancipation at the beginning of the 19th century, the Jews were "integrists": they lived in *shtetl* and ghetto, where theory and practice, belief and behavior, were one. In Europe, until their emigration in the middle of the 19th century, the Irish were "integrists": they lived under colonial rule, where the presence of the enemy shores up one's "identity problem." In both cases, it was American freedom that forced a "double-life" on these two communities; for both, "Americanism" became a heresy, the standing temptation of that religio-cultural apostasy called "assimilation." Each, in its own way, was saying: "America is Exile." With their old European "plausibility structures" either abandoned in Europe or only creakingly surviving here, these minorities lived a double life: the life they lived for themselves *(pour soi)* did not coincide with the life they performed before others *(pour autrui)*. They were culturally "alienated."

As for Catholics, Protestants knew, and Catholics knew that they knew, and Protestants knew that knowing Catholics knew that Protestants knew, that it was "Romanism" which made Catholics "see double" (in the Irish case, Rum was thought to have assisted Rome in this enterprise). Catholics were not real, "integral" Americans the way Protestants were. Catholics, especially Irish Catholics, had their own version of that "moral Marranoism" indigenous to Diaspora Jewry. This was the Protestant prejudice about Catholics and, like all prejudices, it was correct, more or less.

In some contexts this inconsistency was experienced by Catholics as moral hypocrisy, in others as social embarrassment, in still others as shiftiness, sneakiness, and all the other squalid little duplicities. Murray's legitimation, by disembarrassing Catholicism of its unitary church-state theory, aimed to facilitate a Catholic participation in the modernization process ("Americanization") that would be, as he said, "full and free, unreserved and unembarrassed."[124] Catholics would no longer be an ethnic Church paying lip service to the national political society.

When tradition itself is construed, as Murray so construes it, to legitimate modernity (using the Leonine motto: *Vetera novis augere*), the era of the "mental reservation"—*reservatio mentalis*—

is at an end.* This act of legitimation—incorporated later into the Declaration on Religious Liberty of Vatican II—ended, in principle, "the American Catholic dilemma" in its political dimension. Reflections could no longer be legitimately cast on the wholeheartedness of the American Catholic commitment to the democratic process. This "duplicity" had worked against Catholic credibility. To the Protestants, Catholic complaints about "double taxation" for two school systems were but a fiduciary transcription of their dual loyalty. Now, in principle, a separate school system is no longer theoretically justified. Thus, Murray's legitimation will not only have provided cognitive relief for the cognitive dissonance of a Catholic intelligentsia but tax relief for the bourgeois Catholic community.

The social psychological coefficient of these structural strains, a lack of integrity or wholeness ("identity"), is also a concomitant of the modernization process. One does not *wholly* believe in either the primordial faith or in the emergent civil polity. One feels "dishonest" and is ashamed; even careerist anti-Catholics, like Paul Blanshard, are onto something, one begins to realize. A properly sociological psychology would exhibit these felt strains as but the subjective side of systemic tensions in the Catholic belief-system as it settles down in an America enjoying the "high mass consumption" stage of its economic growth. Integrity supervenes on the integration of traditional and primordial sentiments with civil politics.[125] Catholic integration in practice was ahead of Catholic theory; there was a lag between institutionalization and legitimation; Murray's task was to close this gap. In this sense, Murray "made up" (composed) the American Catholic mind.

But to compose the American Catholic mind, Murray had actually to suffer the conflict in his own person. Contemplating Catholic church-state manuals *de jure publico,* authored by European canonists, remarking their cultural illiteracy and obscurantism about America, their blurring of any difference between

---

*I am not here, or elsewhere, implying that Catholics—from Al Smith to John Kennedy—made explicit mental reservations. But I am talking of strains within the Catholic "Thing" and of the strategies for living with them or liquidating them. I am talking about the "underground" life of most American ethnics, the "secret" ethnic, family "understandings" which they knew made them different from the other, invisible ethnics, the WASPs, with their proper, socially invisible "civil religion." I am talking, like any anthropologist, about culture and subculture.

Jacobin and Anglo-Saxon democracy, their confounding of Continental laicist liberalism and the American liberal tradition, their conflating "the sovereignty of the people" in the sense of 1789 with "government of the people, for the people, and by the people" in the sense of Lincoln—Murray confesses: *"Hinc illae lacrimae,* spilled by an American. . . ."*

It was, therefore, almost inevitable that an American theologian, Father Murray, lead the way. Even the profoundest of the European leaders of the Thomist revival clung to the ancient doctrine, seeing no way out. Etienne Gilson, for example, argued, as late as 1954, that though the church deems acquiescence to a factual separation of church and state prudent, "in no case will she ever admit that the Church and State *should* be separate. Their separation remains an evil while, for reasons of expediency, it is being tolerated."[126] The "neo-modernist" fallout from Vatican Council II drove even Jacques Maritain into the camp of the anti-moderns.

Struggling to rescue the Church from the false dilemma of "integralism or liberalism," and rebounding from the Papal condemnation of *L'action française,* Maritain in 1936 had written a book with the famous and oxymoronic title of *L'humanisme intégrale.* † Yet, five years after Murray wrote *We Hold These Truths,* Maritain wrote another pointedly titled book: *The Peasant of the Garonne: An Old Layman Questions Himself About the Present Time.* He begins this his final book as follows: "I turn first to the holy *visible* church [*La sainte Eglise visible*] (she is, I realize, invisible as well).

---

*John Courtney Murray, S.J., "The Problem of 'The Religion of the State,' " p. 337, n. 10. Father George W Shea picks up this *cri de coeur* subsequently in "Catholic Orientations on Church and State" (*American Ecclesiastical Review,* Dec. 1951 [vol. 125, no. 12], p. 416) where he remarks, after quoting certain Spanish and Italian writers on church and state, that though such citation "may strike a neuralgic nerve somewhere in the new school, we refer to them in the belief that there are others who can read Latin without tears." Father Shea's cunning remark should not be allowed to obscure the significance of the spectacle of the leading "de-Romanizer" electing, in the very act of disowning the Roman canonists, to spill his American tears in Virgilian Latin. He plays out a mediatorial role, between tradition and modernity. He is an ethnic intellectual and agonist.

†The title of the translation—by M. R. Anderson (London: Geoffrey Bles, Ltd., 1938) —*True Humanism,* misses the shock Maritain delivers to the reactionaries by linking their sacred wholeness-word, "integralism," with a word in such good repute with the liberal secularists as "humanism." Wholeness-words and wholeness-hunger are endemic to resistance to modernity on the part of Protestants, Catholics, and Jews. Belloc's "Zionist" Catholic irredentism—"Europe is the Faith, the Faith is Europe"—comes to mind. The recent resurgence in Israel of Biblical Zionism is another case in point.

. . . And in beholding [*regardant*] the Church, I kneel . . . in profound thanksgiving."[127] Whatever their sophistication, Maritain and Murray were of a generation of Catholics that rejected liberal or invisible Christianity, "Harnack's wraith-like *Wesen des Christentums,*" in Murray's words. They adored a visible Church, something that had happened within history not as an "idea" or an "essence" but, in Murray's words, as "an existence, a Thing, a *visible* institution that occupied ground in this world at the same time it asserted an astounding new freedom on a title not of this world"[128]—Chesterton's "The Thing."

But if Murray was able to settle his accounts with civility and the civil religion, Maritain was not. The whole point of his title is to resist the neo-modernism of the post-conciliar Church, to identify his Catholicism with the rustic primitive simplicity of the faith of a peasant for whom the Church is as much visible as invisible. (Maritain's "peasant" is the equivalent of what, for Jews, would be an *ostjude.*) Maritain, a man of exquisite urbanity and courtesy, significantly ends his theological career by placing the religious problem of tradition and modernity in some curious relation to politeness and impoliteness. The Church will not survive, he argues, without a willingness to be uncouth. In the end, truth is an incivil thing. Paulette Martin, writing from Paris at the time of the "scandal" created by Maritain's *Peasant of the Garonne,* notes that "the 'peasant', as Maritain styles himself in the title, is someone with no standards of politeness to keep him from upsetting the applecart, or, as the French say, 'putting his feet in the plate.' "[129]

"A prescient friend," the English Redemptorist Martin Jarrett-Kerr writes, "said thirty years ago, 'God help the Church of England if the Church of Rome ever learns manners'. . . ."[130] The point here is that the Church of Rome preserves fidelity to apostolic truth, but that it puts people off by its lack of charity, its arrogant "one true church" incivility. But that if it can only add manners to its truth, all England will flock to it. But suppose, in the constant conflict of truth (candor) and civility (love), love wins? In the end, then, there may be faith, hope, and charity, but if—as the apostle says—the greatest of these is charity, charity will end by devouring truth. And love will be all in all.

Chapter 5

JEW:
RABBI ARTHUR
HERTZBERG AND THE
METAPHORICALITY
OF JEWISH
CHOSENNESS

The essence of Judaism is the affirmation that the Jews are the chosen people; all else is commentary.
—*Rabbi Arthur Hertzberg*
The Condition of Jewish Belief

You will break through time itself . . . and dare to be barbaric, twice barbaric indeed, because of coming after the humane, after . . . bourgeois raffinement.
—*Thomas Mann*
Doctor Faustus

The survival of Judaism in America is endangered by many things; but I believe that its single greatest enemy is vulgarity. . . . [There must be] an end to vulgarity in [Jewish] communal affairs.
—*Rabbi Arthur Hertzberg*
"Dangers of Vulgarity"

Not surprisingly, English is a Christian language. When I write English, I live in Christendom.
—*Cynthia Ozick*
Bloodshed and Three Novellas

Judaism, it was now maintained chiefly by Jewish historians, had always been superior to other religions in that it believed in human equality and tolerance. . . . this self-deceiving theory, accompanied by the belief that the Jewish people had always been the passive,

suffering object of Christian persecutions, actually amounted to a prolongation and modernization of the old myth of chosenness. . . .   —*Hannah Arendt*
Antisemitism

What distinguished the Jews from other immigrants, then, was their image of themselves, however morbid or self-elected that was. They differed in believing that they differed. . . . Indeed, no historian who fails to deal with the deeply ingrained self-image of the Jews will ever understand them. . . . Jewishness has always been a form of consciousness . . . the conviction that he [the Jew] was at [world-history's] center, the unique agent or victim of its design . . . possessed of a special vantage point on the world. . . . The absolute significance which Jews had [in Europe] attached to their fate . . . was not possible [in America] in a [pluralistic] situation for which they can no longer claim even to themselves that they are intrinsically at [America's] center. Nor, for that matter, could anti-Semites.
                                                      —*Leon Weiseltier*
                        review of Irving Howe's World of Our Fathers

Replying to the charge of Rabbi Arthur Hertzberg that he and his brother Percival omit to mention, in their asseverations of their Jewishness, "the main point," viz., Covenantal "chosenness," the late Paul Goodman replies: *"Now as to missing the main point of the creed, the Covenant, I too am aware that I never do set it down. And do you know what I think? I think that this article is something that one does not say; nay, more, it is not an article, it is something that one also does not think, except after the event, the deed; nay, more more, to the extent that it is the case, one does not think of it either before or after, it is simply the case, to the extent that it is the case. . . ."*   —*Paul Goodman*
                                                      letter to Commentary

Jews—most Jews—are modern, enlightened. Judaism isn't.
                                                      —*Milton Himmelfarb*
                                        "Paganism, Religion and Modernity"

I.

Outer Westernization:

The European Background

More than either Protestant Reinhold Niebuhr or Catholic John Courtney Murray, Rabbi Arthur Hertzberg sees clearly that the price paid by the classical religions in America is a promise to *behave* properly in the theological arena. The price Protestants, Catholics, and Jews pay for entry into the First New Nation

—the First Amendment—is identical to the price paid for modernization: the splitting of life into private experience and public behavior. The unseemly special claims of Protestants, Catholics and Jews that, in their own eyes, entitled them to privileged public status—that they were the one true biblical revelation, the one true church, the one chosen people, respectively—forced them to evacuate the public realm and to retreat to private home and house of worship.

These proud ancestral religions were forced to swallow their pride. They had, in effect, to promise, that however unique and superior in the privacy of their hearts and homes they *believed* themselves to be, in public they would *behave* themselves. The First Amendment, in other words, not only separated church from state, it divorced theological conviction from religious behavior, traditional religions from civil religion. Rabbi Hertzberg's chief claim to our attention—as the third of my "case studies" in the influence of civil religion, taking the form of the religion of civility, on historical religion—is his candid confession of this behavioral fact. With the election of a Catholic President in 1960, Catholicism, like Protestantism and Judaism, Hertzberg writes, promised "to abide by the self-limiting tradition of the sects in America, that is, to *behave* in actual *practice* as one among many churches. Thus the inevitable price was 'paid' for full entry into American society."[1] The historic religions had been made to promise that, when they sallied forth into public places, their bearing and their carriage—their public behavior—would express a decent respect for the plural opinions of Americans. They would, they promised, be respectful and therefore respectable. They would not wear the old time religion on their sleeves.

The "yoke" that civil religion in America imposes on its immigrant religions—the civil demeanor of being merely one among many—has two sources. It is a secularization of the evangelical humility that is so important a feature in Christianity's self-conception from the earliest days of the primitive church. But it also stems from the secularization of this idea in the Enlightenment of the eighteenth century. Rabbi Hertzberg, in his *The French Enlightenment and the Jews,* pays particular attention to how the *philosophes,* as they built their "heavenly city" with its decorous God of Reason, set out "to teach the religions the truth about themselves that they did not know *and a new way to behave in light of that truth.*"[2] The Marquis d'Argens averred that there could be good Jews, but "the good were by definition those who had entered polished and reasonable Christian society. . . ." D'Argens rejected the idea that anti-Semitism was a religious prejudice. "He insisted that its real source was in the bad conduct of Jews. D'Argens argued that the Jews were hated for their avarice and bad faith, so that those among them who were honest were punished for the sins of the guilty."[3] But it was in religious extremism that the *philosophes* of the Enlightenment located the darkness they wished to dispel. "They are, all of them," Voltaire wrote of the Jews of his time, "born with raging fanaticism in their hearts, just as the Bretons and the Germans are born with blond hair. I would not be in the least surprised," he concludes in 1771, "if these people would not some day become deadly to the human race."[4]

What later in America would become a concern for the behavior of *religions* had begun in the eighteenth century as a concern for the importance of the deportment and behavior of religious *believers* for entry into modern civil societies. " 'Are the Jews *congenitally* unsociable and rude, or are they this way as a result of having been segregated into ghettos?' Such," the Franco-Jewish historian Léon Poliakov tells us, "was the form of the question over which argument raged in the Eighteenth Century, on the eve of the [Jewish] Emancipation."[5] Like d'Argens, Diderot was concerned with conduct. "He gave an account of a visit to the Jewish quarter of Amsterdam and to its synagogues," Hertzberg notes. "He disliked what he saw at the synagogue because of its noise and lack of decorum."[6] The Enlightenment, Hertzberg finds, was obsessed with the idea of "remaking men to fit *properly* into the new society. . . ."[7]

As a consequence, since the Enlightenment was to be the "sponsor" of Jewish Emancipation, the idea of public decorum was to haunt the discussion of Emancipation in Europe as later the discussion of Americanization in the New World. Rabbi Hertzberg has a lively sense of the crucial if neglected role played by esthetic considerations in the discussion of the Jewish question. As a condition of Jewish Emancipation at the end of the eighteenth century, Hertzberg asks, did the Jews need to prove that "they were the quickest to abandon all their ancient traditions and adopt the cult of civic virtue? Was it enough to be *decently inconspicuous in public* by removing all marks of Jewish ritual distinctiveness outside the home?"[8] A man in the street— a gentleman, a *bourgeois gentilhomme* in the street—a Jew at home?

It is clear that something momentous is being demanded of Jews, or of any traditionally religious people, when, as the price of their entry into modern civil society, they are required to *behave* in public places and do their *living* at home. "America is different," Hertzberg writes. How is it different? Europe had exacted its price: the differentiation of a private from a public realm, an inner "real" world from an outer public appearance. Emancipating Jewry in Europe gave a largely external assent to this basic differentiation of modernity. Few Jews accepted the premise of Isaac de Pinto that *"inner* Westernization was a precondition for the attainment of equality by the Jews."[9] The question Jews asked themselves at the time of Emancipation, and the question Jews—and, as we have seen, Protestants and Catholics—would later ask themselves in America was: Can we religiously (Jewishly) valorize the distinction between outer, public, civil appearances and inner Jewish commitment, or do we accept this bifurcation of our lives merely provisionally, defensively, apologetically, as an accommodation, as a utilitarian "bargain"? Until the Messiah comes?

When Napoleon in 1807 convened at Paris a new Sanhedrin of French and Italian rabbis and Jewish notables, he forced on Jewry in Diaspora a distinction between citizen and believer, between secular and sacred. This distinction, of strictly Christian provenance, was accepted by the Sanhedrin only defensively, in reluctant exchange for civic equality. It was experienced as a "brutal bargain." "This defensive distinction between civic duty and religion, which means the severing of the religious and national elements of Judaism," Hertzberg writes, "was to have a long career in the nineteenth century. In its Orthodox form—which was what the majority of the rabbinic leaders of the Sanhedrin had undoubtedly intended—it meant a marriage between punctilious observance of the Law and maintaining the hope of the Prophets for a miraculous 'end of

days,' on the one hand, and *outward assimilation* to the surrounding secular life and culture, on the other."[10]

II.

Inner Westernization?

The American Foreground

And America? In a curious way, America upped the ante. It
demanded, but it did not say that it demanded, *inner* assimilation, inner Westernization, "interior assent." John Courtney
Murray had felt this pressure when he made his Catholic "settlement" with the First Amendment. America, as Chesterton had
seen, is a kind of "church," requiring "belief." Because, he
wrote, "it has no type it needs to have a test."[11] Is the test of
loyalty inner assent to the First Amendment? Does the Constitution, indeed, consist of articles of faith to be *believed*—as certain
Durkheimian Protestants maintained—or of articles of peace to
be *observed,* as Murray contended?

The work of Rabbi Arthur Hertzberg, current president
(1977–78) of the American Jewish Congress, examines the
effects of the civility implicit in civil religion on the three historical religions of the American tri-faith consensus. In his famous
study of 1963—"America Is Different"[12] he spelled out a vocabulary for the analysis of Jewry's coming to terms with the American pluralistic situation and its First Amendment legitimation.
He tackled the problem of the "un-American" element in Judaism, its claim to be a "chosen people," in its two dimensions: the
election of Israel and the ethnicity of Judaism. The election
claim is the claim to be chosen and it is anomalous in the American context—"heretical"—exactly as the Protestant claim to be
the one true revelation and the Catholic claim to be the one true
church are "heretical." That the claim to religious election involves the chosenness of a particular ethnic people merely dou-
bles the religio-cultural deviance.

Hertzberg's contribution (in 1963), unlike that of Niebuhr

and Murray, had the benefit of hindsight: he wrote of the Jewish "case" on the background of the "settlements" Reinhold Niebuhr and John Courtney Murray had already negotiated in their attempts to come to terms with the pluralistic situation, the First Amendment and the civil religion. He notes that the exorbitant claims of each had been forced to yield ground to the concept of "a religious consensus." Reinhold Niebuhr's position, as one of the architects of this new stance, Hertzberg writes, was to propose a consensus consonant with his 1958 proposal "that Christianity cease all missionary activity among the Jews and accept the notion that each of the two biblical faiths is an equally valid divine revelation for its believers."[13] Niebuhr's proposal was offered not as a contribution to the theory of religious consensus and civil religion, but as a device for implementing civil religion in practice, or, in our words, as a way of turning civil religion into religious civility. "A new theology thus was created," Hertzberg writes, "to provide a basis for consensus *in practice.* "[14] Civil religion, in other words, is the offspring of the religion of civility.

The critics of Niebuhr's revolutionary proposal, Hertzberg observes, "who were in the majority among theologians, did not accept the change in theology that he suggested. They were, and are, loath to part with the idea that in an ultimate sense Christianity is the true faith for *all* men. They pointed out, negatively, that such views would inevitably have to stretch further to end the missions to all the other major faiths, thus leaving Christianity *permanently* as one among many religions"[15] (as a self-acknowledged "henotheism," as I noted earlier). Despite the theological pains Niebuhr had taken to ground his "acceptance" of pluralism—symbolized for him by Judaism—in the *indigenous* Protestant religious value of humility and contrite-heartedness, this legitimation cuts no ice with Hertzberg. He views it as a forced, inevitable, and pragmatic accommodation to reality: a forced conversion. "Whatever may be the theological virtues, or lack of them, of Niebuhr's views" (Hertzberg, of course, is highly skeptical of Niebuhr's claim to ground his "live-and-let-live" theological civility in classical Christianity) "they are the only possible non-Barthian approach to living with a plurality of sects in the world. It is a pragmatic, *American* kind of answer to the 'foreign policy' question posed for Christianity in the post-war world."[16]

Hertzberg is keenly alive to what Niebuhr has surrendered. America tells the historic religions that "within the *private* confines of each [voluntary] denomination it may deal in absolutist terms with those who freely elect to accept its discipline." But, Hertzberg adds, aware—like Georg Simmel—of the absolutist claim of radical monotheism to be the God of the non-believer also: "Each of [the denominations] must, however, renounce any action affecting others which it would have a *right* to only if its truth were absolute, that is, valid for the non-believer, even though he does not yet know it, or very likely may never acknowledge it. In sum," Hertzberg concludes, acknowledging the *practicing* henotheism—or, religion of civility—that America exacts from its historical religions, "the American experiment asked, and continues to ask, something previously unknown and almost unthinkable of the religions: that they become split personalities." With this "split," which America asks in the names of modernity and modernity's civil religion, "each sect is to remain the one true and revealed faith for itself and in private, but each must *behave in the public arena as if* its truth were as tentative as an esthetic opinion or a scientific theory."[17] How deep does this "as if" *persona* of civil religion go? With Niebuhr we may speculate that the *als ob* of the religion of civility resulted finally not merely in a practicing but in a believed henotheism. John Courtney Murray is something else again. He is "far too much of a Catholic classicist even to imagine that, theologically, there is any religion other than his own that is ultimately true," Hertzberg acknowledges.[18]

Father Murray labored hard for years not only to defend the First Amendment "on theological grounds," Hertzberg writes, "but almost to lay claim to it. Father Murray would deny that this arrangement contains an ideology of its own: 'We have to abandon the poetry of those who would make a religion out of freedom of religion [Murray writes] and a dogma out of separation of church and state. We have to talk prose, the prose of the Constitution itself, which is an ordinary legal prose having nothing to do with doctrinaire theories . . .' The American Catholic can therefore, according to Father Murray, in good conscience live with and within the American state, which has no ideology of its own, whereas French Catholics had no choice but to fight the Jacobins in the French Revolution and the aggressively lay state of the Third Republic."[19] But can the Jew live in good conscience with the American "Thing"?

Before we come to the special strain that the Jewish doctrine of Election—the "chosen people" doctrine—introduces in the context of American religious voluntarism (or, as Sidney Mead and Joseph Blau call it, "voluntaryism,") and denominational pluralism, I must first spell out three more general strains between the values of Eastern European Judaism and the vague but curiously intransigent Protestant values embodied in American civil religion.

III.

The Three Disjunctions

of Culture and Social Structure

The first is on the level of the values of the two cultures themselves. American Protestant values, like individualism, free association, voluntarism, and achievement clash point for point with the values inherited from the *shtetl* culture of Jewish *Yiddishkeit*. All these conflicts come to a head at the highest value levels of the cultures themselves, in, namely, their own self-definitions of their religious community. The values locked into these self-definitions of religious membership and identity, in turn, boil down to one question: can you get up and leave? If so, how do you quit? (For too long conditions of *entry* or conversion have fudged the sharper and more revealing question of the conditions of *exit*.) "There is, and can be, no provision made whereby disaffected Jews might leave the fold with dignity and self-respect."[20] Tribal, rather than civil, Jewish culture issues no exit visas. To leave is an act not of reason but of treachery; to apostatize is to betray. To be a Jew, then, is to occupy an ascribed status in an involuntary association. It is, as the character Bernard says in Isaac Rosenfeld's *Passage from Home,* to "accept a sentence that had been passed generations ago, whose terms were still binding though its occasion had long been forgotten."[21] In contrast, Christianity—especially American, denominational Protestant Christianity—is a voluntary association, i.e., you can leave simply by changing your mind, your belief, or your suburb. You can leave with dignity and self-respect.

Of course, these differing exit conditions* correlate highly with the entry conditions, the way one becomes a Jew or a Christian. One becomes a Jew by being born one, by having a Jewish mother: that remains the halachic norm of *belonging* in the community's own self-definition of its religious boundaries (that is, the East European self-definition). "Regardless of what a Jew may do with his life, regardless of what he may affirm or deny, a Jew is someone who is born of a Jewish mother. It seems to me," Hertzberg observes, "that the *crucial* difference between Jewish and Christian identity is to be found here. Christianity arose as a fellowship of believers and, in our age of great pluralism of belief, the sense of fellowship, freely chosen seems, at least to the outsider, to remain the basic Christian category of identity. But," he concludes, "you do not choose your family; you are born into it. . . ."[22]

The collision, then, of the East European Jewish self-definition with the Protestant American denominational self-definition takes place at the highest level, namely, of the values that are institutionalized in the norms governing the entry and exit criteria of membership. It is a crucial factor in this disjunction of culture and subculture that it coincides, point for point, with the values at stake in the collision of modernization with traditionary cultures, as these adversary values are codified in lapidary form by Talcott Parsons's pattern alternatives of value-orientation: specificity vs. diffuseness, universalism vs. particularism, affectivity vs. restraint, self-orientation vs. collectivity-orientation, and achievement vs. ascription.[23] In the East European Jewish community, then,

---

*The Soviet Union is, of course, an ideologically closed society (Marxism-Leninism being "the one true ideology"). The current effort on behalf of Soviet Jewry takes the historically ironic form of insisting on the right of Soviet subjects to exit visas.

replenished continually by immigration, America has had, in its own backyard, so to speak, its own internal "colony," an experiment in "delayed modernization"[24] exhibiting all the features structural to the modernization process as it occurs in the underdeveloped countries. It is under the impact of this process and the crisis it brings, caught "between tradition and modernity," that the second generation writes its poetry, novels, criticism, and sociology. Some, like Rosenfeld's *Passage from Home,* embody both loyalty to the past and the "will to be modern," and issue as a *cri de coeur* representative of the "sensitive" intellectual elite everywhere as it suffers the assaults and promises of modernization.

Two more disjunctions of the East European subculture with American society focus on the level of the social system, rather than the cultural value commitments. As the young, modernizing Jew passes into the larger society, he encounters, long before "religious pluralism" at the cultural level has any meaning, much less attraction, for him, the phenomenon of "role pluralism"[25] on the level of the institutionalized social system. *Any* society has plural roles (one is both a son and a father, for example, in the kinship role-system) but in relatively modernized societies role pluralism becomes so prevalent that "quantity changes into quality," and the whole "feel" of the society radiates "role pluralism." Each concrete individual becomes the point of intersection for multiple roles (union member/householder / conservationist / stockholder, Republican/Catholic or Jew, etc.). This "role-theory" commonplace has some remarkable social psychological consequences for the identity of the ethnic. His identity, being a concrete, total, fused, monolithic "thing," must become his "secret"; he can neither leave it at home (it is not yet a "privatized" identity) nor carry it conspicuously into the public social system (in which he works, walks, buys, sells, etc). So in public places it goes "underground"—"in the 'public interest.'"

There are other cases where role pluralism is experienced, social-psychologically, as restraint, rather than as suppression. Buying a pack of cigarettes in a midtown drugstore during lunch hour on a day when everything's gone wrong, one must restrain one's complaint; the clerk is not a friend; your role is that of customer, and *kvetching* (ideal-typically, anyway) is ruled out by the values that pattern that particular relationship. "It is the person in role, not the total concrete individual, who is a member of the collectivity, even the societal community," writes Parsons.[26] Parsons has been criticized for making the lowest unit of his action theory the role, or the person in role, instead of the whole, concrete person; he has even apologized for its violation of "common sense." But, on the contrary, there are now few if any roles (were there ever?) in which one can act holistically. G. H. Mead's "mes" are multiplied, mated to the expectations of an increasingly complex social environment. The search begins (if one is that kind of a person) for the *I* ("identity crisis") which turns out to be systematically elusive. One becomes more cultivated, "elaborated," subtle, precise, functionally specific and (alas!) refined. As one makes more distinctions in self and environment, one becomes more distinguished, more insistent on distinguishing this from that, relevant from irrelevant. It is a researchable hypothesis that refinements of thought and refinements of manner occur *pari passu.*

Here again, there is a cost, and some terribly complicated people end up praying for the advent of *les terribles simplificateurs.* As in other instances, modernization drives a hard bargain. It is a relatively "total phenomenon," and you cannot pick and choose when and in what respect you welcome modernization. Traditionary subcultures, in the person of their front-running elites, feel the cost before they reap the benefits they dreamed of. In dreams begin responsibilities.

One final point of disarticulation between the East European subcultural ethos and the American social structure must be mentioned. Throughout the society, and paralleling the tolerance of ideological differences institutionalized in its religious pluralism and political dualism (the "two-party" system), there is a more fluid form of tolerance called "civility" which circulates informally if imperiously throughout the system. It is a generalized role, learned rudimentarily in primary socialization (ideally) and reinforced through the institutions of secondary socialization. This is a vast, and unresearched, subject. In a sense, civility operates in a manner paralleling the role Durkheim assigns to restitutive law in his *Division of Labor in Society:* it moderates private differences, it promotes—and is the index of—a solidarity that is not vehement and of the heart (like punitive law) and, like the prescriptions of administrative and procedural law, those of civility do not necessarily "correspond to any sentiment in us" and are "born in very ex-centric regions. . . ."[27] In a sense, civility is Simmel's "sociability" divested of the odor of the Berlin salons (where he encountered it) and let loose in the streets as a generalized medium of social interchange. The prescriptions of its code—like Deuteronomy—are largely negative. From its first axiom—the duty of civil inattention—all the others may be unpacked. It is civility's restraint that keeps the emotional temperature of public places cool.

The evolution of the code of public behavior has been from the positive content of gallantry and chivalry (incorporating particular notions of the role of women) through courtesy and politeness—which retained hierarchical and aristocratic components of *noblesse oblige*—all the way to the current code of civility. Civil behavior approximates a neutral medium for the exchange of those intangible gifts ("civilities") in the civic culture. These civilities are taken at face but, when the occasional crisis demands, are backed up—as is paper money—by the hard coin of genuine affect.

But the whole point of civility is that it creates, maintains, expresses, and celebrates—like the elementary forms of religious rites—a solidarity no less genuine for being a solidarity of the surface.[28] The traditional consensus of the ethnic group, the primordial ties of tribe, village, and family constitute a solidarity of the depths, anchored in affect. To the traditionalist background the solidarity of the surface constituted and legitimated by civility must seem, indeed, a mere "pretension to community." (There are also "mechanical" solidarities in Durkheim's sense in the civic culture but these are along vertical lines of leadership and political authority.) The ethnic, passing from home into the larger society, runs smack into that curious surface consensus called "civility" (or "bourgeois niceness" or "agreeableness" or whatever name you give it) and is appalled; if he belongs to the second generation there is a certain amount of fascination mingled with his dismay.

But the strain remains. The doctrine of Jewish election, on the religious level, symbolizes many of the socio-cultural strains that accompany the Jewish presence on the American pluralistic scene.

IV.

Chosenness as *Religious* Impropriety

If Protestants and Catholics, as we have seen in Reinhold Niebuhr and John Courtney Murray, experience the theological equality implicit in the First Amendment as something of a trial, the Jewish member of the tri-faith system experiences this theological status as social and even cultural upward mobility. Writing of that present-day ceremonial of American civil religion—in Robert Bellah's meaning of "civil religion"—the Presidential inauguration, when clergymen of all three faiths deliver invocations, Rabbi Hertzberg writes that it is indeed "no secret" that Jews are "much more uplifted by the presence of rabbis on that occasion than their Christian counterparts are by the participation of bishops," for the Jewish presence "at the most sacred moment of American civic life" constitutes, for Jews, *"visual* proof that they are indeed equal, in every sense, and that they do belong as full *co-owners* of American culture."*

Unlike Catholics, who built their separate parochial school system, Jews have cherished the public school system because it is the major place where Jews "visibly experience" their integration into America.[29] Rabbi Hertzberg goes on to say that the longing of the American Jew for *"a truly equal status in American culture"* is "his deepest and most messianic need."[30]

Correctly or incorrectly, this same "messianic need" for status is imputed to Catholics who, in the person of John F. Kennedy

*Apropos the word "co-owners," words such as *"possession* and *dispossession, takeover, cultural ethnocentrism, spiritual heirs,* and the like—terms that reflect a property-making or -claiming tendei.y in criticism," notes sociologist S. A. Longstaff, "began creeping into cultural journalism in the forties and have since become a staple in the field." "Literature and American Pluralism: Sociological Implications of the Jewish Breakthrough in American Letters" (unpublished paper delivered at the Society for the Study of Social Problems, Aug., 1976).

(Hertzberg is writing during the Kennedy administration), "will allow no one to tell them that they are less American than the descendants of an older majority" and who, in the interests of this need, seek to "remake American society" in such a way as "to remove from public life anything that suggests that they are less at home here than Cabots—or Kennedys."[31] Though there is some doubt whether the Kennedys and the Catholics were, or are, quite that grim in endeavoring to excise from public life "anything" that even "suggests" that the Loyolas are less than the Cabots, nevertheless, it may be assumed that Rabbi Hertzberg is a pretty good witness as to the deeper aspirations of his own community.

It is Rabbi Hertzberg's contention that two things stand in the way of this need of total "acceptance in [American] society"[32] by third and fourth generation members of the Jewish community, viz., a religious claim and a behavioral fact: the claim to be "chosen" and a certain vulgarity in behavior. Judaism's claim to be religiously "chosen" violates the ethos of American civil religion—the Protestant Etiquette—as much as does Catholicism's claim to be the one true church; there is—there always has been in the West—a pervasive pressure on Judaism to "reconstruct" and soft-pedal its doctrine of election. Judaism's belief in its own chosenness adds up, in the American milieu, to a kind of cultural "misbehavior." Protestantism's implied claim to be "superior" to Judaism (its "mission to the Jews"), Catholicism's implied claim to be "superior" to Protestantism (its "one true church" doctrine), and now Judaism's implied claim to be "superior" to both (its "chosen people" doctrine) all place the ideology of American pluralism under considerable strain. In the eyes of civil religion, these elitist claims are not only heresies but, in their self-indulgent self-regard, they are vulgarities, and not unrelated—as we shall see later—to Rabbi Hertzberg's observation that "the survival of Judaism in America is endangered by many things; but I believe that its single greatest enemy is vulgarity. . . ."[33]

From the beginning of the Diaspora, Judaism was saddled with the problem of finding non-Jewish legitimations for its belief in its own election (chosenness). What occurred to post-Emancipation nineteenth-century Judaism was this: seeking a

Western legitimation of the doctrine of its own election, Jewry, delving into Western cultural values, came up with an aristocratic recension of its own chosenness. This *noblesse oblige* explanation, merging with the "Hebraism" *vs.* "Hellenism" ideology, opted for a kind of spiritual elitism: Judaism was an aristocracy of the spirit "burdened" with a "mission" to the West. In the end, the reinterpretation boomeranged. As Western culture democratized itself, the component of condescension implicit in the Reform Jewish vocabulary of "mission" and "service" was thrown into relief. In the West itself, at that very moment, aristocratic courtesy was losing out to democratic civility. The Christian, modernizing West could only experience Judaism's claim that "more was expected of it because more had been given to it," not as humble acknowledgment, but as theological arrogance in questionable taste. In twentieth century America it must appear even more "offensive." Rabbi Harold M. Schulweis, in finding such reinterpretations of "chosenness" utterly unconvincing, is making a convincing case for Judaism's membership in the civic culture. The *noblesse oblige* claim to higher spiritual obligation, he writes, remains "an aristocratic conceit which demeans all other peoples by lowering our moral expectation of *their* behavior." Rabbi Schulweis finds that a further twist in the *noblesse oblige* machinery, the modern suggestion that God's choosing of Israel "really means" Israel's choosing of God, is as invalid an inversion as "turning X's owing Y money into Y's owing X money. The propositions are clearly not symmetrical."[34]

As with Father Murray, if one belongs to an historical religion with sacred texts, to change is to legitimate, to legitimate is to construe texts, and to construe is to *construct* a canopy over "what's happening." The hermeneutic of legitimation can go in two directions: it can delve into its own indigenous religious tradition for the terms with which to legitimate the "outside" world it is acculturating towards, thus building a sacred canopy over a secular world (this, generally, was the enterprise of Reinhold Niebuhr and John Courtney Murray); or it can "rob the Egyptians," using values drawn from the outside, secular world, such as *noblesse oblige,* constructing secular canopies over sacred things. This latter alternative has, in general, been the course chosen by Judaism. For Christianity, the secular West is a version of itself in mufti, in a condition of secularity; it has only to look "inside" to find the lexicon of legitimation for what it finds "outside." But minority Judaism was long an enclave. What was autochthonous to the House of Israel, despite the current artifacts of interfaith courtesy—such as "Judeo-Christian"—articulated poorly with the world Jewry found when ghetto walls crumbled. It struggled, it still struggles, to find Western-Christian ways of talking about what it means to be Jewish.

The struggle centered, it still centers, on the doctrine of the "chosen people." No Jewish religionist can affirm the doctrine without hastening to add instant modulations and refinements. In this way conceptual misbehavior is atoned for. To Westernize, to Christianize, is to become—in a non-trivial sense—refined. Judaism has struggled with the important *olenu l'shabeach la' Adon hakol* part of the prayer service (where Jews thank and praise God "for not having made them like the other nations [*goyim*]")[35] exactly as an embarrassed and liberalizing Catholicism—they are one and the same thing—has struggled to take the thunder out of the *extra ecclesiam* doctrine. Both claims violate the spiritual decorum of the West. Both legitimate the "ostentation" of visibility and separateness. Both call attention to themselves. Both make a religio-cultural "scene" that offends against the "civil inattention"[36] the West wishes to accord them. But Catholic "truth" and Jewish "Torah" remain, so far, incompletely broken to the authority of that Christian "yoke," the *halakah* of the protestant West, decorum and civility. Catholic "pride" and Eastern European Jewish *"chutzpah"* have not yet been refined away.

The Jewish psyche suffered a trauma, J. L. Talmon writes, "when the Jewish belief in chosenness sustained the terrible shock of national disaster and exile."[37] This trauma was renewed by Emancipation in the nineteenth century. If, as Professor Talmon writes, Jews "could hardly be absorbed by the amorphous barbarians in whose midst they found themselves in the early Middle Ages,"[38] nineteenth century Europe was another matter; and twentieth century America still another. Now the shoe was on the other foot. The Jewish movement of "Reconstructionism" was an American-Jewish effort to reconstruct "chosenness."

The whole of the Reconstructionist movement in Judaism—

a naturalistic interpretation of Judaism "as a religious civilization"—is an elaborate ideological machine for avoiding the appearance of national and ethnic conceit imputable to the "chosenness" doctrine. The best way to answer the charge that the
chosen-people doctrine has been "the model" for theories of
national and racial superiority, and to demonstrate the non-
privileged character of Judaism, writes Reconstructionism's
founder, Mordecai M. Kaplan, "is to eliminate that doctrine
from the Jewish liturgy,"[39] and so the Reconstructionist Prayer
Book duly deletes the prayer thanking and praising God for not
having made Israel like unto the *goyim.*

But Reconstructionism happened between the wars. In post-
war America the Jewish doctrine of chosenness no longer has to
be laundered so assiduously. In fact, "young turks" like Arthur
Cohen and Rabbis Steven Schwarzschild and Richard Rubenstein have reconstructed chosenness right back into their (often
rather esoteric) versions of Judaism. In a kind of theological
Judaica irredenta, these restorationists reclaim the "scandalous"
doctrine of chosenness for Judaism, looking back in anger at
what they take to have been the pusillanimous capitulations of
Reconstruction and Reform Judaism. But these thinkers do not
"represent" the Jewish community in the eyes of the general
Gentile culture. For them to re-embrace the "chosen people"
doctrine was thus a more or less private act, publicly embarrassing.

Rabbi Arthur Hertzberg is a more interesting figure in this
connection precisely because, as rabbi of a Conservative synagogue in Englewood, New Jersey, he maintains a vital exoteric
connection to the middle-class suburban Jewish community.
Thus, he is "representative." Also, he is an "academic," teaching at Columbia in Salo Baron's Institute. And he maintains
relations with the secular Jewish intellectuals (he officiated at the
marriage of Norman Podhoretz and Midge Decter, for example). And, as president of the American Jewish Congress, he is
in constant attendance, as Jewish delegate, at the continuing
interfaith summit. His ecumenical credentials are in good order,
for a time he turned out a monthly column, "The Jewish
World," for the activist Catholic weekly, *National Catholic Reporter.* And yet, as we have seen, he too finds Judaism "incon-

ceivable" without its "truest key," the chosen people doctrine.

What has happened in America, then, according to Hertzberg, is that the doctrine of election in Judaism—and its correlate, the ethnic ingredient in Judaism—were forced to retreat from the public domain, and a "split personality" was forced on Jews as the price for their acceptance as one of the religions acceptable to the civil religion consensus. Judaism, for decades, not unlike many Jews, "passed" as a religious denomination "like any other" religious denomination. Ethnicity and chosenness were kept in the closet. The general public image of Judaism was, in effect, a religious fiction.

V.

Religious Fictions and Legal Fictions: Cunning

Catalysts of Modernization

Behavior in public places is governed, as Erving Goffman details for us, by the exigencies of the situational proprieties governing the times, places, and circumstances of that public behavior. The ground rules of Anglo-American freedom create the "space" in which social behavior can appear; and as we have seen, the "price" of that freedom is the sundering of public from private, i.e., the emergence from familial and tribal "realities" of "behavior" itself, i.e., the decorum of social action "appearing" in public. What a religion "really is" for itself is thus, in fully developed "modern" societies, privatized. It retires from public view; any of the traces that remain in public of its old monopolistic cockiness that haven't as yet been discreetly brought in off the streets into the living room (or bedroom) are carefully, civilly inattended to. In a word, it has disappeared.[40]

Behavior (yes, in the sense of decent, "nice," good behavior) introduces an inner-outer split that is, at the same time, a private-public split. Behavior systematically introduces an *als ob* into human action: the religions (and, of course, the actors who are their carriers) must "behave" in public "as if" their truth were tentative and not absolute. What happens, then, with the emergence of the civic culture and its civility (which is the *outer*-worldly behavioral coefficient of the protestant *inner*-worldly ethic immanent in modern industrial societies) is that all the squalid "double-lives" and dual loyalties of the immigrant Jews and Catholics (and others) emerging from their traditional and primordial milieux are traded in for the one, great, tidy, *legitimate* dualism of modernity, viz., the private-public, invisible-visible split. It is with traces of aggrieved regret that Rabbi Hertzberg laments this "split personality"[41] forced on religions by the freedom, religious pluralism, and, we should add, the "dialectic of civility" that is abroad in our land. Rather might he rejoice, as perhaps part of him does, that, by a curious turn of events, civility tries to make Marranos of us all.

Hertzberg's point should be clear: to allow the very label "religion" to be applied to itself, and by "coming on" in public as if it were one of the tri-faith established "religions" as Western Christendom understands a religion to be a religion, is, in Hertzberg's eyes, hypocrisy. The oxymoronic concept of an "ethnic church" simply won't wash in Western terms. Hertzberg blames the American Jewish Establishment for promoting and presiding over this aspect of the "brutal bargain." The jewel of Jewish chosenness has been traded for social acceptability. Judaism (and Jews) must henceforth pretend in public that they are like the *goyim*, whatever *reservatio mentalis* they may retain in private. The stance of the American Jewish Establishment, he writes, has been dictated by the "peculiar hope" that *"all other* Americans will believe that Jews are indeed 'just like everybody else,' but that the Jewish young *themselves* will know differently in their secret hearts."[42] Rabbi Hertzberg interprets the public muting of Jewish difference moralistically as a form of hypocrisy (when he is not employing the business metaphor of the "bargain"). "The protective coloration of likeness has appeared to the [Jewish] Establishment to be an indispensable tool with which to create safety [read: invisibility] for the Jew. . . ."[43]

Hertzberg remarks that in America today as in nineteenth century Germany, beneath this Reform, denominational, religious, *protestant,* voluntarist, universalistic definition of the Jew, there lurk "far different and more specific emotions about the uniqueness of Jewish identity."[44] He warns the Jewish Establishment that "what is happening" is really the reverse of what they want, viz., the *Gentile majority* being courted by the religious, Reform-type definition of Judaism is not prepared really "to behave as if" the definition of Jewish identity as a religious identity were completely true, while the *younger Jews,* taking it at face, "are refusing to be any kind of Marrano within democracy . . ." and are thus emigrating from the Jewish community.[45] What Hertzberg perceives moralistically as pretense and hypocrisy is more accurately identified by an outsider as a fictive (or appearance) component in the civic culture, viz., what Eliezer Livneh calls "the persistently maintained *fiction* that the Jews are a religious community, just like the other groups. . . ."[46] The Jewish self-image today demands religious affiliation as the identifying characteristic because, as Sklare notes, "nothing else can be defended in American terms."[47] Religious fictions enable traditional religions to grow gracefully. Like legal fictions—see Lon Fuller's brilliant *Legal Fictions*[48]—they are midwives of modernization. Civil religion and American civic culture not only coerce all differences into religious differences because religious differences are the only legitimate, non-stigmatic group differences, but civility converts the old, intransigent, religious substances into interesting "adjectives" which will "pass." Young Jews on campus, Norman E. Frimer writes, "see themselves as counterparts of their non-Jewish friends—members with an adjectival religious badge. . . ."[49]

A Jew with any memory or piety at all must swallow hard as he hears himself say "I happen to be Jewish." This pregnant phrase, "happen to be Jewish," is the everyday, routine formula of what passes for the knowledge of what a Jew is, and which is enshrined and legitimated by Jewish membership in the tri-faith religious establishment. To be but another "denomination" is to avow that a contingent relation exists between you and your religious community: you "happen to be Jewish" has the air of "I might have been Methodist" about it. An area of empirical research opens up here for the sociology of knowledge, since commonsense knowledge of what passes for Jewish identity is itself constructed as a means of Jewish "passing."

Religious pluralism thus has become, for Jews, a legitimate avenue of assimilation. By accepting as self-image the religiously defined label of "Jewish," they qualify as Americans. But the paradox remains: Gentiles have established securely a taken-for-granted Jewish identity as "religious" that, for Jews themselves, remains problematic, and that facilitates assimilation. Thus many ironies attend the consequences of what Norman Podhoretz speaks of as "the effort of the Jewish organizations to have Judaism officially recognized as one of the three major American faiths."[50]

Is survival jeopardized by success? Has "making it" as one of the three equi-legitimate expressions of American religiosity perhaps begun the "unmaking" of the Jew? Has the tri-faith ideology of Jewishness-as-a-religion *reversed* at last, for Jews, the confidence trick that Berger and Luckmann see society playing on the child in primary socialization, viz., "to make appear as necessity what is in fact a bundle of contingencies,"[51] so that the traditionally disadvantageous social fate of being born a Jew is exorcised at last, and the formerly fatal ingnominies of ascriptivism yield to achievement, voluntary affiliation, and the public civility resident in the locution "happen to be"?

It would seem, indeed, that the Jewish "religious" identity acquired in secondary socialization has begun to supplant the older, earlier, "ethnic" identity of primary socialization, and that—in the American context—the accident of a Jew's birth is today made meaningful only by being defined precisely as an accident (i.e., as "meaningless": I only "happen" to be Jewish). For the first time, younger Jews are able to enjoy the "inner emigration" of a certain "role distance" from their Jewishness as they could not when it was uniquely embedded in their massive primordial socialization. The late stand-up comic, Lenny Bruce, brought this form of "working the system" of *both* Jewish identities, and playing them against each other, to the stature of a performing art. Many of his "bits" could have been titled "Games Ethnics Play."

The institutionalization of Judaism and Jewry as the third "official" religious division of American society has largely taken place, as noted above, since the war. As there was a "price" for Emancipation in Europe in the 19th century, so there is a price-tag on "official recognition" as one of the three official religions in twentieth century America. This institutionalization of the Jews has clearly been a policy, Professor Dennis Wrong observes, on the part of "powerful elite groups in government at all levels, the political parties, the churches, professional associations and the mass communications industries. . . . It is, of course," he notes, "as a *religious* group that the Jews have been recognized"[52] and it is as such that America has underwritten their survival.* Jews, he notes, are now not merely regarded by others as a religious group, "but they increasingly so regard themselves" and thus, in this respect, appear to have completed a full cycle, returning, with the acculturation of the East European immigrants, "to the outlook of the late nineteenth century American Jewish community of largely German origin and Reform persuasion. . . ."[53]

The sheer structural fact of the institutionalization of Judaism as one of a *triad* of religions is important. Judaism, in its historical self-conception in the West, has always related to the Christians as "those others." But a dyadic relation doesn't civilize: the two members of the dyad either get along or they don't. "Two" is company or enemy, but three—pluralism—is a crowd. What the American philosopher Charles Sanders Peirce called "thirdness" involves (Hegelian) mediation, that is, it involves overcoming the sheer otherness of a dyad of "confrontation" or the sheer togetherness of a dyad of symbiosis. In a cultural as in a cognitive context, a trialogue means that at least one member is always "audience," at any given time, for the other two's dialogue. Thus, the rotating dialogues are always being overheard and monitored by a built-in third, which functions as the generalized "other" or "conscience" of the first two. There is therefore a tendency for any two members of the trialogue to listen carefully to each other, sensitively taking the role of the second in the presence of the vigilant third. The role of the third party to the pluralism, be it referee, conscience, or judge, is played in turn by each member of the trialogue. This role, with its serially alternating incumbents, tends to internalize each member of the pluralistic set to the other. Each is no longer merely "situational" to the actions and interests of the others, to be used as means to ends. As instrumental-relations abate,

---

*A complex change gets under way after the 1967 Arab-Israeli War, in which American policy begins to underwrite Israeli *national* survival as a way of ensuring American Jewish *religious* survival. American civil religion can thus maintain the fiction of a split in Judaism between ethnicity and religion by relocating ("displacing") the "material" or ethnic component of Judaism in the Mideast. This story must await another time.

the ceremony of civility quickens. This is another sense, we contend, in which pluralism civilizes.

Thus, left to themselves, Rabbi Hertzberg remarks, the major faiths of the Western world "would not have thought about each other very much, except as objects of conversion. Implicit within the American stance on freedom of religion is pressure on the various groups to presume that the others are here to stay." The American tradition, despite the vaunted "neutrality" of the state vis-à-vis its religions, actually "shaped the religions in America"; and that it did so "by more than providing them with blank space in which to expand and collide seems undeniable," concludes Rabbi Hertzberg.[54] The public space of social encounter provided by the civic culture is a part of the *pays réel;* it is not the empty *tabula rasa* of the *pays légale* taught by the civics textbooks; it is an ambience dense with the funded ground rules of Western freedom and the informal coercions of propriety.

We have encountered earlier one of these informal coercions of propriety: Rabbi Hertzberg calls it the "pressure to presume" that the other parties to the trialogue are here to stay. The act by which Reinhold Niebuhr abandoned the Christian mission to the Jews was at the same time an act that legitimated the existence of the Jews. It was a conversion experience, i.e., it was a *religious* legitimation of Jewry. And if it involved abandoning essential components of Christianity, it also drew on other equally essential Christian components. To be a religious legitimation it must be a *free* act. Niebuhr, writing before Murray had completed his church-state breakthrough, notes that Catholicism frankly accepts the situation of religious diversity in America "only under the *compulsion* of history . . . [it] regards this situation as provisional."[55] "Obviously," he concludes, "this position is in conflict with the presuppositions of a free society."

Just as the political rules of the two-party system, as we shall see in chapter 7, are subjected to considerable strain by a totalitarian party which accepts the rule of free speech and minority rights *provisionally*, intending, on achieving its own majority, to deny these rights to its own minority, so also to practice toleration of another religion only provisionally (until it is converted) is not to accept either the toleration rule, or the other fellow, internally and as one's own. To the degree that the other is accepted on sufferance, to that degree one is anomic to the culture: the rules are "for the other fellow."

True civility, in other words, can never be temporary (if it is, it is expedience, i.e., a means to an end). True civility, in fact, never defines the other person or religion in *temporal* terms, as a historical stage in one's own development (for instance, Judaism as a *preparation for* Christianity, as *praeparatio evangelica*). True civility's vision tends to be spatial and parataxic: the religions are sitting side by side, or across the table from one another ("the civilization of the dialogue"), or, if they are moving, marching *together* till the end of time or, as in the parable of the tares, growing together till the harvest (Murray's legitimating evangelical trope). The civic culture thus puts an end to the *Interims*-etiquette of theological condescension. The "preamble" role Christians ascribe to Jews is ended. The Catholic "wrong turn" historiography of the Reformation is over. We are all here to stay, not only *de facto* but *de jure*. Each has a right to be here as one-among-many. Each accepts the others not in a provisionary and cautious way, not with stipulations and hidden provisos, and "for the time being," and "subject to change without notice," but permanently, unconditionally, wholeheartedly.

To accept and internalize such values is, in the end, to change one's outer appearance as much as one's inner disposition. The "look" of civic niceness takes over the human face, as it does the face each religion turns toward its public. Fanatical conviction is relativized and relegated like a private orgy to the home. What I call the "one-among-many-mien" is born and spreads itself across the democratic countenance. The American denomination, with its civil demeanor, is coming into being.

VI.

Words and Deeds: The Unanticipated Consequences of a Forensic Identity

If Catholic "good behavior" was rewarded and sealed by the election of John F. Kennedy, the Jewish problem remains stubbornly unresolved. Jewish assimilation will be consummated not politically but by the religious event of becoming a religion "like" the other religions. Judaism took part in the "religious revival" following World War II, but the Jewish version of the post-war "religious revival" was not, I think, due to the operation of any Hansen's law (the hypothesis that the grandson embraces what the grandparent rejects) nor even to Judaism's establishment as one of America's *three* religions, but rather to its official recognition as one of America's three *religions*. This religious label, at best misleading, has tended as we have seen, to invert the reality it putatively describes. It is a case of what Robert K. Merton calls "the self-fulfilling prophecy," where an initially false definition of a situation evokes new behavior which makes the originally false conception come true.[56] Situations defined as religious, to echo W. I. Thomas, become religious in their consequences. One of these consequences is the phenomenon of the "Jewish Center" in the suburban metropolitan areas. In these "gilded ghettoes," as Kramer and Levantman call them, the child is, indeed, "the meaning of this life," and "leads" his parents back into the synagogue. If the religious label is a kind of anticipatory socialization of the child, equipping him for integration into the American "way," the child—perhaps especially in the Jewish case—supplies a kind of retroactive socialization for the parent.* "And a little child shall lead them" indeed.

Another consequence of this religious labeling of Jews is that the religious definition enters the commonsense world of both Gentile and Jew becoming, on the pre-theoretical level, "what everybody knows about Jews." Just as the locutions of psychoanalytical theory "re-enter everyday life"[57] enabling the victims of urban malaise to construct a plausible neurosis "in conformity with the recognized symptomatology,"[58] so the tri-faith "construct" of pulpit and subway poster is anchoring itself in the routine consciousness of both Jew and Gentile. To research

*The Father of Princeton historian and Presidential adviser Eric Goldman, after giving his only son the un-Jewish name of Eric, turned around and adopted Eric as his own middle name, thus becoming—in Eric Goldman's words—"the only father in the U.S. named after his own son." This is a form of acculturation-assimilation by means of what anthropologists call "technonymy." Fern Marja Eckman, "Closeup," *New York Post*, Feb. 9, 1964.

the extent to which the three-religion formula is experienced, for Jews, as a misnomer, and the generational differences in the use of religious labeling in Jewish self-identity, would constitute an interesting task for the sociology of knowledge. Our hypothesis would be that while the older generations would mostly find such religious self-definition factitious and forced, the younger ones would, mostly, "believe" it. An inter-generational figure such as Rabbi Arthur Hertzberg is interesting precisely because he has enough memory of the old, ethnic "chosenness" definition of Jewry to be contemptuous of the new religious definition, but enough status and cultural aspiration to be helpless before the cultural opportunities afforded by "working the tri-faith system." We know, Martin E. Marty writes, "that Jews sometimes stress the religious, sometimes the secular character of their community and its alliances."[59] (Marty's very religious-secular formulation, of course, betrays its Western Christian provenance.)

This facultative definition of Judaism—with its built-in options: a forensic, public, religious definition for the Gentiles, and a familial, private, "peoplehood" definition for themselves—has its advantages, but also its embarrassments. Nathan Glazer, from within Judaism, speaks of American Jews living in a society that "expects to see their ethnic particularity ultimately abandoned." The regime of civil religion is so coercive that, even to describe this situation, is to be driven to use the language of social shame and embarrassment. The ethnicity of Judaism, Glazer writes, inevitably leads to "a certain embarrassment among American Jews. . . ."[60] It is not only "the embarrassing shackles" of the complex code of Talmudic legislation,[61] it is not only that, in the third generation suburbs, "it is embarrassing to have the children playing outside while the Christian children go to Sunday school and church,"[62] but there is an "embarrassing dilemma," viz., the question *whether* the Jewish religion *"is* a religion or a means of preserving the Jewish nation."[63] This "embarrassing split between group loyalty and religious faith,"[64] this "conflict between Judaism and Jewishness" was still, in the 1950s when Glazer wrote, unresolved.[65]

"Unresolved," but lived with. Each subgroup evolves

strategies for living with its own internal contradictions, and with the contradictions between its own "sub-universe of meaning" and the larger, environing culture. In the Catholic case, as we have seen, its assimilation in fact ran far ahead of the theoretical legitimation-machinery available to justify it. Catholics were very "American," occupying visible and public positions in the society (from politics to bar-tending), fighting its wars, even hounding its "un-Americans." It is questionable that many Americans feared what John F. Kennedy would *do* if he won the Presidency. Did they really think he would "take orders from" the Pope, violate the Constitution, even press for Federal aid to parochial schools? Some, doubtless, did, but most sensed correctly that the real dilemma was between words and deeds, ideas and behavior, and that Kennedy, when challenged, might be forced back into *talking* the language of the pre-modern, Latin, unitary church-state theory. It was Catholic theory which was saddled with particularism, and American Catholic behavior which was universalistic. John Courtney Murray, as we have seen, tried to bridge that legitimation-credibility gap.

The Jewish case, as it seems to me, is the mirror inverse of the Catholic dilemma. The respondents in the 1968 Marshall Sklare and Joseph Greenblum study of the Jewish community of "Lakeville" (a suburb of a Midwest metropolis),[66] when asked what they considered essential to being a good Jew, answered overwhelmingly in universalistic, humanitarian, "liberal" terms ("leading an ethical and moral life," promoting "good causes and civic betterment," helping the underprivileged, etc.). And yet, notes Professor Glazer in his review-article of the Lakeville study, if we were to conclude that the essentials of Jewishness had been reduced by the respondents to "a series of platitudinous, humanitarian sentiments, we would be quite wrong. This set of responses, after all, represents what people *say*. . . ." What they *do*, as described in the bulk of the study, argues strongly that being a good Jew also (or rather?) consists for them in giving their children a Jewish education, joining a synagogue, supporting Jewish causes (especially Israel), and showing concern over intermarriage.[67] Thus, if we begin from choices on a check list, we get a universalistic picture of the content of Jewish commitment in America; but if we begin with actual Jewish behavior, a different, considerably more particularistic, picture emerges.[68]

Stabilized at a relatively low, even minimal, level of religious observance and synagogue attendance, it is clear to Glazer that it is the ethnic character of the Jewish community that is "one of the major, or perhaps the major, prop to the maintenance of Jewish identity" and that the *specifically* religious elements in Jewish life, if there are such, play a very small role in maintaining the community. In Lakeville, Jews are kept together "by family links, common cultural traits, certain special interests, and a distinct emotional atmosphere . . ." and by negative plausibility structures that keep their self-definition going: they disapprove of intermarriage, seven out of ten belong to Jewish organizations not sponsored by a synagogue, and "the great majority of Jews in Lakeville (and this is a community of professionals and businessmen with a median family income in 1966 of $18,000) have no close friends other than Jews."[69]

The Jewish paradox, we have noted, is the reverse of the Catholic paradox. This is one more aspect of the "double-life" lived by many an ethnic immigrant. In the Jewish case, the verbal-theoretical universalism has served to obscure observation of the particularism of Jewish group action. In the corresponding Catholic case, traditionalist-particularist verbal and theological rigor have served to obscure a certain universalism in practice. Sklare writes that "at the present moment the Lakeville Jews remain considerably more Jewish in action than in thought"[70] and, we should add, the religious definition of Jewishness inflates this forensic character of public Jewish identity even more. It adds a further note of universalism, bifurcating even more radically Jewish thought from Jewish action, Jews as they are for themselves and Jews as they "publicly relate" for others, Jewishness *pour soi* and Jewishness *pour autrui*. This is clear, Glazer writes, from the fact of Lakeville Jewish participation in synagogue "despite the 'universalism' of their *stated* religious views, from the fact that most of their philanthropic contributions go into Jewish channels despite their *stated* distaste for the parochial, and from their uneasiness over the possibility of intermarriage despite their [*stated*] commitment to the primacy of romantic love and human equality. . . . Obviously, there is something of a contradiction here. . . ."[71]

The "contradiction" consists in construing Jewish identity in terms drawn from the larger culture, in constructing a "secular" canopy over a "sacred" thing, in universalizing for others what remains a stubborn particularity for oneself (and, yes, in the end, for others too: the Reform apologetics "works" only "by courtesy" of the Gentile civil culture). The social engineering (in terms of plausibility) and the identity-management (in terms of psychic morale) and, lest we forget, the kind of rhetoric and public relations required to maintain the precarious equilibrium of such a contradictory identity, is something of a feat. Some of the Jewish penchant for public relations may have its origin in the strategies required for impression-managing this forensic Jewish identity. "Indeed," the late Will Herberg noted, "public relations seems to be more anxiously, and skillfully, cultivated by American Jewry than by either the Catholics or the Protestants; nothing that any Jewish community agency does, whatever may be its intrinsic nature or value, is ever without its public relations angle."[72] The social construction of such a defensive and forensic identity would have been impossible without anti-Semitism, and their half-knowledge of this fact gives to the strenuous efforts of Jewish defense organizations and others to eliminate anti-Semitism an ironic cast: they half-fear that they are digging their own grave, and that when the last anti-Semite finally disappears, the last Semite will quickly follow.[73]

An unintended consequence of this Jewish "optional" identity (as ethnic community and as universal religion) surfaced during the "Six-Day" Arab-Israeli War of June 1967. After several decades of public relations, arguing to the American people that the Jews were a religious denomination like any other (Protestant) denomination, many Gentile Americans understandably took the Jewish Establishment at its word (as did many of the younger generation of Jewry, as Rabbi Hertzberg noted above). Then, with the 1967 Arab-Israeli war, came the *volte face:* Christians, defining the war politically, and making many shades of response—to be sure, mostly pro-Israeli—were chided for not realizing that, for the Jew, the war was a religious war since *Kol Yisroel hem chaverim:* All Jews are brothers. The Six-Day War had turned American Jewry publicly, openly, into an ethnic *Gemein-*

schaft again. Even Reform Jewish journals hailed the war as the end of the "merely" religious definition of Judaism. In America, *Dimensions* magazine editorialized, many Jews had been tempted "to define themselves as a mere religious denomination—like Protestants or Catholics. The crisis exploded this . . . Jews are not like other religious groups. We are—and the crisis demonstrated it anew—different and unique, defying the pigeonholes of history and sociology. . . . The trauma and triumph of 1967 healed many breaches."[74] Soon, once more, in Jewish publications, there was talk of Jewish "peoplehood" (the respectable rhetorical form for "chosenness") and ethnic community. Religion, which had long functioned as a polite surrogate for Jewishness, came under increasing attack. Judaism began to be publicly re-ethnicized. An "instant theology" appeared, with Rabbi Richard L. Rubenstein telling his audiences, as early as September 1967, that Jewish theology had been reshaped from "exile" to "homecoming": " 'place' has now supplanted time in Jewish religious sentiment and God is experienced primarily as a God of earth and nature."[75]

A month later, Reform Rabbi Balfour Brickner was charging that Christians dragged their feet on helping Israel by treating the war as a political issue. The first topic on the agenda for dialogue with Christians in the future, he remarked in hurt tones, is going to be "the meaning of Jewish peoplehood, not all this esoteric stuff about conscience and family. We've got to go back to basics, to real solid basics, of what we are and what we mean to one another."[76] With that statement Reform Judaism had come full cycle: now the "mystique" of peoplehood becomes the "real solid basic," the ethical themes of classical Reform become mystical and "esoteric stuff"!

With such an about-face, Americans who were anti-Israeli in the war, or who were neutral, or who perhaps were pro-Israel but not wholeheartedly enough, were "coerced"—for social reality is a "thing"—to *experience* their (to them, political) position as a form of anti-Semitism. The "New Left" refused this "definition of the situation" and split from the "Old Left." Dwight Macdonald, for example, called the ardent ethnic solidarity sparked by the war, with its "callousness" to Arab rights, "disgraceful and disgusting, and let my anti-anti-Semitic friends make the most of it."[77]

But if Macdonald felt manipulated by the anti-anti-Semitic
ethos, a real specter *had* been haunting American (and other
Diaspora) Jewries: assimilation, disappearance. And the *Te
Deum*s that Rabbi Hertzberg, Milton Himmelfarb, Robert Alter,
and a hundred others sang were as much in gratitude that the
Six-Day War had shored up a tottering American Jewish identity
as they were in celebration of an Israeli military victory. Their
joy, if understandably "overdetermined," was not mindless.
Jewish survivalism could now take a new lease on life, shaking
that bland monkey "religion" from its ancient back. American
Jewish ethnic identity was in business again.

A further unanticipated consequence of the religious self-
definition of Jewry was the return, on the part of a new breed
of Jewish religionists, to the touchy doctrine of Jewish "chosenness" (as noted earlier). It is not altogether clear whether this
is merely the Jewish version of the post-war "religious revival"
with its "rediscovery of confessional heritages" or a move "in
the game of marginal differentiation that pluralism engen-
ders."[78] More important, perhaps, for the Jewish "rediscovery"
than either the intra-Jewish need for marginal differentiation or
the inter-religious workings of the "economics of ecumenics"
was what I shall call "introjective Judaism."

VII.

The Return of the Chosen People Doctrine:

Baptized, Pedigreed, Secularized

The palmary example of the working of this "introjective
Judaism" mechanism is Arthur A. Cohen. As ordinary, everyday
Jewry more and more—up until the Six-Day War anyway—acculturated itself into the American "religious" definition of the
Jewish community, Arthur Cohen carried the process, on the
plane of religious thought, one step further: he became ac-
quainted, while at the University of Chicago, with Thomism; he
ended by taking, as a datum of his Jewish experience, the fact
that Christianity believes that the Jews are chosen. Cohen's ca-

reer has been an attempt to assimilate that datum into contemporary Judaism, making it *de jure* there. It is as though the Jewish chosenness doctrine had survived in respectable form only as a residue in Catholic and Christian theology. Cohen, in any case, encounters it there in the early fifties. Instead of a conversion to Christianity, to which, for a time, he was enormously attracted, Cohen decided—with the aid of Rabbi Milton Steinberg of the Park Avenue Synagogue—to introject the high theological *yichus** in which Judaism was held in Catholic and Christian circles. Phrases out of Jacques Maritain—the "mystery of Israel," "the scandal of particularity," etc.—turn up more and more in his writings of the 1950s. The very term "theology" in his usage is of "high" Thomist provenance. Just as Will Herberg theologizes out of Niebuhr, Cohen does so out of Maritain, Tillich and the Existentialists, with touches of Buber.

What you get then is a Judaism *à rebours,* and Cohen's willed theological effort may be seen as the attempt to "fill the bill," to flesh out with a theology the post-war billing of Judaism as "one-of-the-three-major-American-faiths." Just as the tri-faith dictum functions as a kind of involuntary gift made to the Jewish people by the *goyim,* so the role Jews are depicted as playing in Catholicism's "salvation history" becomes the means by which Cohen legitimates the absolutist theological claims of Judaism. The theological legitimacy and status that Catholicism (and Protestantism) accord Judaism is retrojected back into "domestic" Judaism. It is my contention that this "feedback Judaism" begins on the everyday life plane of tri-religion pluralism, where it is promoted by the Jewish Establishment as a means of ethnic survival. But, by the dialectics of the self-fulfilling prophecy, Jews—especially Conservative Jews, as Marshall Sklare notes—are "forced into 'making good' on the stereotype. . . . Additionally, the [religious] stereotype—once it is successfully established—reacts back on the Jew himself. . . . At this juncture, the Jews may find themselves propelled into fulfilling the image [in his everyday behavior] projected by the Gentile. Although he himself may not actually *believe* the stereotype to be wholly valid," concludes Sklare, "he feels that he must *act like* the type of 'good Jew' which the Gentile imagines—the Jew who is loyal

*Pedigree, status.

to his rabbi, interested in his synagogue."[79] Here again we note the "brutal bargain" which forces an *als ob* (he must *"act like* the type of 'good [i.e., religious] Jew' which the Gentile imagines") onto Jewish behavior and *mauvaise foi* into Jewish consciousness. The civility of the civic culture provides a kind of moratorium, in the privacy of which the ethnic immigrant can work through the crisis of his identity, in preparation for full entry into the modernizing West. During this "probationary" period he behaves in public as the "imaginary Jew" of the Gentile imagination.

These macrosociological events have their microsociological counterparts. Arthur Cohen returned to Jewish chosenness by courtesy of Catholic Christianity. In his grand assault on Jewish Reconstruction's naturalism and traditionlessness—his review-article of Eugene Kohn's *Religion and Humanity* in 1954—it is Catholicism that Cohen uses against Kohn's attack on Jewish chosenness: "It is quite clear that all the neuroses which are supposed to attend the Gentile world upon the election of Israel are non-existent. Ironically," he writes, "all serious Christian theology is adamant that Israel is elected, that, more than elected, it is the most mysterious and divine community in the world. . . ." Cohen continues, fairly purring: ". . . the Christian Churches . . . are insistent that Israel has not only a vocation, but is chosen [citing Berdyaev, Maritain, Bloy, Péguy]." To forestall the appearance of servility, he concludes by reminding his readers that this election is not "a gratuity of the Christian world. It is a fact of belief . . . a datum of the Jewish religious experience."[80]

By 1959, Cohen had moved his revival of the Jewish chosenness doctrine from inhouse Jewish to mass circulation secular journals. It was in *Harper's* for August of that year that his manifesto, "Why I Choose to Be a Jew," would appear. Judaism was now no longer fated chosenness, a given ethnicity, but more like a gathered church, a properly protestant voluntary association. Belloc's famous jingle—"How odd of God/to choose the Jews" —became instantly obsolete as Cohen made up his mind whether to choose God. The Israeli philosopher who observed of Franz Rosenzweig (1886–1929) that he was the last Jewish thinker who would ever be able to think of history as waiting until he had decided whether or not he wished to remain a Jew, had, apparently, never heard of New York's Arthur Cohen.

In this *Harper's* essay it is notable that the egalitarianism of American civil religion forces on Cohen a fractured rhetoric for the public discussion of Jewish chosenness. "Judaism is exclusive," Cohen tells us, "only in the sense that we affirm we possess important truth which is available to all—everyone can join but only on *our* terms. . . ."[81] Cohen is here discreetly mentioning the unmentionable. Ira Eisenstein, son-in-law of the founder of Jewish Reconstructionism (Mordecai Kaplan), had warned that "we ought not to *say* that God gave the Torah to us and to nobody else, particularly at a time when mankind seeks to foster the sense of the equality of peoples." Eisenstein is here suggesting, Charles S. Liebman comments, "that though Jews *are* at least *unique,* it is *bad taste* to *talk* about it. The American influence," he concludes, "is in the very marrow of Reconstructionism."[82] The American civil religion brings the triumphful religions to heel by impeaching their taste.

It was also in 1959 that Philip Roth's story "The Conversion of the Jews" appeared, in which young Ozzie Freedman—*aet.* 13 — wants to know *how* Rabbi Binder can call the Jews "The Chosen People" "if the Declaration of Independence claimed all men to be created equal," and in which Ozzie refuses, as an evasion, the rabbi's effort, in reply, to distinguish between "political equality and spiritual legitimacy."[83] Clearly, Ozzie is on his way to becoming a good Reconstructionist and completely rejecting any American Jewish obnubilation of the chosenness doctrine.

But not so his creator, Philip Roth. Roth has brilliant things to say about the vicissitudes in America—and not only in America—of the doctrine of Jewish chosenness. If in nineteenth century Europe, Judaism was secularized, as Hannah Arendt shows, as psychological "Jewishness,"[84] in twentieth century America Judaism was inherited as psychological *specialness.* What a Jewish child inherited, Roth writes, was "no body of law, no body of learning and no language, and finally, no Lord—which seems to me a significant thing to be missing." But what one *did* receive "was a psychology, not a culture and not a history in its totality. What one received *whole,* however, what one feels whole, is a

kind of psychology; and the psychology can be translated into
three words—'Jews are better.' This is what I knew from the
beginning: somehow Jews were better. I'm saying this as a point
of psychology; I'm not pronouncing it as a fact."[85] Situations
defined as real, runs the dictum of sociologist W. I. Thomas,
become real in their consequences. Jews self-defined as "better
than," become better in their performances.

The sociologist of religion, Marshall Sklare of Brandeis University, was one of the first Americans to note this fact, what I
call "the metaphoricality of Jewish chosenness." This is the
insight that Jewish *religious* chosenness secularizes in Diaspora
from a spiritual claim, becoming a metaphor for moral, intellectual, cultural, literary, entrepreneurial, or even national claims.
Jews, Sklare noted in 1955,

> still possess a feeling of superiority, although more in the moral and
> intellectual realms *now* than in the area of spiritual affairs. While the
> [Jewish] feeling of superiority is a factor which has received com-
> paratively little attention from the students of the problem [of ex-
> plaining Jewish survival], it is of crucial importance because it oper-
> ates to retard assimilation. Leaving the group . . . is viewed not as
> an advancement, but as cutting oneself off from a claim to superior-
> ity. (*Conservative Judaism: An American Religious Movement* [Glencoe,
> Illinois: The Free Press, 1955], p. 34. My italics.)

Clearly, this is not the "one-among-many" mien we found
"unconsciously" inculcated by the pluralism of the American
civil religion and the American civic culture. Just as the forensic
definition of Jews as "religious" unwittingly urged them to
"make good" in public on the religious definition of Jewishness,
so the lineal secularized descendants of Jewish religious chosenness—Philip Roth's the Jew as "better than"—forced at least the
more gifted among them into making good on individualizing
this generic variable "betterness." As Philip Roth explained in
1963 to the "Second Dialogue in Israel" panel:

> So one had to, then, I think . . . begin to create a moral character
> for oneself. That is, one had to invent a Jew . . . There was a sense
> of specialness and from then on it was up to you to invent your
> specialness;* to invent, as it were, your betterness . . . invent a
> character for [yourself], or invent certain moral responses, invent

attitudes . . . there was, I think [in Jewish writers], that striving and yearning to be special, . . . the blessing and burden of having been brought up in America [in contrast to Israel]—was to have been given a psychology *without a content,* or with only the remains of a content, and then to invent off of that.[86]

These psychological "remains," in *Galut,* of the content of the doctrine of chosenness constitute a Jewish variant of the secularization process. But relativization has proceeded only so far. The consciousness remains comparative: "better than." The relation to others remains dyadic, not pluralistic: "there were reminders constantly that one was a Jew," writes Roth of his upbringing, "and that there were *goyim out there.* As a friend of mine recently wrote in *Commentary,* he heard the word *goy* hundredfold and he heard the word "kike" maybe once in his life. I haven't heard it used against me yet, but I've heard *goy* used against Gentiles a good deal."[87]

Hovering over everything is a fact: the fact that Protestant dissenting Christianity and its value-system made it not only wrong and sinful but unseemly and in bad taste to claim to be "chosen," to lay claim to being *legally* (via ancient privilege) *or morally or spiritually* "better than." The decorum of American civil religion expresses this religious taste and, consequently, proscribes, as intolerable pride and vainglory, the open claim to be "elect" or "elite."

It is, significantly, acculturated Jewish rabbis like Arthur Hertzberg and acculturated Jewish philosophers like Albert Hofstadter who continually rediscover, in countries and cultures indebted to the Protestant ethic, the commanding role played by (what I call) the Protestant esthetic—especially in seemingly unrelated fields, like theology and morality. Civil religion embodies this esthetic and hence taboos as vulgar ostentation any claim to be special or superior, be it the Catholic "one true church" or Jewish "one chosen people." It even taboos as bad taste the secularized residues of these ancient claims and privileges.

---

*Is there a foreign policy analogue to Roth's "specialness" idea in the frequently heard notion that between America and Israel there exists an unquestioned "special" relationship, albeit undefined? Is the rhetoric of "specialness" perhaps an American recension and secularization of (European) "privilege"?

When, for example, Rabbi Hertzberg cries out that "the survival of Judaism in America is endangered by many things; but I believe that its single greatest enemy is vulgarity . . ." and concludes with a call for "an end to vulgarity in [Jewish] communal affairs,"[88] he speaks out of his acculturation in American civil religion and civic culture. In this value-system, both egocentrism and ethnocentrism are not only immoral (ethically) but vulgar (socially and esthetically). And the opposite is equally true: to be vulgar and ostentatious is to be selfish and inward-turning, proud and unaware of how one's self or one's group may *appear* to others, offending their rights, needs, or sensitivities. Good taste, in this context, is secularized Christianity.

Albert Hofstadter, for example, commenting on a passage in Saint Augustine's *Confessions*—chapter: "The Sin of Pride"—where Augustine calls such pride a *foeda iactantia,* an "unseemly ostentation,"[89] insists that only if one grasps the "ostentatious unseemliness of spiritual pride in the very way in which it is *experienced as such* in Christian life can he understand the spirit of Christian morality (insofar as it is manifested in this detail)."[90] In Western Christendom (post-Christian or otherwise) the *nexus* between spiritual humility and spiritual decorum is no "detail." It is of the essence. And it is the imperious coerciveness of this normative equation that, forbidding "ascribed" *spiritual* "specialness," forces latter-day Jewish chosenness to secularize itself into the very American "achievement" channels of economic success, social importunity, Roth's psychological "better thanness," and intellectual-artistic ambition.

One of the few culturally "respectable" ways open to revivalists of Jewish chosenness, as I have indicated in the case of Arthur A. Cohen, is, ironically, to legitimate the doctrine via Christianity itself. Other legitimation routes have been taken, however. Rabbi Richard L. Rubenstein struggles to redeem "chosenness" out of Camus, calling it an "absurd given," while Jacob Neusner announces that "Our chosenness is vindicated by our suffering. This," he hastens to assure the reader, "has nothing to do with tribalism."[91] Norman Podhoretz at a Jewish Museum lecture proposed Jewish chosenness—only, it appeared, half-humorously—as an empirical hypothesis to account for the disproportionate achievement of Jewish genius and the "miracle" of Jewish survival. But the culturally preferred means for legitimating Judaism's "chosen people" claim is, ironically, as we have seen, Christianity. "Already, in fact, *Christian* emphasis on the Jews' special election by God is causing liberal Jews to re-examine the meaning of the Mosaic covenant," noted *Newsweek,* commenting on the U.S. Roman Catholic hierarchy's ecumenical "guidelines for Catholic-Jewish Relations." Instead of shying away from the concept of "an elected people," such liberals are now increasingly tempted to reaffirm it. "It is ironic," concludes Reform Rabbi Balfour Brickner, "that truly theological dialogue with Christians might be the catalyst which helps Jews stay alive Jewishly."[92]

It *is* ironic that it is the Christians and especially the Catholics who are today legitimating Jewish particularism. Post-conciliar Catholics, scandalized by their own particularity, celebrate the "thinginess" *(choséité)* of Jewishness. The second issue of *SIDIC* *(Service international de documentation judeo-chrétienne)* devotes itself unashamedly to a discussion of the "fundamental yet shocking" fact of the "bond between the people of the Covenant and the land of their fathers." This is no *"accidental* aspect of their faith,"as it is with Catholics, but "an *essential* part of their existence as a people."[93] How odd, how perverse, even, it must seem to some, that Catholics, in the same era in which the more modernizing of them insist on "spiritualizing" even the Eucharist—finding the particularism of the transubstantiation doctrine theologically *infra dignitatem* and ecumenically embarrassing—how odd that these same modernizers should be the very ones putting their hands to long, painstaking, scrupulously theological celebrations of Jewish chosenness and particularity, writing for *SIDIC* articles with titles such as "Eretz Yisrael and the Jews," "Blessed Are the Meek" (for they shall inherit the earth —i.e., the "land" of Israel), "The Land of Israel in Jewish Liturgy," etc.[94] Odd or not, the explanation is not far to seek. Some of it lies in "self-hate." Some of it lies in the fact that, its own triumphalism having been evicted by civil religion, Catholics must content themselves with celebrating a vicarious triumphalism: the phenomenon of vicarious particularism is very American. But most of the explanation lies in that Christian charity, civility, and courtesy that "seeks not its own," that turns the

other cheek, that never takes its own side in a quarrel. It lies in
that Christian decorum of self-effacement whereby, with con-
summate tact, rather than "offend" with its truth, Catholicism
chooses to give no offense and to disappear through its altru-
ism.[95]

VIII.

Hertzberg and the End of Zionist Ideology: Jewish Chosenness Secularized into the "Special Relation" to Israel, the Land of Unlikeness; or, The Normalization of the Abnormal

Rabbi Hertzberg has never wavered in his conviction of the
centrality of the Jewish doctrine of election: "The essence of
Judaism is the affirmation that the Jews are the chosen people;
all else is commentary." But there has been an evolution in his
view of how best to legitimate this pre-modern conviction in a
modernizing world and before the bar of American civil religion.

In 1963, as we have seen, in "America Is Different," just
exiting from the "consensus" 1950s, and treating as an equal
with such partners to the "tri-faith" ecumenical dialogue as
Reinhold Niebuhr and John Courtney Murray, Hertzberg has
seemed if not to soften at least to bifurcate the chosen people
doctrine: it was a private matter for Jews to believe—not a public
matter to act on. A year later, in a column "American Experience Shows the Way to Amity," he seemed to codify this position. Despite the fact that "our various theologies are absolu-
tists," *in practice* we avoid anything that is a "real religious
offense to others." How much, we must ask, is this a mere matter
of expedient accommodation, and how much is it an internal
change in Judaism's self-conception? The latter, it would seem,
for Hertzberg writes of each religion—including Judaism—as

"consistently acting on the presumption that the concerns of the other major religious faiths are, in a *very deep sense,* present and voting in *our internal* deliberations."[96]

But the voting metaphor is troubling. The earlier "America Is Different" piece had used a business metaphor for Jewry's relation to the American separation of church and state doctrine and to the American pluralistic civil religion: it was a "brutal bargain," this "deal" by which we Jews and others "privatize" our deepest convictions. Clearly, the Jewish accommodation is in the instrumental mode. A year later, Hertzberg is using a "voting model" metaphor: the other major faiths are "present and voting" in our internal deliberations. This still smacks of a very pragmatic relation to those other religions as chiefly part of the environment of Jewish social policy and action (as either obstacles or facilities).

Then in 1964 he wrote—significantly, for the *Jewish Frontier*—his resounding "America Is *Galut* [Exile]." In this piece, only three years prior to the "Six-Day War" of 1967, he hews to the hard line. He deliberately chose the word *Galut* to describe the situation of Jews in America. He takes the Jewish "establishment" to task, chiding them for pusillanimously evading the socio-cultural implications of the "chosen people" doctrine, viz., that Jews in America ought to be different, unique, incommensurable, unlike, apart. The Jewish establishment, he argued, had to chose between safety and survival. Myopically preoccupied only with safety, it stressed Jewish likeness to other American religious groups, thus jeopardizing survival. "The protective coloration of likeness has appeared to the Establishment," he declares, "to be an indispensable tool with which to create safety for the Jew. . . ."[97]

As the sixties open, then, Hertzberg is sounding the alarm, telling the Jewish Establishment that while the older generation may accept as politic the fiction that Jews and Judaism are "a religion *like* any other religion," "younger Jews are refusing to be any kind of Marrano within democracy."[98] He claimed that it was the youngsters—some of whom were in the course of being "lost" to the New Left—who refused to live this double life, who realized that beneath this "Conservative" and "Reform" forensic definition of Jewishness there existed "far different and more specific emotions about the uniqueness of Jewish identity."[99]

Hertzberg, in 1964, thus pleaded with the Jewish establishment to admit—to the American public, to their own children—that Jewish identity was not just a third and variant form of a general American "religious" identity—as in the Protestant-Catholic-Jew formula—but was something that simply "cannot be expressed in conventional Western terms. . . ."[100] Hertzberg also noted the Jewish Establishment's "discontinuity between theory and practise," viz., that "in *practise* it has behaved uniquely . . ." even while talking the rhetoric of "Jews are just like everybody else, only more so." "Its stance has been the peculiar hope that all other Americans"—but not, of course, the Jews themselves—"will believe that Jews are indeed 'just like everybody else' . . ."[101] Even some Jews, Hertzberg warns, are beginning to believe this.

Jews, Hertzberg insisted in 1964, are a people apart. But the religious core of Jewish apartness has eroded in the civil society of modern and tolerant America. "Apartness must have content," he insists. "For such content we can only wait." But where is this apartness-content to come from? Perhaps, he proposes, the uniqueness of Jewish identity, so euphemized and etiolated in America, can be shored up by our expatriation to Israel. We can end the danger to our Jewish identity, he argues, by starting to think seriously "for the first time since adolescence, of *aliyah* [emigration]: at the very least," he concludes, "the *aliyah* of our children."[102]

The 1967 Arab-Israeli War—the "Six-Day War"—gave to the generality of American Jewry and Rabbi Hertzberg the "content" American Jewish identity had been waiting for. The secular Judaism of American Jews became, almost overnight, as we have seen, the special obligation to support Israel in every way possible.

Soon after the founding of Israel, Hertzberg recalls, he had tried to formulate for himself the assumptions upon which Israel's leader, David Ben-Gurion—a pronounced secularist—was operating. These assumptions added up to a paradox: "There is no God, but He has a unique relationship to the Jews,* whom he chose to be his very own and to whom He gave the land of

Israel. The command was *aliyah,* the resettlement in the Land.
... [*Aliyah*] was the lawful heir of all the 613 *mitzvot* [commanded
deeds].... Once again, from underneath the shaven face of the
modern Jew the beard of his grandfather was staring at me."[103]

Rabbi Hertzberg is here the historian of secularized, metaphorical and allotropic forms of the ancient doctrine of Jewish
chosenness. This religious doctrine endures beneath even the
secular identity of the modern Jew. It perhaps is at the root of
American Jewry's "special" attachment to Israel. "I thus became
convinced that there is no secular Jewish identity in the modern
era. ... What is almost never denied, even by such super-
modern Jews, is one essential assertion—in my view *the essential
assertion*—of the religious tradition, the doctrine of the chosenness of Israel."[104] Modern Jewish secularism, in a word, "has
simply substituted for the ultimate sin of religion, rebellion
against God, a new definition: betrayal of the community. ...
[God] has been heard by these secularists as enjoining at the
very least the chosenness of Israel."[105] Hidden underneath the
secularist rhetoric, Hertzberg concludes, the ancient belief in
the chosenness of Jewry survives. This is the "content" Hertzberg had waited for in the sixties, and that had surfaced with the
1967 War.

Hertzberg is here advancing a view of Jewish chosenness that
I call "the metaphoricality of Jewish chosenness."† Not unlike
the "Jewish identity" of Philip Roth we examined earlier—
where Jewishness was a "better than" variable, taking on many
values—Hertzberg's "chosen people" doctrine reveals a metaphorical openness to the specifications supplied by changing
Jewish history. It now means: the chosenness-specialness of Is-

---

*There is an unmistakable echo here of the tag once applied to the Spanish-American
ex-Catholic philosopher, George Santayana: "He believes that there is no God, and that
Mary is His mother."

†I adapt here Alvin W. Gouldner's essay "The Metaphoricality of Marxism and the
Context-Freeing Grammar of Socialism," in which the important clue to the survival of
Marxism as politics—despite its failure as economic theory—is found in "the underlying
rules for metaphoric switching that it employs" for its key terms, viz., "proletariat" and
"socialism" (e.g., the interchangeability of proletariat, peasantry, and people). This
metaphoricality has enabled Marxism "to survive countless reversals of party line, fal-
sified predictions, and political defeats." Thanks to an analogous metaphoricality, the
doctrine of Jewish chosenness "succeeds" in metaphorical forms despite its "failure" or
superannuation as religious belief.[106]

rael among the nations. Henceforth, American Jews and America itself, will observe a "special relation" to Israel.

It was a solemn moment when, a year after writing this, in Jerusalem, on a Tuesday evening, June 29, 1976, Arthur Hertzberg, president of the American Jewish Congress, addressed as opening speaker the assembly of notables and American and Israeli intellectuals gathered to discuss the contemporary meaning of Zionism and Israel. After greetings from Teddy Kollek, Mayor of Jerusalem, and before the next speaker, former Israeli Foreign Minister, Abba Eban, Rabbi Hertzberg began:

> Classical Zionism asserted that it understood and could tame anti-Semitism; that it could either sustain or make an end of the Diaspora; and that at the very least, it would create in Israel a normal nation among the nations. As a matter of fact, all of these propositions have been disproved by history. Since it is impolitic to say such things out loud, Zionist discussion has been sterile in recent years.[107]

It is a moving moment. Twenty years earlier Daniel Bell had declared the end of the ideology of Marxist socialism.[108] Here now is Rabbi Hertzberg, the historian of Zionism, declaring, in Jerusalem, the end of the ideology of Zionism. (In fact, *all* the ideologies that constitute the tradition and *"paideia"* of intellectual Jewry in Galut—Marxism, Zionism, Freudianism—and that were fashioned as critiques of Emancipation and as remedial "explanations" for post-Emancipation Jewish behavior and Gentile anti-Semitism, are in the process of being disproved by history.[109]) With what, then, does Hertzberg propose to replace classical Zionist ideology? Pragmatism. "The only way Zionism can be defined for all Jewry today," he proposes, "is pragmatically."[110]

Israel, Hertzberg is saying, is not—as was classically desiderated—"a normal nation among nations." Hertzberg does not lament this historical eventuality because he sees it as providing (among other things) precisely that "content" for Diaspora Jewish chosenness/apartness/uniqueness that religious Judaism was no longer able to supply. In 1964, in "America Is Galut," he had looked upon the relatively empty "form" of Jewish sociocultural apartness and found it lacking in "content." "For such content," he had concluded, "we can only wait."[111] It is precisely in the abnormality—in the *anomaly* of Israel among the nations as a "land of unlikeness" (to use the late Robert Lowell's title)—that Hertzberg sees the survivalist possibilities for Diaspora and American Jewry. This "content" is now the very anomalousness—the uniqueness, oddness ("how odd of God to choose the Jews"), "chosenness"—of the state of Israel itself. It is the very abnormality of Israel that will keep Diaspora Jewish identity in business. Strenuous pragmatic efforts on behalf of Israel's survival will keep the Jews of the Diaspora different from other groups, guaranteeing their apartness now and in the future, giving new "unique" content to their identity.*

Classical Zionist ideologists like secularist Theodor Herzl and "Diaspora Zionist" Ahad ha'Am never imagined the Israel history has created. What is more, they would have found the present Jewish Diaspora—especially in America—totally surprising. *"Neither* of them imagined a Diaspora which would have the opportunity to emigrate to a Jewish state and would choose not to; which would have the opportunity to affirm a serious Jewish culture and would largely neglect that opportunity; and which would, paradoxically, make of its labors on behalf of the Jewish state—fund-raising, political support, emotional involvement—the dominant *content* of its Jewish life."[112]

The missing "content" that Hertzberg was "waiting for" in 1964 had now arrived. He cannot quite believe his own eyes. The "content" which classical Zionist ideology, in all its variants, believed a "Jewish homeland" would furnish to the Jews of the Diaspora, this content has been supplied instead by the Diaspora itself—especially the American Jewish community.

---

*Earlier, Rabbi Eugene Borowitz had noted that because of Jewry's acculturation in the Diaspora to a universalistic idea of humanity and, I would add, under pressure from the egalitarianism of civil religion, "the average American Jew rejects the traditional notion of the Chosen People, that God chose the Jews, making them, implicitly, superior to all other peoples" (p. 577). Instead, religious chosenness is secularized, metaphoricized, displaced. "If we look carefully, we can trace in secularists a displaced religiosity, which comes out particularly in [among other things] . . . intense involvement in the behavior of the State of Israel" [Precis, p. 553]. Of the sociological legitimating function of this new "Covenantal sense of Jewish uniqueness," Rabbi Borowitz, anticipating Rabbi Hertzberg, concludes: "I think I can say that it *justifies* the separateness of being a Jew in the United States of America" (p. 568). Borowitz, "The Chosen People Concept as It Affects Life in the Diaspora," *Journal of Ecumenical Studies,* Fall 1975 (vol. 12, no. 4). My italics.

Hertzberg is carrying unprecedented news to Jerusalem, news of a stunning reversal of history, and he is exasperated by the fact that his auditors are not fully aware of how astonishing it is. What neither Herzl nor Ahad ha'Am imagined, nor can you here realize for the momentous event that it is, he tells his audience that Tuesday night, "is a Diaspora which would *give itself content* and at-homeness in freedom by the very verve of its political and economic efforts for the State of Israel, and which would, indeed,"—and this is his crucial insight—"become a great success in the eyes of America precisely because of these efforts."[113]

The old American bugaboo of "dual loyalty," Hertzberg is announcing, has been defeated—at least in the case of the Jews. It is now *legitimate* in America for Jews to act on, if not to acknowledge, a "dual loyalty" (to America, to Israel). Americans now accept this anomaly. Even more (Hertzberg doesn't quite bring himself to say this, but it is implied): it is now legitimate in America for American Jews as Jews—and their allies—to support publicly an Israeli foreign policy even when that policy would appear to be (even on a generous interpretation) at odds with an American foreign policy (perhaps, at odds even with an American national interest).* Thus, for example, after a delegation of Jewish members of Congress and supporters of Israel met with President Carter to calm their worries about his continued commitment to Israel, Representative Jonathan Bingham —husband of June Rossbach Bingham, author of *The Courage to Change* (our chief source on Niebuhr in chapter 3)—reported only one remaining misgiving: "You cannot question his sincerity. The only question is whether he perceives what's good for Israel the way the Israelis perceive it."† If assessments such as Bingham's are now routinely accepted as legitimate, this is unprecedented news indeed. It is this news that Hertzberg brought to Jerusalem in the summer of 1976. If true, this news of a new and anomalous Diaspora more than matches the anomaly that

---

Newsweek's "Periscope" (Aug. 29, 1977, p. 14) informs us that the Carter Administration has ordered up "a weekly roundup of Jewish publications. Modeled after the President's regular daily news summary, the roundup reviews all U.S. Jewish publications and The Jerusalem Post. The summary which carries a blue Star of David logo, is sent to Carter and a handful of his senior staffers."

†Martin Tolchin, "Carter Assures Representatives on Israel; Calls Koch 'My Friend,' " *New York Times*, Oct. 7, 1977, p. A3.

Israel (for classical Zionist ideology) has become.

Within the American *Jewish* community there is no question that the change has occurred. The 613 *mizvot*—or duties and offenses—have been boiled down to one. Hertzberg writes:

> The only offenses for which Jews can be "excommunicated" in the U.S. today is not to participate in those efforts [in behalf of Israel]. Intermarriage, ignorance in the Jewish heritage or lack of faith do not keep anyone from leadership in the American Jewish community today. Being against Israel or apathetic in its support does.[114]

Many or most of Hertzberg's interlocutors in the Jerusalem dialogue concede Hertzberg's analysis with reference to the American *Jewish* community. Stephen Lerner, editor of *Conservative Judaism,* avers, for example, that "I think Rabbi Hertzberg is correct in stating that support for Israel is the religion of much of American Jewry."[115]

But it is the other news that Hertzberg brings that creates disbelief, even resentment. He tells his Jerusalem colleagues that the *general* American community, the American civil religion itself validates, at long last, Jewish specialness, anomaly, oddness, uniqueness, and chosenness, the Jewish "right to live out their unconventional lives."[116] This assessment bothers his audience; it does not bother Hertzberg; he glories in this change, in this acceptance. Jews in the United States, he tells Israel's Jews,

> have beaten down all the charges that the intensity of their concern for Israel is a form of dual loyalty. That indeed, has been their greatest internal political victory in the last generation—to make America accept the idea that its Jewish minority, convoked primarily in politics as a pro-Israel pressure group, has the *right* to that activity. In the U.S. today, every other pressure group exists in order to achieve some domestic objective. Only the Jews exist as a recognizable pressure group united on a foreign policy issue.[117]

It is this unacknowledged "greatest internal political victory in the last generation" that has enabled the American Jewish community pragmatically to refute classical Jewish Zionism. It is precisely because Israel is *not* the classically Zionist "state among the states," that the American Jewish community can

"blow its cover" and . . . come out "unabashedly as a group *not*
analogous to any other."[118] Everything in Zionism is now
changed, changed utterly. In fact, "to be *anti*-Jewish means *today*
to demand that the Jews be more 'normal'; to be *pro*-Jewish, or
positively Jewish, means to accept the notion that the Jews have
the right to live out their unconventional [read: particularistic]
lives."[119] In fact, even the charge that "Zionism is racism" is, in
Hertzberg's formulation, "really an attack on the *sui generis* nature of the Jewish people."[120] If the Jews weren't chosen, Hertzberg would seem to be arguing, Zionism would indeed be racism.

Shock waves of uneasiness in the audience forced Hertzberg
to return later to his central point: that Jews are the only American minority with their own foreign policy, and that their greatest victory was to "make America accept" this idea as legitimate.
Traditionally, any American Jewish position on what American
policy should be toward Israel has always been very carefully
couched in terms of the *American* national interest. It is because
Hertzberg seems to go beyond this formulation that he arouses
uneasiness in Jerusalem. In reply to the president of the World
Jewish Congress, Nahum Goldman, who acknowledged that the
creation of Israel regettably *"has* raised for Jews outside of Israel
the specter of dual loyalty,"[121] Hertzberg, the president of the
American Jewish Congress, replied that "in the era of the end
of [Jewish] political passivity I am less afraid than Dr. Goldman
of the charge of dual loyalty in the U.S." "I am not afraid that
the issue will be raised—I think the issue has been killed." He
went on:

> The great political victory of American Jewry is to have established
> the proposition that we are the only minority in America that exerts
> pressure on foreign policy. Why was Brzezinski in Jerusalem today
> [June 30, 1976] on behalf of [presidential candidate] Carter? He is
> in Jerusalem because everybody knows that Israel is the issue for the
> American Jewish community.[122]

Today, Hertzberg is claiming, American Jews are accorded *de
facto* group rights, rights as Jews in foreign policy matters. Traditionally, in the United States, and unlike Europe, as Lucy S.
Dawidowicz notes, "only *individual* rights are constitutionally

guaranteed; religious, ethnic, and racial *groups,* in relation to each other and to the larger society, have no formal recognition. They function in the informal social structures, not through official government channels."[123] This, Hertzberg would appear to be telling his Jerusalem audience, may be true in the civics textbooks, but it is not true in the realities of American politics and foreign policy. In foreign policy, the special group interest of American Jews in the fate of Israel is today recognized through official government channels *de facto,* if not *de jure.* President Carter forgathers openly and formally with groups of Jewish notables to receive advice on American foreign policy toward Israel.*

Hertzberg contends that in contemporary America the Jewish group is recognized as unique and *sui generis;* he is arguing that America at long last accords a *de facto* recognition to the anomalousness of the American Jewish community, which anomalousness is the secularized form that chosenness takes. His language comes close to connoting that the Jewish minority is not only different from but perhaps superior to the other minorities:

> It is a fact that in the perception of America as a whole the Jews are not one of a half dozen plural minorities. As a matter of fact, the American community as a whole knows that all other minorities are convoked for one or another *domestic* reason; the American Jewish minority is convoked for *world* Jewish reasons.[124]

At that point, Hertzberg was interrupted from the floor: "You have said this a number of times," a member of the audience interjects. "How about the Greek and Turkish lobbies in the U.S.?" "Nonsense," Hertzberg retorted. "The Greek and Turkish lobbies are a one generational affair with immediate immigrants; the Jewish lobby is a third and forth generational

*Professor Dawidowicz in the aforementioned review chides Professor Celia Heller for her "anachronistic" assimilation of a "fuzzy" American and twentieth century concept of pluralism to the nineteenth century recognition of plural national minorities (as was the pattern in the Habsburg Empire). But Professor Heller's "anachronism" is perfectly understandable; *in practice,* if not in theory, American Jews *are* related to governmentally as a group on a pattern not too dissimilar from that of nineteenth century Europe. Heller writes out of the massive sociological reality of this "informal" American "recognition." Such group realities and their lobbies in America are not in the least "fuzzy."

affair."[125] At long last, "the civilized world accepts the notion that 'the house of Israel is not like all other nations.' "[126]*

IX.

Status as "Messianic Need": Hertzberg and the Conflict Resolution of the Second Generation Jewish Intellectual

Those of us who have followed Arthur Hertzberg through the years, in his writings, in his TV and radio appearances, or who have been privileged, as I have, to audit his history classes at Columbia University, know that in whatever he says or does—he is frequently deliberately shocking—he is always seeking status for Judaism in American culture. Whereas Niebuhr and Murray argued the merits of justice and equality for their respective religions in American *society*, Hertzberg is a seeker for status in American *culture*. Not unlike American ethnic intellectuals generally, he is fanatically importunate of cultural *yichus*. He is Judaism's status-seeker.

Jews are already religiously equal in American society (in tax exemption status, on state occasions, etc.). "In these areas the Jews really are equal in all respects to all other denominations in America, and no pressure of the majority or of its faith is being exercised upon them," Hertzberg writes.[127] Politically and legally the separation of church and state has produced for American Jews a truly equal status in American society. But,

---

*Thus, for example, when the American Jewish community vehemently disapproved of the joint declaration the U.S. Secretary of State, Cyrus Vance, and the Soviet Union had worked out on convening a Geneva peace conference, there was nothing surprising in the Jewish community selecting Vance's counterpart, Israeli Foreign Minister Moshe Dayan, to argue the Israeli position with the American Jewish community. "The Conference of Presidents of Major American Jewish Organizations, which represents 32 national groups, met at its headquarters at 15 Park Avenue," we read on page one of the *New York Times* (Oct. 4, 1977), "and decided to send its chairman, Rabbi Alexander M. Schindler, along with Foreign Minister Dayan to Chicago, Atlanta and Los Angeles at the end of the week to assess Jewish reaction."

Hertzberg adds, in what must be one of the strangest sentences ever penned by a rabbi, the American Jew's "deepest and most *messianic* need is not a completely secular American state; it is a truly equal status in American culture"[128] (Hertzberg's italics).

The civil religion by legitimating religiously "cultural pluralism" meant, Hertzberg writes, "that each American would live in two cultures, the public culture common to all and the subculture of his own particular ethnic tradition."[129] This civil religion in America in effect separates belief and action. Its vision postulates "a secular public culture shared by all Americans, who will differ only by belonging to three coexisting and equal enclaves of private religiosity."[130]

But Hertzberg knows that the civil religion, which decides the rules by which the denominations interact, is itself a secularized form of Protestant Christianity. If Judaism is inherently communal, it cannot be privatized—"protestantized"—leaving the public realm open to the public behavior of the civil religion. Judaism must "behave" its religion Jewishly. But the only religious behavior legitimated for the public sector ("public places") in this "nation of behavers" is the *halakah* of Protestant Christianity's civil religion: the rites—or civilities—of the Protestant Etiquette or the religion of civility.

For Judaism to have a "truly equal status," then, in this culture, would be for it to be able to command a deference and respect, from the whole culture, for its very difference from Christianity and *because* it is different, "deviant," unique, chosen. This wish of the American Jew, this "need" for status of the second generation Jewish intellectual—Hertzberg is obviously telling us about himself and his cohort—is clearly a need that is deep, "overdetermined," exorbitant, and—of course—impossible. It is the ultimate, repressed wish that fueled nineteenth century Jewish Emancipation. So impossible of fulfillment is this wish that Hertzberg openly acknowledges its religious provenance. Hence he calls it a "messianic" need for a certain kind of "status" in American "culture."

As the sociologists Kramer and Levantman demonstrate, if the first generation of American Jews were overwhelmingly preoccupied with survival, and the second with success, the third generation is preoccupied with status.[131] It is my contention that the ethnic intellectual syncopates and skips a step in the normal development of the rank and file members of his community. The immigrant intellectual becomes overwhelmingly preoccupied with status-issues prematurely, so to speak. The younger third (and even forth) generation of Jews is today preoccupied with status.

What has happened is that Israeli Jewry is living a first generation survival problem, and that the third (and fourth) generation of American Jewry is making *that* survival problem the content of *its* status problem. American Diaspora Jewry is living through a first generation problem—survival—vicariously. The Israeli quest for survival becomes the content of the Diaspora quest for status, with both living off the "making it" or success (economic and political) of the second generation. Rabbi Hertzberg recapitulates in his own personality this curious conflation of differing generational needs. Status factors enter into the choice of survival as the chief issue (even exaggerating it sometimes into an ideology: survivalism). And "success" lies to hand as a facility for both status and survival.

Switching to Mideast foreign policy—the reason the status of Jerusalem is such an irreconcilable issue is precisely because it is a status issue. All Israeli foreign policy issues are, for both Israeli and American Jews, couched in terms of security, strategic need, and, ultimately, survival itself. All issues, that is, except the future status of the city of Jerusalem (occupied in 1967). As *National Review* magazine, with its generally supportive and pro-Israeli policy, comments: "There is a special feature to the Jerusalem issue. In general, the Israelis justify their stand—on the Golan Heights, West Bank, Sinai, etc.—by their need for territorial security. Whether or not their arguments along that line are valid in any given case, the basis of such a position—a nation's need for security—is accepted by all nations, and permits a rational discussion in the light of the facts. But the political status of Jerusalem has no significant bearing on Israel's territorial security. It is for Israelis an ideological issue. Israel wants sole sovereignty over Jerusalem not to improve her territorial security but to fulfill what many Israelis believe to be religious destiny. Obviously this consideration is irrelevant to anyone who does not share this religious and ideological conviction. The question of Jerusalem's political status can be rationally discussed and fruitfully negotiated only if it is de-ideologized. . . ."[132]

The "new chosenness," then, represents the convergence on a single target of the three "s's" of three generations of American and immigrant Jewry: "survival," "success," and "status." The existential situation of Israeli Jewry together with the overdetermined motivation of Diaspora Jews generate an unprecedented anxiety that is also experienced as an unprecedented opportunity: a "messianic need" for status couches itself in the vehement realism of a rhetoric of survival.

It is, in conclusion, the fact that Arthur Hertzberg embodies the actualities of this convergence in both his ideas and in his person that I selected him for my Jewish "case study." It is Judaism's status in the American diaspora as it is Israel's survival in the Mideast that, jointly, most concern him. To maintain and elevate Judaism's cultural and social status in America is Hertzberg's "deepest and most messianic need," to apply to himself a phrase we have seen him use of American Jewry. Judaism, he is convinced, will cut a distinctive figure in Western culture only to the degree that it is conspicuously, ostentatiously, *chutzpahdically*—and hence, inevitably, incivilly—*not* Christianity. "The essence of Judaism," he declares, as we have seen, "is the affirmation that the Jews are the chosen people; all else is commentary."[133]

In a recent talk before Columbia's "University Seminar on Studies in Religion" titled "Why Judaism Is Not Christianity" Rabbi Hertzberg performed a virtual *midrash* on his own declaration of Jewish chosenness. He spelled out in bleeding detail the religious, communal and national coefficients of this declaration. He reiterated all his old positions: the widespread, "Judeo-Christian," mythical assumption that both Judaism and Christianity share a biblical text in common—the so-called "Old Testament"—which sends scholars in quest of a non-existent genus of which Judaism and Christianity are "differing" variants; Zionism is as essential a national expression of Judaism as evangelism is of Christianity; Judaism is inherently communal as Christianity is inherently individualistic ("Religion is what the individual does with his own solitariness," declares A. N. White-head, betraying his subtle conditioning in Christendom); Judaism and Christianity must be understood in their utter alienation from each other; Judaism secularizes into Zionism as Christianity secularizes into Marxism; since the Six-Day War (1967), Israel has become the religion of American Jews.

But, as always with Rabbi Hertzberg, revealing touches in his rhetoric (recalling his book on the French Enlightenment) betrayed the polemical orientation of his position: Judaism's adversary, in his conception, is the Western Christian Protestant *halakah*, the demanding proprieties of the universalistic civility of the civil religion. Jewish nationalism and Zionism were thus something "we Jews as a 'proper religion' ought supposedly to play down"; a "proper religion behaves in a certain way"; Judaism's *halachic* residues are presumably scandalous "and ought not to be introduced into polite society."

The assembled scholars, both Jewish and Gentile, sat there in various stages of dismayed disagreement. Was this a Jewish Marcionism in which Jews and Christians don't even share a God in common? The Chairman went around the table, polling the auditors who, one after the other, expressed their varying demurrals. When my turn came, the Minutes of the Meeting state: "Professor Cuddihy found himself in sufficient agreement with the speaker not to wish to comment."[134]

One final word. In Hertzberg's *apologia pro vita sua Judaica*—to invoke a more complex presence—we must note one striking omission: in his account of the current general American acceptation of Jewish anomaly and "chosenness," of Jewish specialness and of the "special relation" to Israel, Hertzberg credits the "victory" entirely to the "achievement" of American Jews—*"their* greatest internal political victory in the last generation." He thus neglects a salient and obtrusive fact of the American culture: he is unmindful, in his conviction that this is a unilateral "achievement" of American Jews, of the indispensable role played by the American secularized Christian culture. American Jews "have beaten down all the charges" of the anti-Semitic component of the culture, as he puts it. No positive contribution from the general Gentile society is acknowledged.

But the "achievement" of such an American Jewish "special status" was notoriously a two-way street. What Hertzberg describes as an earned or "achieved status," to use the language of sociologist Talcott Parsons, is, in fact, also an imputed or "ascribed status," a gift of the philo-Semitic component in Christendom. True, American Jewry did much to "achieve" this special status for Israel; but it must not be forgotten that American culture—precisely as a secularized Christian culture—felt constrained to validate this "achievement" with a religiously available though now secularized "ascribed" status: "the special relation" to Israel. For complex reasons, then, America has never treated Israel unpreferentially or "like all other nations" —*k'khol ha-goyim.* In practice, if not in theory, it acknowledges "chosenness."

Chapter 6

———— ◆◆◆◆ ————

POSTSCRIPT TO THE
CASE STUDIES:
LITTELL, BOZELL,
KAHANE AND
MENAHEM BEGIN

———— ◆◆◆◆ ————

. . . the conception of the church, which implied the fundamental break with the Jewish law which Paul made final, constituted the differentiation of Christianity as a religious system (a cultural system) from the conception of a "people" as a social system.
—*Talcott Parsons*
Sociological Theory and Modern Society

Each of the three religions has produced a later generation of theologians who have radicalized even further the innovations of Niebuhr, the resistance of Feeney, and the problems of Hertzberg. Dr. Franklin H. Littell—as well as Dr. A. Roy Eckardt—began their work where Niebuhr had ended. Not only was the mission to the Jews called off, but the whole relation of Christianity to Judaism was reargued on the premise of the necessary incredibility of Christianity to Jews.[1]

In September 1966, L. Brent Bozell published the first issue of a magazine called *Triumph*. In a sense, it may be viewed as the lineal descendant of Father Feeney's *From the Housetops*. Its inaugural editorial, while promising a "civilized, lively, and profitable conversation with serious Protestants and Jews,"[2] also told its readers to expect "some unirenic thinking about pluralism."[3] *Triumph*, like its title, was deliberately, ostentatiously, unfash-

ionably "triumphalist." It aimed to convert the unbeliever and
the backslider; it fought abortion; it supported beleaguered car-
dinals and bishops in their efforts to enforce Pope Paul's *Huma-
nae Vitae* encyclical (banning artificial birth control) on their
dissident clergy. Bozell attacked, with bravura and brilliant sociological insight, the snobbery of the liberal Catholic "establishment."*

But gradually, structurally, inevitably, *Triumph* became incivil.
By January 1969, it announced itself, and the Catholic church it
sponsored, as at war. "This is a good war, as most truly religious
wars are. It will require, on our part, courage, chivalry, charity
and good will. Its purpose, of course, is to convert the heathen
scum."[4] The bishops were attacked for their tepidity and *pro
forma* opposition to abortion legislation. "Where the bishops are
not silent, they are discreet, polite, very proper participants in
the American political order." "What if our shepherds were to
become *fierce?*"[5] The wife of the editor, as if in enactment of this
possibility, does, in fact, publicly slap the face of Ti Grace Atkin-
son for what she takes to be an insult to the Blessed Virgin Mary.

Finally, in the summer of 1970, as if to signal its abandonment
of civility, *Triumph* deliberately adopted tribal language, describing its adherents as "The Confessional Tribe."[6] The whole "settlement" worked out by John Courtney Murray in the language
of civility is explicitly repudiated. Not insignificantly, in this
same issue, the proper understanding of the "No salvation outside the Church" formula, so central to Father Feeney's crusade,
is once more opened up for debate. In April 1973, *Triumph* in
an editorial quotes Anne Roiphe: " 'Maybe it's . . . better to be
tribal and ethnocentric than urbane and adrift' [Anne Roiphe]
proposes. Anyone who has to think even for a moment about the
answer to that one is already too urbane, too adrift," *Triumph*
comments.[7] *Triumph* ceased publication in 1977.†

The Jewish maximalist position—on chosenness as on Israel
—is voiced by Rabbi Meir Kahane who writes a column for the

*See, for example, the editorial "The Little Foxes," *Triumph*, Jan. 1967 (vol. 2, no.
1), p. 38.
†For an up-to-date assessment of the current, post-Vatican II state of American
Catholicism, see my review of Andrew M. Greeley, *The American Catholic: A Social Portrait*
in the *New York Times Book Review*, Mar. 6, 1977, pp. 3, 18.

weekly newspaper *The Jewish Press.* Week after week he repudiates the Jewish "sell-out" by "the Jewish Establishment" to the civility and gentility of the "general culture" of the *goyim.* The Jewish Defense League (JDL), inspired by Rabbi Kahane, engages in violent harassment of Soviet personnel in the United States. Bozell's *Triumph* magazine welcomed Kahane's crusade against civility. "The JDL, at least, doesn't stand by wringing its hands," *Triumph* editorialized. "It has started to shift the burden and the hurt to the Soviets, and has done so by violent or quasi-violent means. Rabbi still means 'teacher.' "[8] Kahane, with his extreme ethnocentrism, is shocked when Jew testifies— "informs"—against Jew when JDL members are brought to trial. He views himself as a reincarnation of Vladimir Jabotinsky.[9]

On May 18, 1977, Israel elected the Biblical fundamentalist, Manahem Begin, as its prime minister. Believing the Jews have been chosen by God to inherit Biblical Palestine, the prime minister shifted policy on the occupied West Bank, calling it "liberated" Judea and Samaria. The Orthodox religious bloc, in order to form a coalition, and because its views are much closer to Begin's than to those of the former Labor Party leader, Yitzhak Rabin, was given many pledges. One of these pledges, recalling my chapter on Niebuhr, was to seek legislation "to prohibit Christian missionary activity among Jews."[10]

Begin's election represented a strong resurgence of religious nationalism. As such, it was both troubling and exhilarating to America's Jews. "Troubling" because, as largely secular civil libertarians by profession, they were being now asked, as Israeli supporters, to underwrite—if only vicariously, in Israel—a shift toward theocracy in the modern world. "Exhilarating" because, as I said relative to Meir Kahane, in the case of most American Jews, if they probe down a couple of strata in their psyches— which is to say, back a couple of generations in time—they will encounter a Kahane and a Begin.

As American Jewry anxiously awaited the arrival of Prime Minister Begin for his first talks with President Carter, this ambivalence in American Jews between the ancient, precivil, old-world fanatical Judaism of Begin and the more assimilated, suburban, civil Judaism of American Jews, was brilliantly rendered by Seymour Krim, himself an American Jewish intellectual, in an Op-Ed piece written for *The New York Times*. Begin had gone directly from Europe—"the mother of fanaticism," as I called it in the Introduction—to Palestine, with no interlude of immersion in the American civil culture. "Here is the intact, unashamed, brilliant and sometimes scathing old-world relative [American Jews have] done their best to forget," Seymour Krim writes in the *Times*. "He is a Majority Jew," Krim says "not a Minority one like his American cousins, and he doesn't have to look over his shoulder to check out what the goyish [gentile] crowd is thinking. . . ." He is "a throwback to American Jews who have been here for more than a generation. . . . He slaps down stupid questions like flies. He suffers fools ungladly. He believes in what he believes to the point of contempt."[11] Begin is Jewish religious triumphalism incarnate.

To be a Minority Jew, that is, an *American* Jew (or an American Catholic or American Lutheran) is to be part of the pluralistic "settlement" depicted in this study. To be a Minority religionist in America is constantly to have "to look over your shoulder to check out what the goyish [or Jewish or Catholic or Episcopal] crowd is thinking." Krim: "Some American Jews—who can blame them?—will want no identification with this embodiment of all the conspicuous 'Jewish traits' that made them fight shame as young Americans. . . . Others will undergo reconversion, feel that they have betrayed the solid Jew in themselves with mod disguises. . . ."

Begin's election and visit to America, in other words, confronts the assimilating American Jew and American civil Judaism with a "roots" problem: "Menahem is in holy touch with roots they've let wither. . . . Menahem's pointing finger goes all the way down to the most protected personal depths. Ex-Prime Minister Rabin seemed an imitation American compared to this implacable gent."

Central to Begin's visit to America, then, is less the fear of his political confrontation with Carter than the American Jewish anxiety about their psychic confrontation with a suppressed part of themselves. In this ethnic psychodrama, Krim writes, "The Jew, suppressed in all of us, steps forward, alert . . . Mr. Raw Conscience [rather: Mr. Scripture-hawk—J. M. C.] is coming to America to put all middle-class American Jews on the existential spot. . . . He will enter each one," Krim concludes, "like an avenging ghost you can't keep out."[12]

He will be a "ghost" because, unlike David Ben-Gurion, Golda Meir, Yitzhak Rabin—all of whom were touched, in varying degrees, by the civil societies of the Diaspora—Begin comes directly from East Europe to Palestine. He is the unreconstructed *ostjude*.

"In a very real sense," writes Amos Perlmutter, Israeli-born professor of political science at American University in Washington, "Begin is the first *Jewish* leader of Israel. He is the first one to believe—in the traditional sense—in the God of Israel. . . . In his view [the Jewish] state will not be fully established until *all* of the world's gentiles—or at least the sane and decent ones —have been persuaded of the *special* nature of the Jewish case and the rightness of the Jewish claim to all of Palestine."[13]

The view of Prime Minister Begin's foreign minister, General Moshe Dayan, is identical in this respect. In August 1967 he declared: "If one possesses the Bible, if one considers oneself as the people of the Bible, one should also possess the Biblical lands, those of the Judges and the Patriarchs of Jerusalem, of Hebron, of Jericho and other places as well. I do not thereby set forth a political programme but, what is more important, the means of realizing the ancestral dream of a people. The foreigner must understand that, aside from all the strategic importance for Israel of the Sinai, of the Golan Heights, to the Straits of Tiran, and of the mountains to the west of the Jordan, these regions are situated at the heart of the Jewish history."[14]

The ancient belief of Jews in their own religious chosenness, it may be argued, has thus returned in the more respectable, secularized form of a metaphor for the *"special* nature" of the Jewish case and in the rightness of the Jewish claim, as Perlmutter sees it, "to all of Palestine." It is because he pressed this claim with President Carter that, subsequent to Prime Minister Begin's visit, U.S.-Israeli relations have been under strain. In the thirty years since the United States became the first nation to extend formal recognition to the state of Israel, Washington and Jerusalem, Terence Smith of *The New York Times* writes, "have been linked in an unwritten alliance that may be unique in the modern history of nations. This 'special relationship,' as it is often called, has survived the strains of an oil embargo, four Middle Eastern wars, seven American administrations. . . . Its tangible expression has been awesome: $12.7 billion in economic and military aid, including an arsenal of modern weaponry, and political support that has included the use of the United States veto in the United Nations Security Council six times in the last five years."[15]

How are we to account for a "special relationship" of such tangible and intangible dimensions? The cynical explanation one often hears, couched in terms of the political and economic clout of the American Jewish voter, is, I contend, inadequate. America's exceptional and economically costly relation to Israel is a standing refutation of the "economic interpretation of history." The explanation must be sought, rather, in terms of the American generosity for a people conceived in terms of the religious category of victim, in American guilt over the Holocaust,* in the underrated phenomenon of philo-Semitism and, lastly, in the fact that in the Israeli claim to a "special" relation and "special" treatment, the secularized Christianity of the American civil religion hears secular echoes of the ancient claim to religious chosenness and, suspending the evenhandedness implicit in the universalism of its own religion, responds.

The "special relation" to Israel, then, is no more a simple surrender to Jewish "pressure," as some contend, than the United States Civil Rights Act of 1964 was a surrender to Black "pressure." Guilt over slavery and its consequences is as crucial to legitimating the latter as guilt over the Holocaust is to legitimating the former. Both policies stand or fall on the strength of their argument from historical uniqueness. In fact, it is not unreasonable to foresee that history will one day look back and view America's "special relation" to Israel as having been a foreign policy equivalent of what, in domestic politics, was known as "affirmative action."

---

*See my forthcoming book on the Holocaust.

Chapter 7

———◆◄●►◆———

AMERICAN CIVIL POLITICS AND THE "CONVERSION" OF EUROPEAN CLASS STRUGGLE INTO INSTITUTIONAL CONFLICT

———◆◄●►◆———

The political system rests on a sociological generalization and on an ethical commitment: that there is diversity and that this is normally good.   *—Bernard Crick*
In Defense of Politics

The ethos of American civil politics tames European political ideologies in exactly the same way as civil religion tames the European religious theologies. As the three-party system of religious pluralism works by virtue of its member religions' commitment to civil religion, so party politics and the two-party system work thanks to the commitment to civil politics. As civil religion is born out of the acceptance of plurality and the recognition that religious pluralism is both permanent and normal, so American civil politics—politics itself—is, as Bernard Crick writes, "fundamentally a descriptive recognition of diversity [pluralism of interests] plus an ethical recognition that this should be normal. . . ."[1] Civil politics issues from accepting "the problem of diversity"[2] as civil religion arises from interior assent to the fact of irreducible and irrecusable religious pluralism.

We have seen how the story of religion in America involves two phases: an early cognitive phase, in which each religion on arrival "learns" of the existence of the diverse other religions, and accommodates to them in a provisional, grudging, "utilitarian" way (as one acknowledges a physical obstacle in the situation of one's intended action); and a later, ethical phase, in which this diversity and pluralism is gradually, internally accepted, as somehow not only inevitable, but also right and meaningful, and good: what was merely descriptive of an external situation becomes normative and religiously legitimate. The change is from *"you* are *there,* and *we* are *here"* to "it is good for all of *us* to be *here."*

This inner acceptance of a religiously loyal opposition—the plural American "religious system"—matches point for point the American "political system." Ideological politics, imported from Europe—like classical theology—begins by accepting the diversity and pluralism only provisionally. But civil politics in America finally forces fanaticism out of the public arena just as civil religion in America privatizes the *soi-disant* absolutisms of religion. Civil politics as "the open canvassing of rival interests" abhors secrecy. "Palace politics is private politics, almost a contradiction in terms. The unique character of political activity lies, quite literally, in its publicity."[3] In the ideology of class struggle—the "rational" terror of communism—as in the ideology of racial struggle—the "irrational" terror of nazism—there was "a fanatic rejection of the [bourgeois] compromises of mere 'politics'. . . ."[4] In the civil politics of a free society, the moral consensus, as Crick demonstrates, is not something "mysteriously prior to or above politics: it is the activity (the civilizing activity) of politics itself."[5] The only basic consensus in a civil political regime is the agreement "to use political means."[6] The fierce perfectionism of fanatical ideology detests the imperfection of civil politics, its slovenly community, its half-way covenant, its "untidy elegance [and] rough civility," the interminable jaw-jaw of its parliaments and its pride in "conflict become discussion."[7]

Bourgeois liberal democracy in America, with its civil religion and its civil politics, does not banish the ideologies of communism and socialism (any more than it outlaws the "one true church" or the "one chosen people" theologies). Neither does it argue them out of existence by proving them false. As Robert Bellah remarks in his brilliant book on civil religion, the American repudiation of socialism "goes deeper than rational argument."[8] Rather, civil and bourgeois America finds ideology to be an obsession, and the greatest triumph of the bourgeois is to have "brought obsession into disrepute."[9] In America, the great Marxist obsession with Armageddon and with power, class, and conflict, like the great parousiatic religious triumphalisms, are brought into disrepute by two subversive influences: civility, flowing in from all sides and, from below, the infrastructure of role pluralism and criss-cross which work their remorseless deflations. Fanatical obsessions, both religious and political, are not refuted; they are discredited, ultimately, by civil religion and Protestant taste.

I.

Naked Struggle or Legitimate Opposition?

Socialism never got off the ground in America. The sheer existence of the American "thing" has always constituted an intellectual embarrassment to European social thinkers of Marxist and neo-Marxist persuasion. Rather than re-think Marxism—the power-conflict model of society—from the ground up, the theory was patched up with ad hoc band-aids to account for the eccentric social motions of the "new world." This was the well-known thesis of "American exceptionalism." America's lack of a feudal past (the theme of political scientist Louis Hartz), its constantly receding geographical "frontier" (identified by historian Frederick Jackson Turner), its pervasive upward mobility (as a conflict-regulator), its ever-renewed pool of proletariat stumbling up out of immigrant steerage—these and other matters were and are the social safety-valves cited to make plausible the lack of radical social cleavage and class conflict on the American social scene, which, in turn, makes sense—so it is argued—of the intellectual scandal of socialist Marxism's egregious irrelevance to the United States.

"The oft-repeated question of Sombart," the German sociologist Ralf Dahrendorf writes, " 'Why is there no socialism in the United States?' finds an answer not in the vague notion of the 'American way of life' but in the generally *positive* value attached to conflict in the United States."[10] (The "American way of life" reply to the "why no socialism" question is a layman's facile version of the value-consensus theory, and it is this theory that Dahrendorf seeks to rebut.) But Dahrendorf is correct in his analysis: it is precisely the very American and Protestant power of "positive" thinking about conflict that renders the conflict-theory of the traditionally "oppositional" intelligentsia moot in America. For it is in Puritan America that naked class-conflict has been clothed—institutionalized—in the adversary relationship of collective bargaining. This power of the "American thing" to institutionalize conflicts of interest (conflicts of economic interest in labor-management negotiations, conflicts of political, regional, and ethnic interest in a two-party political system, conflicts of religion in a three-religion "system") has at last got through to, and instructed the new generation of European neo-Marxists, like Dahrendorf. But this "power of positive thinking" still drives the older Frankfurt socialists up the wall. The whole of the Marcusean *"J'accuse"* against America could be summed up in his cry of "cooptation." This is a code word, and should be unpacked to read: "institutionalization."

The Anglo-American civic culture has succeeded in moderating the ancient malignant conflicts of the Continent. "The intensity of social conflict is at a minimum," Dahrendorf writes, "where the conflict *as such* is taken seriously and is pursued most energetically, as, for example, in U.S. industry. Conversely, all attempts to erase the lines of conflict . . . threaten, contrary to their intent, to sharpen conflict."[11] Dahrendorf, while noting the fact of de-intensification, misses the role of institutionalization in its creation. The idea of collective bargaining and the trade union movement emerged in the teeth of violent social conflict. The change occurred when the parties to the conflict accepted the adversary relationship as inevitable, continuing, and unavoidable. At that "moment" opposition was accepted "inwardly" as legitimate. That is the "moment" when social inventiveness came into play, and new institutions were created: the trade union *movement* passed into a collective-bargaining *institution* (a Gompers and the IWW gave birth to a George Meany and the AFL-CIO).

The same thing occurred in American politics. Up to the eighteenth century and earlier, political opposition was unlegitimated or only quasi-legitimate. But a change took place from anti-party thought to the idea of an opposition party: to a *system* of *permanent* and *recognized* partisan opposition. "The emergence of *legitimate* party opposition and of a theory of politics that accepted it," writes the late Columbia historian, Richard Hofstadter, "was something new in the history of the world; it required a bold new act of understanding. . . ."[12] (The idea of a culturally legitimate religious opposition—pluralism—operating under the norm of church-state separation, was something equally unprecedented in world history.) It was this pivotal cultural idea and the social institutions which embodied it that cast the shadow of illegitimacy—and unrespectability (the same thing in this, the bourgeois era)—on all third-party-type movements, and that turned socialism in America into a merely agitational, utopian, and "non-responsible" opposition or, at best, an "educational" but not a political force (parts of FDR's "New Deal" were thus "educated" by earlier "movements").

The importance of the idea of "system" must not be neglected in this analysis. In every institutionalization of conflict, be it economic, political, or religious, we hear the echo of the legal system, the Anglo-Saxon "adversary system." Earlier I wrote of the crucial moment when capital and labor accept each other as "parties" to a permanent conflict. In fact, they became such "parties" only in the act of inwardly accepting each other as "representing" legitimate if adversary interests—in other words, as *parts* of a larger whole or "system." Parties are self-defined as parts. The traditional political campaign, as Parsons notes, far from being a meaningless "ritual," functions to "reinforce the generalization of support" for the supra-party *system.* Power changes hands: long live the system! "Naturally," he continues, "this depends on definite institutional conditions, notably the acceptance of electoral results by the losing side without impairment of basic loyalties, and the restraint of winners from using their power to suppress opposition. It depends overwhelmingly," he concludes, "on the firm institutionalization of such 'rules of the game.' "[13] (The controlling image behind the power-conflict "school" is of an oppositional dyad in a zero-sum struggle; the image behind the value-consensus "school" is of [at least] a triad of independent and interdependent "parts.")

Our liberal era—which Talcott Parsons calls the denominational or pluralistic era of Western Christian civilization—has witnessed the addition of a third conflict-institutionalization (to the political and socio-economic), viz., the institutionalized ecumenism of the three-party religious system of Protestantism, Catholicism, and Judaism. Beginning with the "separation of church and state" (a political decision to take religion out of politics) it has moved, as we have seen, to an inward acceptance of each other by former religious adversaries. No longer putting up with each other with *de facto* sufferance, each inwardly acknowledges and accepts the other as *de jure,* as a legitimate and "loyal" opposition that is here to stay, and has a right to stay. This religious "settlement" reflects itself in the ecumenical editorial mastheads of religious journals, in the membership of the almost continually convened interfaith summit meetings on Educational TV. (Locutions like "Judeo-Christian" reflect this as yet informal institutionalization.)

The short phrase "the *agreement* to disagree" sums up all these changes. One lives, and lets live. One "goes along to get along." Compromise is at the heart of the Anglo-American adversary institutions of the Civic Culture (as Gabriel Almond and Sydney Verba call it); and compromise presupposes consensus. Marx, the fountainhead of all conflict theory in the West, refused to enter the bourgeois *Gesellschaft* which is the Christian European West. Marx—and Hegel—were correct, Walt Whitman Rostow writes, "in asserting that history moves forward by the clash of conflicting interests and outlooks; but the outcome of conflict in a regularly growing society is likely to be governed by ultimate considerations of communal continuity which a Boston lawyer,

Charles Curtis—old in the ways of advocacy and compromise—recently put as follows:

> I suggest [he said] that things get done gradually only between opposing forces. There is no such thing as self-restraint in people. What looks like it is indecision. . . . It may be that truth is best sought in the market of free speech, but the best decisions are neither bought nor sold. They are the result of disagreement, where the last word is not 'I admit you're right,' but 'I've got to live with the son of a bitch, haven't I.' "

To this Rostow adds: "This ultimate human solvent, Karl Marx —a lonely man, profoundly isolated from his fellows—never understood. He regarded it, in fact, as cowardice and betrayal, not the minimum condition for organized social life, any time, anywhere."[14] Talcott Parsons has been our greatest student of this "ultimate human solvent" and of the ways it transforms social cleavage not into consensus but into conflict.

II.

Parsons: Conflict-Theory vs. Cleavage-Theory

The mythical Talcott Parsons of conflict-theory ideology and polemics is a Panglossian* *idiot savant,* bland as he sits in benign audition of the harmonious music subsystems make as they serenely mesh in pre-established social-system copulation with their member subsystems in the frictionless symphony that constitutes our social life. The mythical Parsons is a Cambridge Candide, rounding out a 50-year ego-trip on the littoral of the Charles, ripe for the pen of another Voltaire. The mythical Parsons is blessedly immune, as only a WASP can be, to the facts of suffering, pain, power, poverty, sex, conflict and war. The mythical Parsons stands in dire need of an Alvin Gouldner to instruct him in the realities of social earthquakes, of an Irving

---

*Professor Lewis Coser, for example, speaks of "the Panglossian view that underlies much of Talcott Parsons' vision of the world." "Lewis Coser on Social Thought, *New Republic,* Nov. 27, 1976, p. 24.

Louis Horowitz to remind him that one of the Seven Deadly Sins is greed. The mythical Parsons is, in short, invincibly ignorant.

But from the real Parsons, the Parsons, that is, whose words are open to inspection—if by some chance we should care to read those words—we learn a very different view of personality and society. We learn, for example, that personality development is a "painfully built up step by step" process, and that "the essential point" and "crucial problem" presented by the early phases of this development "is not how to get commitment to the 'right' values, but how to get commitment to *any* values."[15] "The basis of this view," Parsons concludes, "is the *conviction* of how very precarious a truly human level of personality development *in any sense* is."[16] Leibniz is never recorded as having declared any such "conviction." An essay remains to be written titled "The Precarious Vision of Talcott Parsons."

Furthermore, Parsons's vision of society is precisely comparable to his vision of human personality. Edward C. Devereux, Jr., for example, writes that for Parsons "society is a veritable powder keg of conflicting forces, pushing and hauling in all ways at once. That *any* sort of equilibrium is achieved at all . . . thus represents for Parsons something both of miracle and challenge. Far from taking societal equilibrium for granted," Devereux concludes, "he sees it as a central problem demanding detailed analysis and explanation."[17] It is this vision of the precariousness of both personality and society that alone makes understandable Parsons's life-long obsession—for it is nothing less than that—with the Hobbesian problem of order. A descendant of John Calvin does not have to be told that, with a slight change or two, life could very easily become "nasty, brutish, and short."

The Parsonian difference with the Marxist wing of the power-conflict school, then, is not that, due to his WASP impercipience and incorrigible *goyisher-kop*-itude, all conflict has absconded from his theory. Rather, he has genuine, bona fide empirical and theoretical differences with the Marxists over the nature, extent, and consequences of the conflicts manifestly present in modern industrial societies. They claim to have found, and in any case consider it their office to promote, one putative line of cleavage that radically rends the socio-economic fabric of all industrial, capitalistic societies. The classical Marxian concept of "class" denotes the central axis of this cleavage, subsuming all other conflict situations under its hegemony. Parsons and his followers, on the other hand, claim that modern (especially American) society exhibits no such single monolithic cleavage but rather multiple lines of crisscrossing conflict on more than one axis. They claim, further, that such crisscross, far from splitting society, tends to promote its solidarity (the cutoff point, in any given case, where conflict promoting integration passes over into conflict creating malintegration, remains an empirical question).

A confusing element is introduced into this whole question by a certain vicissitude in American intellectual history: a whole cohort of Americans committed—for one reason or another—to Marxian socialism have entered the academic profession of sociology and may have done so—adding another dimension to the confusion—under the aegis of Parsonian sociology! What may appear as a curious byway in the sociology of knowledge will, in fact, give us access to the intellectual ancestry of some of the issues at stake in the controversy between the value-consensus and power-conflict theories of modern society. In this way the ground will be prepared for an account of how a sort of synthesis of the two positions emerges in the post-war American sociology influenced by Parsons. In this way, also, we can almost observe the internal diversity and pluralism of the American community in the process of inscribing its diversity and complexity in those who study it. Civility gradually evicts ideology; civil politics replaces ideological politics.

III.

Socialism Passes Into Sociology

(And Out Again?)

For a whole generation of second generation immigrant intellectuals, Karl Mannheim—especially his *Ideology and Utopia*—constituted the intervening intellectual variable between socialism and sociology. Louis Wirth went from writing *The Ghetto* (1928) to translating, with Edward Shils, *Ideology and Utopia* (1936) to exploring the city as a permanent settlement of "socially heterogeneous individuals" (1938).[18] The heterogeneity and pluralism of Western society was a striking and massive fact. Soon, sociological awareness of heterogeneity as social environment would deepen into awareness of the internalization of heterogeneity in each individual, taking the form of role pluralism, multiple reference groups (Merton), and the resultant cross-pressures of crisscross.

When Seymour Martin Lipset contributed a kind of sociological memoir to *Sociological Self-Images: A Collective Portrait,* he called it "From Socialism to Sociology."[19] Similarly, Robert Merton had made earlier, in his Mannheimian "sociology of knowledge essays," a settlement of his accounts with the appeal of the ideology of Marxism. In each case the crucial element in the shift from socialism to sociology was the distinction between social conflict in Europe, where all conflicts nested and reinforced each other into a basic cleavage, and conflict in America, where differences did not overlap and accumulate but, on the contrary, tended to crisscross and cancel each other out. "The prolonged intensity of class conflict in many continental nations," Lipset observes, "was owing to the overlap of economic class conflict with 'moral' issues of religion, aristocracy, and status. Because moral issues involve basic concepts of right and wrong, they are more likely than economic matters to result in civil war or at least class cleavage."[20]

Lewis Coser wrote his *Functions of Social Conflict* under Merton at Columbia. A slow attenuation of Marxist-socialist ideology was at work. Coser, as Dahrendorf noted of America generally, was thinking "positively" about conflict. Conflict is good for you, Coser maintained. In fact, it promotes consensus and meliorist social change. In fact, it is the prophylaxis for revolutionary change. Coser and the "alienated" socialists of *Dissent* magazine still talked about class, but not class war. Soon they talked mostly of status, as the classic Marxist concept of class fell into disrepute. Clearly, modernization, with its attendant mobility and role-pluralism, had become the solvent of socialism as it had become the solvent of socialist identity. Primordial identities were being differentiated into modern personality systems. An end of ideology was in the offing.

European Marxists also, like the late J. P. Nettl, as they came slowly under the influence of American (i.e., Parsonian) sociology were quick to focus on "the whole notion of cross-pressures" as the crucial variable in the civic societies of the modernized world that *directly* "negates the type of [Marxist] postulate about what society is like," and on which postulate Rosa Luxemburg and her contemporaries had two distinguishable polarized *classes* locked in cosmic combat.[21] Theodor Geiger also notes that "free development of the personality appears to be closely related to the individual's being located at the intersection of several social circles. By constantly changing roles between his various social circles, the individual gains a certain distance to them all, increasing his consciousness of being an independent person."[22] Such insights made the irrelevance of ideological politics in America increasingly obvious.

The influence of Max Weber, "the bourgeois Marx," also grew, as did the influence of Parsons. The socialists began cashing in their one big ideological Cleavage and their ideological Cleaver—Marx—for the small change of a lot of little (or littler) conflicts that answered more accurately to their American experience. Their socio-political commitments shifted as their acculturation deepened. Crucial to this change was the Viennese Paul F. Lazarsfeld and the Bureau of Applied Social Research. His "panel method" operationalized the insight into crisscross experienced by his generation in the course of its translation to America. By 1948 he was announcing that "the study of people under cross-pressures is one of the major concerns of social science today," and citing the Everett C. Hughes study, *French Canada in Transition* (p. 86), in which the English Catholic must choose between ethnic affiliation and religion, i.e., either to study with Protestant ethnic fellows at McGill—the usual choice —or to resolve the conflict by studying with Quebeçois at, say, Laval. He wrote: "The understanding of what actually transpires in such [cross-pressured] situations will make for tremendous gains in the understanding of social change."[23] Fourteen years later, in the course of his *Voting: A Study of Opinion Formation in a Presidential Campaign* (written with Berelson and McPhee) he offered his classic formulation, viz., that "an individual who is characterized by any type of cross-pressure is likely to change his mind in the course of the campaign, to make up his mind late, to leave the field and not to vote at all" (p. 284).

By the 1950s the idea of crisscross and the functions of crisscross had become common property. Robin Williams, Jr., observing in 1951 that American society is "simply riddled with cleavages"—note the plural—goes on to identify a "remarkable phenomenon," viz., "the extent to which the various differences 'cancel out'—are non-cumulative in their incidence."[24] By the mid-fifties anthropologist Max Gluckman was demonstrating the fertility of crisscross by applying it to *Custom and Conflict in Africa*. Declaring that "the central theme of my lectures is cross-pressures," he found forms of mutuality in the color bar itself. He explores the paradoxes of crisscross: the bonds of conflict, the competitive money economy binding black to white, alliances *across* the color line, norms of reciprocity irrepressibly developing (pp. 137–165). The mid-fifties also witness the conflation, in people like Lenski, of crisscross theory with "status crystallization" and non-vertical dimensions of status (*ASR*, 1954, p. 405). By 1960 John Galtung was calling the idea of multiple loyalties a "pillar of criss-cross theory" and spoke of "institutionalized guarantees against polarization—at least up to a certain level of conflict intensity." People under cross-pressures, he noted, "have difficulties choosing sides since they would share one status with either side; . . . according to some findings [recently questioned, by the way—J.M.C.] this should lead to withdrawal, and in the withdrawal lies a reservoir of manpower for keeping the structure going so as to minimize the effect of the conflict and contain it" [Marcuse's "cooptation"—J.M.C.].[25]

In my reckoning, the theory of crisscross is dealing with a core question: what kind of "social cement" integrates modern, industrial, liberal, "bourgeois" societies? What kind of solidarity obtains between members of the modernized *Gesellschaft?* Marxian power-conflict theorists find radical polarization papered over by the ideology of value-consensus. The Parsonian value-consensus theorists find multiple and frequently "hidden" interconnectedness, often obfuscated by the ideology of the conflict-theorists. Again: just as the Marxists not only *discover* "scientifically" the fact of ultimate class conflict, but also *promote* a praxis that will activate and intensify this cleavage, so the Parsonian theorists of the liberal society not only discover "scientifically" multiple cross-cutting conflicts and therefore no radical cleavage, but they promote a liberal praxis that increases integration by promoting conflict. "Hence," Galtung writes, "the paradox: to increase integration, activate a second dimension that is not perfectly correlated with the first so as to get both links and split loyalties to the extent that there are people in dissonant combinations."[26] These "institutionalized guarantees against polarization" are, it seems to me, inherent in the modernization process itself, and hence make modern societies proof against Marxist takeover and *fully* modernized intellectuals immune to Marxist ideology. On the whole, only relatively "backward" personality systems within the highly developed industrial societies take to Marxist ideology. These Marxist ideologues might thus be construed as supplying independent confirmation for a paradox of Marxism: its success in the underdeveloped countries.*

Goode in 1960 conceptualizes this same phenomenon of cross-pressure in his "Theory of Role Strain." Since the individual's "total role obligations are overdemanding," role strain is normal[27] just as, years earlier, Durkheim found that crime is normal. Conflict, in other words, is built-in, pluralized, crisscrossed, hence moderated. Conflict exists, but attenuated, deintensified, de-fanaticized. Pre-modern ideology is ended. Each role-incumbent is a conflict-manager, playing off the felt strain of one role-cost against another, bargaining, negotiating, distantiating (this is the provenance of Goffman's role-distance concept). In a society such as ours, Goode writes, "each individual has a very complex role system and . . . numerous individuals have a relatively low intensity of norm commitment to many of their role obligations. . . ."[28] There is a kind of sociological casuistry involved in fitting *ideal* role obligations to the *real* demands of one's alters in the role. Parsonian role theory is

---

*Cf. Robert G. Wesson's brilliant *Why Marxism? The Continuing Success of Failed Theory* (New York: Basic Books, 1976).

marvelously sensitive to the ubiquity of conflict in this as in other domains.

"The most creative group of American sociologists," Lewis Feuer noted some years back, in the course of reviewing C. Wright Mills's *The Sociological Imagination*, "has evolved from youthful radicalism to adherence to (what a sardonic critic might call) the 'allrightnik' view of American society."[29] As they became increasingly intimate with the American experience, as they became "inward" to American society, their erstwhile Marxism became increasingly irrelevant. The growth of the social sciences, and especially sociology, and especially the Parsonian theory of action, invited them to reconceptualize their American experience in non-ideological terms. Edward Shils, a member of the generation in question, argues that the emergence of the social sciences as subjects of university research and teaching "constitutes a major factor in the tarnishing of Marxism" which has lost its allure because it is "too simplistic, too threadbare intellectually and morally, too often just wrong or irrelevant. . . ."[30]

Thus did many of this group drag themselves, kicking and screaming, from socialism into sociology, from the commitment to ideology to the commitment to knowledge, from Marx to Weber and Parsons. The story of this "intellectual assimilation" has yet to be told. But any teller of the tale will have to give a featured place to the role of "crisscross" in the radicals' discovery of the liberal society. And the role of Parsons (sometimes through his student, Merton, the first one to cross over the bridge) is uncontestable. If Hannah Arendt can write that Rahel Varnhagen "assimilated by way of Fichte's *Addresses to the German Nation*,"[31] surely many of this group may be said to have "assimilated by way of Parsons's *Social System*." Intellectuals assimilate via the cultural system, as non-intellectuals assimilate in social system, everyday-life terms.

But some, especially among the first generation, refused to budge from their commitment to the power-conflict theory. Meyer Schapiro, for example, was already attacking in 1945 those admirers of Weber who try to "present him as a major prophet for our time and [what is much worse!—J.M.C.] set him beside Marx and Trotsky, men of an altogether different and much greater historical significance."[32]

And some others, among the second and third generations, are notably restive garbed as academic *Berufsmenschen,* mere sociologists, would-be intellectuals. Having betrayed their youthful idealism [read: socialism] and having "sold out" in the fifties to "academic sociology" [read: structural-functionalism], they now, with a fillip received from the New Left in the sixties, are busily translating their sociology back into socialism. Alvin Gouldner comes first to mind.[33] But then there is Norman Birnbaum, revved up once more by the "humanism" of the Manuscripts of 1844. And Irving Louis Horowitz's twistings and turnings, and his mentor, the late C. Wright Mills (that "caretaker of the socialist polemical tradition"[34]) who led the power-conflict theorists into battle against Parsons's "grand theory" of consensus in the fifties by transforming sociology back into socialism. What Lipset writes of the late George Lichtheim in "The Sociology of Marxism" may be applied *mutatis mutandis* to this whole group, lapsing from sociology to "critical sociology" and socialism again: "This is a tortured book," he tells us, writing of Lichtheim's *Marxism: An Historical and Critical Study,* "tortured because Lichtheim seems torn between past attachment to Marxism as the best form of sociological and political analysis, and current rejection of everything it stands for. On the one hand," Lipset continues, "he refuses to acknowledge the possibility that latter-day sociology is superior to Marxism in any way, or even that it could possibly incorporate any of its approach. Consequently there are the snide remarks about sociology both for criticizing Marxism and for accepting it. On the other hand, he feels it necessary to deny to others, sociologists or not, the possibility of applying any part of the Marxist analysis."[35] This is the fate of the second generation ex-radical intellectual, "born between two worlds, the one dead, the other powerless to be born" (Matthew Arnold). Lichtheim and his cohort are situated between socialism and sociology, between ideology and science, between the power-conflict and the value-consensus theories, between Marx and Weber (or Parsons). Toward Marx they exhibit the proprietary attitude of the reluctant apostate, tenderly protective of a lost love. Toward Weber (or Parsons) they exhibit the contempt of the *Luftmensch* intellectual for the *Berufsmensch* professional. Toward both, they are deeply ambivalent.[36]

Daniel Bell spoke for a good many members of this ex-radical group when, at the end of the 1950s, he wrote *The End of Ideology: On the Exhaustion of Political Ideas in the Fifties.*[37] Socialism for many, though, was not so much exhausted as repressed in the interests of "making it" in academic sociology. Gouldner, clearly, is speaking for himself when he writes: "One might say that in the United States Marxism was part of the suppressed 'underculture' of academic sociology, particularly for those who matured during the 1930s."[38] As Bell's book summed up the fifties for many of the CCNY-Brooklyn College cohort that matured in the thirties and who had, as they thought, given their Socialist identity honorable burial in Sociology, so Gouldner's book, coming at the close of the sixties, codified the socialist backlash, the "return of the repressed." Inside every "oversocialized" academic sociologist (of this group) in the fifties there was an "undersocialized" socialist screaming to get out. In the sixties, with the advent of a New Left youth movement casting itself as a new proletariat, they saw their chance and began crawling out of their carrels. Gouldner's *Coming Crisis* is the belated Manifesto of this curious *vernissage.* The buried appeal of ideology had proved overpowering. Neither civil politics nor civil religion had been able to touch it, much less tame it.

IV.

The Covert Appeal of Marx's Conflict Model

When Ralf Dahrendorf, in his joust with Parsons, praises Thrasymachus's definition of justice he adds, as he does elsewhere, that "whereas I have little sympathy with the content of Thrasymachus' argument in defense of the 'right of the strongest,' I have every sympathy with his insistence. . . ."[39] Far from being a Socratic utopian, though, Parsons would not take exception to the claim that conflict is ubiquitous, that might often suppresses right, nor would he—or Davis and Moore—find unacceptable, provided it was properly nuanced, Dahrendorf's insistence that "the fundamental inequality of social structure, and the lasting determinant of social conflict, is the inequality

of power *and authority* which inevitably accompanies social organization."[40] It is only the lingering element of the Marxist
"grand theory" of conflict that Parsons finds objectionable.

Marx (it is equally true of his followers) was "so dominated by
the 'logic of dichotomies,'" Parsons remarked,[41] that he was
"virtually oblivious to the elements of what may be called pluralization that were already developing in the society of his day,
especially in the England in which he lived."[42] Pluralization has
been characterized by a whole "series of emerging solidarities
that cross-cut the basic Marxian dichotomy. . . ." To call support
for trade-union organization and "welfare state" legislation
"false consciousness" "smacks very much of the notorious 'ad
hoc hypothesis,'"[43] and is Marxism's own brand of ideology.
Marx confined the process of structural differentiation in modernizing societies to the polarization of two inherently antago-
nistic classes whereas, in fact, the dominant trend has been "that
of 'pluralization' through further structural differentiation on
lines cross-cutting the two-class polarization. . . ."[44] Ideology
may be defined as the refusal to accept pluralization—Crick's
"diversity"—and differentiation as inseparable from modern industrial democratic society.

It is my contention that the middle-range theory of crisscross
(of the continuities in the theory of which I have been giving
some indication) is empirically responsive to the actual conflicts
observable in our society, finding them plural, cross-cutting,
and multidimensional. This theory constitutes a kind of synthesis of the conflict and consensus views, but not of the Marxist
version of the conflict theory. This theory recognizes enough
conflict in society to satisfy any ordinary appetite; it does not
recognize the Marxian socialist class cleavage simply because it
does not find it there. This apocalyptic class war is not accessible
to scientific observation or theory; it is a product of the ideological imagination. For Marxist reductionism, all conflicts are epi-
phenomena of class conflict; all are mini-conflicts in a great
macroscopic class struggle. What is the covert appeal of this
version of the power-conflict theory?

It is possible, Parsons maintains, "to identify components of
Marxian theory that have survived primarily because of their
special appeal to politically activist and radical intellectuals. The

first of these is the relatively radical devaluation of existing societies in which most of these intellectuals are involved, combined with an optimistic activity oriented toward changing societies in the desired direction." Secondly, and perhaps more latently, it provides a focus of blame for "the parlous state of society." Dichotomous thinking is *dramatic* thinking; Marxian ideology solicits the imagination. "In all this," Parsons continues, "the drama of dichotomy between the obstructors and the promoters of progress, the exploiters and the exploited, in short, the bad guys and the good guys, is clearly crucial ideologically." Beneath even this drama, lies the high cultural prestige (in the West) of the victim-role, and of those who garner "innocence by association" with accredited victims. (For three decades latter-day Marxists have constituted themselves as a kind of "victim search committee" since the disappearance by embourgeoisement of the classical Marxist victim, the proletariat. In the '60s, academic "critical sociologists" settled on their militant middle-class student clientele as candidate for this office. The social mobility we call "aging" has now expropriated them of their chosen victim-vanguard. Age stratification cross-cuts socio-economic stratification; were its findings not *infra dig* to them, the literature of age stratification could tell the socialist sociologists where they might find their absconded "New Left.") There is thus, Parsons continues, "a deep vested interest in the conception of a *two*-class system, one class of which is wrongfully in the ascendancy but, it is held, will legitimately be displaced by the previously oppressed" (Parsons's italics).

It can thus be seen, Parsons adds, "that Marxism gives the intellectual groups, especially in underdeveloped societies, first, a basis for committing themselves to modernization. . . . It also justifies a sharp break with the patterns of the traditional society in question."[45]

Three years earlier, in another context, Parsons had identified a third element in Marxism that accounted for its appeal to the intellectual. This is its covert appeal, not to the intellectual's commitment to modernization, but to the other side of his ambivalence, his longing for the pre-modern *Gemeinschaft* of his past. "In this light," he wrote, "Communist ideology may be interpreted as a statement of the symbolic values of modernization, in which symbolic *covert* gestures of reconciliation are made toward both the past and the future, within the framework of expected conflict. The first of these gestures involves the attempt to *preserve the integrity of the premodern system;* and I believe that this is *the primary significance of the symbol, socialism.* In essence, the purpose of this device is to [re-]assure us that the process of differentiation which is inherent in modernization need not jeopardize the integrity of preindustrial community solidarity. . . . I would further interpret this aspect of Communist ideology," he concluded, "as defensive or protectionist in character. . . ."[46] The ethnic intellectual is riddled with *Gemeinschaft-*nostalgia and what Peter Gay calls "wholeness-hunger." The power of Marxist ideology is that it reaches him covertly, touching the secret places of a heart which longs for the old premodern security of mechanical solidarity, when it was all a tribal matter of "them" and "us," the "good guys" and the "bad guys." Marx neglected the "Durkheimian problem," namely, in Parsons's words:

> the problem of the basis of order in a social system in its integration of associational relations and motivations with the normative structure of the society. This is the field we would now call that of the "societal community." For modern societies in particular it is Durkheim's conception of organic solidarity that is crucial—it is the very thing that most sharply inhibited Marx from correctly predicting the main trend of development of the advanced industrial societies. To put it in Durkheimian terms, in place of a developing system of organic solidarity, Marx saw only two antagonistic systems of mechanical solidarity, one for each of the two principal classes of his capitalistic system. Even after the transition to socialism, there is, according to Marxian theory, the sharpest limitation on the kinds of differentiation that could promote an organically-solidary societal community, in favor of a highly authoritarian system of mechanical solidarity.[47]

This commitment of Marxism to (Durkheimian) mechanical solidarity is at the root of its bifurcation of society into two, and only two, groups standing in an unmediatizable adversary relationship to one another. It is the conflict theory of society in its classic form. It is at the root of the Marxist concept of the "objective enemy," that is, the (ideological) conviction that whatever a person's subjective intentions, for example, that nevertheless, what he is doing is "objectively counterrevolution-ary." The adverb "objectively" codifies and operationalizes the mechanical solidarity component in Marxism. It is, furthermore, a researchable hypothesis that it may also account for the dis-proportionate appeal of Marxism for the second generation of East European Jewish intellectuals. Ethnic solidarity and its ac-companying ascriptive identity is of the mechanically solidary type. It is a "tribal," mechanical solidarity and identity rather than a "civil," organic solidarity and identity. There are "objec-tive" friends and "objective" enemies. In fact, this is one of Portnoy's complaints: "I am sick and tired of *goyische* this and *goyische* that! If it's bad it's the *goyim*, if it's good it's the Jews! Can't you see, my dear parents, from whose loins I somehow leaped, that such thinking is a trifle barbaric? That all you are expressing is your *fear?* The very first distinction I learned from you, I'm sure, was not night and day, or hot and cold, but *goyische* and Jewish!"[48]

Roth is obviously exaggerating, and enjoying his role as "in-former to the *goyim*" on the ingroup secrets of ethnic subcul-tures (and of many more than the Jewish) and it *is* "a trifle barbaric," i.e., instilling mechanical and tribal solidarity in a dichotomous "we–they" form. Nevertheless, for children leav-ing their ethnic community and "secularizing" their identity, there is a standing temptation for this "very first distinction" to find a secular functional equivalent in Marx's "very first distinc-tion," the dichotomous class cleavage of his conflict theory. Ethnicity and class are both ascriptive variables; they offer the inner fixed gyroscope of a premodern "tribal" reassurance for those who are lost in the wasteland of the modern *Gesellschaft*. There is no a priori reason why these ascriptive, Durkheimian "mechanical solidarities" should not translate into each other. Moses Hess (1812–1875) pioneered the translation from Marx-ism to Zionism. For this betrayal Marx mocks him in his *Mani-festo*.* This translatability is a researchable hypothesis. For, as James S. Coleman observes in his study of conflict and cleavage,

---

*Cf. Arthur Hertzberg, ed., *The Zionist Idea: A Historical Analysis and Reader* (New York: Meridian Books, 1960), pp. 117–18.

"one of the reasons that Jews have been a major focal point of conflict is that there have seldom been cross-cutting lines of cleavage which *tied* various segments of them to *other* persons in society."[49]

V.

The Synthesis of Power-Conflict

with Systems-Integration Theory

As the conflict theory (especially in its Marxian version) reflects the pre-modern mechanically solidary view of society, so crisscross (the consensus theory) reflects the fact of modern Durkheimian "organic solidarity." Despite the fact that sociologists as early as Simmel saw conflict as a "web" rather than as a "war," crisscross is a very American thing, both in theory and in fact. It is a genuine "synthesis" of all the truth in the conflict theory, leaving out its Marxian ideology, and all the insights of the value-consensus theory. The classic formulation in the literature of crisscross was made almost sixty years ago by the American sociologist E. A. Ross:

> A society, therefore, which is ridden by a dozen oppositions along lines running in every direction may actually be in less danger of being torn with violence or falling to pieces than one split just along one line. For each new cleavage contributes to narrow the cross clefts, so that one might say that *society is sewn together* by its inner conflicts.[50]

If social conflicts converge in a single direction, in other words, and are consolidated along a single axis, their intensity increases, and parties to the conflict become fanatics. It is a contention of this analysis that the mills of the modernization process "grind exceeding small," transforming tendencies to macro-cleavage into mini-conflicts. In this sense, it is the modernization process itself which is the despair of the ideologues of "total conflict." For the cutting edge of the modernization process is structural differentiation with its attendant pluralization. Often, it sunders us from what we love, and sews us into what we hate. It divides us from ourselves. It complicates our lives.

To return to civil politics. Social structural crisscross makes a good fit with our political system: both promote a system of "checks and balances" acting as a break on monolithic consolidations of economic and political power. Crisscross supplies the infrastructure supporting the symbolic media (Parsons) that bind our society into a community (a "societal community"). Crisscross, again, codifies the independent variability of the dimensions of class (money, status, and power). It refuses to reduce them to one. The very title of C. Wright Mills's book in the conflict-theory tradition—*The Power Elite*—collapses two dimensions (power *and* status [= "elite"]) into one.

Perhaps the first thinker to attempt formally a synthesis of power-conflict with consensus theory—which he calls system analysis—is R. A. Schermerhorn. In his *Comparative Ethnic Relations: A Framework for Theory and Research,*[51] he credits Max Gluckman with shifting him from an exclusively power-conflict analysis. His field, the field of ethnic relations, "lends itself so readily to power-conflict analysis" (p. 53). Gluckman's African crisscross analysis woke him from his dogmatic slumber and his allegiance to what he feels is a built-in ideology which he calls the "victimology" (p. 8) of the power-conflict approach. He has moved under Gluckman's influence to what he calls a "more dialectical view" ["dialectical" adds nothing to his analysis—J.M.C.] "in which systems analysis assumes correlative importance." What comes through clearly from Gluckman's analysis in *Custom and Conflict in Africa,*[52] he relates, is that "conflict interactions between groups of unequal power *engender* integrative bonds that have system characteristics. They are not something superadded but an inherent feature of the process of change. Gluckman's portrayal of colonial conquest in South Africa, for example, has so many overtones reminiscent of parallel movements throughout the world, that it furnishes a kind of paradigm for them" (p. 53).

Power-conflict elements, in other words, are necessary to the systems-integration approach. Both personality and society "call for conflict as integral rather than residual features of system" (p. 38). Power, conflict, and change have never been residual categories in Parsons's understanding of the systems (or consensus) integration approach; pattern maintenance for Parsons has always been just that, "maintenance," an *effort* to maintain, to "keep up" value standards in the teeth of everything that tries to tear them down. Consensus is carved out of conflict, play by play, moment by moment. Its victories are instantly vulnerable. Violence dogs decorum. Civilization, spelled out in civility, is a fragile thing.

VI.

The Experience of Crisscross: from "Between" to "Within." Cross-Pressures Civilize.

The experience of crisscross could be called the social psychology of crisscross. Better, it is the sociological psychology of crisscross; it is what happens to the consciousness of people (you, me) as we internalize the crisscrossed web of organic solidarity that constitutes the modernizing world. Crisscross humanizes us. More specifically, it civilizes us. Crisscross theory in social science has intimate, inner connections with the humanistic disciplines. It bridges the "two cultures."

Morton M. Hunt once made his way up to Hastings-on-Hudson to interview, in a large Tudor house, the sociologist Robert Merton, in order to do a profile on him for *The New Yorker*.[53] In the course of that visit Merton, after dinner, pushed a couple of cats off a side table so as to pick up a copy of T. S. Eliot's *Notes Towards the Definition of Culture*. He read to Hunt a passage, that concludes: " 'Numerous cross-divisions favor peace within a nation, by dispersing and confusing animosities.' " And then he defended, for Hunt, the power of sociological jargon, at least when it says much in little: "All very well and clearly said, but a sociologist would only have [had] to write: 'Cross-cutting status-sets reduce the intensity of social conflict in a society.' "[54]

Cross-cutting status-sets also reduce, Merton might have added, the intensity of personality conflict within the individual.[55]

"Perhaps the most important variable having to do with the location of the lines of social cleavage," writes James S. Coleman, in the best analysis yet written on crisscross, "is the level at which these lines crosscut society. By this I mean that the major lines of cleavage may come *within* individuals or *between* individuals. If the lines of cleavage come within the individual, this is tantamount to saying that numerous roles are important to him, and that he will feel cross-pressures when faced with an issue—such as, for example, the issue of released time from public schools for religious instruction." The question "what makes for or against cross-pressures?" reduces to the question, Coleman explains, "what brings the lines of cleavage within individuals or keeps them between individuals? The answer is simple: cross-pressures are absent when the major meaningful kinds of classification coincide."[56] When, for example, ethnicity, religion, and social status coincide, there are few cross-pressures. When Catholics are mostly Irish and Italian and working class, he notes, while Protestants are WASP and white collar, the lines of cleavage coincide. Jews have been a focal point of conflict, as we have seen, through a lack of cross-cutting lines of cleavage which "*tied* various segments of them to *other* persons in society." Group conflicts, Coleman concludes, are at their strongest "when no conflict is felt *within* the person."[57]

But, granting that *group* conflict abates when conflict is brought within the person, precisely what change happens *within* the individual person? Gene Wise, in a remarkable essay on the late historian of Puritanism, Perry Miller, contrasts him with another Puritan historian, Thomas Jefferson Wertenbaker. For both Wertenbaker (who wrote *The Puritan Oligarchy*) and Miller (*The New England Mind*) he concludes, "conflict is basic; but Wertenbaker locates it essentially *between* men, *between* groups, *between* ideas, while Miller views it *within* men, *within* groups, *within* ideas."[58] Again we must ask: with the social relocation of conflict from *between* to *within*, what change occurs in the consciousness of the individual? Wise's title gives the answer away: from an *angry*, embattled consciousness confronting an *external* enemy, the individual becomes an *ironical*, conflicted consciousness confronting an *internal* friend. A civil has replaced a tribal consciousness. He experiences what Valéry called "inner civilization." Internal conflicts multiply. "Multiplicity of conflicts stands in inverse relation to their intensity," Lewis Coser writes.[59] Outer intensity abates, inner intensity increases. We then tend to become the liberal unitarian of Robert Frost's scorn, who can't take his own side in a quarrel. But, as Yeats said, "out of our conflict with others we make rhetoric, out of our conflict with ourselves, poetry." And then the stage is set for a further and higher level of consciousness: how are we to bring about what Charles Williams called "defeated irony" without refanaticizing our consciousness? There is something awry "in the nature of things" if irony is the highest form of consciousness. Children are not ironical.

The Simmel-Ross formulation of crisscross, about the relation of the structure of conflict to the intensity of conflict, Robert Merton observed in a remarkable "Concluding Observation" to his 1959 speech at Louvain, "is an hypothesis *borne out by its own history,* for since it was set forth by Simmel and Ross, it has been taken up or independently originated by scores of sociologists, many of whom take diametrically opposed positions on some of the issues we have reviewed."[60]

VII.

The Two Testaments

of American Civil Religion

At this point, using "civil religion" in the more accustomed sense of Robert Bellah, let us turn for a moment to American history. In roughly the first hundred years of our country's history, the powerful symbols of national solidarity were the bewigged "Founding Fathers": Ben Franklin with his Deism and Providence and his "rebellion to tyrants is obedience to God"; George Washington with his Farewell Address on morality and religion; Thomas Jefferson and the Declaration of Independence. The dominating metaphors all derive from the Mosaic analogy: Americans have left Europe (Egypt) and tyranny for a "promised land," a New Jerusalem, a city upon a hill. The "civil religion" of the Founding Fathers is not specifically Christian. Its tropes and the figures of its rhetoric derive largely from the Old Testament. "The theme of the American Israel was used, almost from the beginning," Robert Bellah observes, "as a justification for the shameful treatment of the Indians so characteristic of our history. It can be overtly or implicitly linked to the idea of manifest destiny that has been used to legitimate several adventures in imperialism since the early nineteenth century."[61] In the first centenary of America's history, then, the American adversary is, generally speaking, "tribal" and external: "out of our conflict with others we make rhetoric." (Yeats.)

The trauma of Civil War creates a "new testament" for American civil religion. America no longer "confronts" an enemy but divides against itself: brother against brother. The rights and wrongs at issue lose something of the earlier easy clarity and self-righteous certainty. Lincoln's second inaugural inaugurates this universalism: "With malice toward none, with charity for all." "The earlier symbolism of the civil religion" Bellah notes, "had been Hebraic without in any specific sense being Jewish."[62] Lincoln's modernity and "bitter resisting mind" change all this: correcting the hybris of the precursor civil religion he now with deliberate irony calls Americans "an almost chosen people." The Gettysburg Address, written on the back of an envelope, seals this change; American civil religion moves from eighteenth century rhetoric to modernist and deathless poetry: "out of our quarrel with ourselves we make poetry." [Yeats]. American civil religion in a time of trial turns itself into poetry.

The Gettysburg Address is high demotic, the American civil prosaic sublime. The late American poet, Robert Lowell (b. March 1, 1917; d. Sept. 12, 1977), commented:

> The Gettysburg Address is a symbolic and sacramental act. Its verbal quality is resonance combined with a logical, matter of fact, prosaic brevity. . . . In his words, Lincoln symbolically died, just as the Union soldiers really died—and as he himself was soon really to die. By his words, he gave the field of battle a symbolic significance

that it had lacked. For us and our country, he left Jefferson's ideals of freedom and equality joined to the Christian sacrificial act of death and rebirth. I believe that this is a meaning that goes beyond sect or religion and beyond peace and war, and is now part of our lives as a challenge, obstacle and hope.[63]

Bellah notes that "the symbolic equation of Lincoln with Jesus was made relatively early. . . . With the Christian archetype in the background, Lincoln, 'our martyred president,' was linked to the war dead, those who 'gave the last full measure of devotion.' The theme of sacrifice," he concludes "was indelibly written into the civil religion."[64] The Civil War, and Lincoln's life and words, had permanently altered the American civil religion. The major "lines of cleavage," to revert once more to James Coleman, would henceforth be indelibly relocated *within* Americans rather than *between* them and non-Americans.

Thus the "internalization" of conflict promoted by the pluralism and "crisscross" of our *socio-economic* modernization coincided with the *cultural* symbolism bequeathed to us by Lincoln and the Civil War. The experience of cross-pressures at once modernizes us, middle-classifies us, and Americanizes us. The experience of crisscross is the social psychological coefficient of the modernization process. It makes us civil. It introverts our consciousness, giving us an inner life to complement the outer differentiations of modernization. Structural differentiation generates crisscross which, in turn, brings into being, in the words of Norman Podhoretz, "the qualities of reasonableness, moderation, compromise, tolerance, sober choice—in short, the anti-apocalyptic style of life. . . ." of the bourgeois era. It is the ambiguous triumph of crisscross to have "brought obsession into disrepute."[65]

Nailed by fate to crisscross, our ego-centric and ethno-centric American selves are excruciated into that form of awareness we call civility. The culture of crisscross is thus converted into consciousness. Crisscross lies at the crossroads of modernity.

Chapter 8

———◆◄●►◆———

HOMELY
PROTESTANT:
A DECORUM OF
IMPERFECTION

———◆◄●►◆———

The imperfect is our paradise.
Note that, in this bitterness, delight,
Since the imperfect is so hot in us,
Lies in flawed words and stubborn sounds.
                                            —*Wallace Stevens*
                                       "The Poems of Our Climate"

. . . the flaw being belatedness. . . .
                                            —*Harold Bloom*
                                            Wallace Stevens

Underlying the overt theme of this book—namely, that the taming and assimilation of European religion and politics in America has involved a religio-cultural conversion on the part of theologians and intellectuals—is another less patent theme: the deepest dimension of this religious change has been a change of taste. America, in requiring that its religious bodies exchange a triumphal demeanor for the civil demeanor of a denomination, is teaching the self-effacing modesty of puritan good taste to its citizenry.

Self-definitions predicated on being "the one true church" or "the chosen people," as we saw earlier, are experienced in America as an unseemly ostentation, as vulgar boasting, puffing, as ridiculous even. Good taste, like St. Paul's charity, "vaunteth not itself, is not puffed up, doth not behave itself unseemly, seeketh not her own" (I Corinthians 13 : 4–5). Modernist good taste is the expressive symbol of the Christian virtue of humility. This taste takes the form of a "decorum of imperfection," a phrase I borrow from the title of an article on the recently "discovered" puritan New England poet and divine, Edward Taylor (1645–1729), by Charles W. Mignon: *Edward Taylor's Preparatory Meditations: A Decorum of Imperfection.* *

Mignon makes clear that Taylor's work is not, as it is often taken to be, in the Anglo-Catholic tradition of the English metaphysical poets. There is an American puritan plainness instead. This is the kind of motivated imperfection William Dean Howells found in Emily Dickinson's poetry. It recalls Santayana on Emerson's poems: "Compositions so prompted are religious exercises; . . . something baffling and uncouth about them offends the merely literary critic. . . ."† It is this kind of American puritan indecorum, and not his frequent French décor, that defines Wallace Stevens, finally, as quintessentially American as Walt Whitman.

"Homely Protestant" of the title is the name of a painting by Robert Motherwell reproduced on the dust jacket of this book. It exists in two versions. It is, Motherwell writes, "possibly my single most important 'figure' painting."†† A "virtual monochrome of subdued but subtly and richly varied ochres," is how Arnason describes it (p. 25) with a kind of "primitive barbarism" (p. 30) and "barbaric splendor" (p. 88). It has a dry, mat, flat, uninflected quality. It is unpretentious, unostentatious, ordinary, civil, plain.

It is this taste, this Puritan plain decorum which has captivated us and which our culture knows as the most "modern" and best good taste. This ineloquence, this understated esthetic of litotes, this decorum of imperfection, is the secular esthetic expressive symbol of the dissenting "Protestant" (i.e., anti-Anglican, anti-Catholic) religious values of the Puritan origins of

---

Publications of the Modern Language Association of America (PMLA), Oct. 1968 (vol. 83, no. 5), pp. 1423–28.

†George Santayana, "Emerson the Poet," in *Santayana on America: Essays, Notes, and Letters on American Life, Literature and Philosophy,* ed. Richard Colton Lyon (New York: Harcourt, Brace & World, 1968), p. 280.

††H. H. Arnason, *Robert Motherwell* (New York: Harry N. Abrams, 1977), Plate #70, p. 103.

American identity. I call it, alluding to Max Weber, the Protestant esthetic. It constructs itself, like "good taste" always does, on restraint: "some do not."

I.

When critic Stanley Kauffmann says of Jane Fonda, daughter of Henry Fonda and the patrician Boston socialite, the late Frances Seymour Brokaw, that she has "thoroughbred gawky grace,"[1] he is talking good taste talk. Grace all by itself, grace unmarked by gawkiness, is too smooth, too easy, too facile, too *"cavalier"* is our language's way of instructing us in the puritan roots of modern good taste. Facility is one of our words for vulgarity. "After the easy elegance of color painting in the 1960s," writes Hilton Kramer of Walter Bannard's paintings, "we see here a new dialogue with the tough styles of the early New York School."[2]

The verbal rightness that matches the fierce elegance of modernist taste is, equally, at war with smooth rhetorical effects. "Imperfect, ruggedly rounded out, and in places appearing almost uncorrected," Clive Jones writes of W. H. Auden's poem "Through the Looking Glass." "The poem creates its effects with a monstrously skilled carelessness that is in every sense superb. . . ."[3] Something that is beautiful because it is "imperfect, ruggedly rounded" and appears "almost uncorrected" is instantiating what we call a "decorum of imperfection." We read in *The New Yorker* "Profile" by Berton Roueché of the young Massachusetts Congregational minister, Edward Hougen, to take another instance, that the writer listened with surprise as the preacher preached: "His voice from the pulpit was not a pulpit voice. It was his natural voice—easy, halting, conversational. He spoke as he had spoken at dinner."[4] Notice that word "halting;" this is one of the stigmata of modernist good taste. If the modernist lyric wrings the neck of rhetoric, as Ezra Pound said, the mod cleric wrings the neck of pulpit unction. Everything is to be bare, uninflected, and painfully yet somehow casually flat.

When a young middle- to upper-middle-class married couple

today takes posession of a new apartment, what happens? The plaster is stripped from the open face brickwork of walls and fireplace; varnish is scraped up off the floor; there are protracted discussions of the differing virtues of various paint removers; ceiling beams are exposed to view. The laminated end-grain massive maple butcher chopping block is installed in all its "authenticity." This modernist taste which strips and reveals is in an adversary relation to an older, bourgeois taste that conceals. In jeans the seams are exposed to view; the other culture concealed the seamy side of clothes from view. "Coarseness, revealing something; vulgarity, concealing something," E. M. Forster wrote.[5] Green River Cemetery way out in Springs, Long Island, where the painters Jackson Pollock and Ad Reinhardt and writers Frank O'Hara and A. J. Liebling are buried, exists in bucolic but not in cultural isolation: dialectically related to bourgeois vulgarity, it is, Grace Glueck writes, the avant-garde's "*answer* to Forest Lawn. Unlike that manicured park full of Hollywood celebrities, Green River's grounds are rough, its monuments unostentatious, and its setting far from picturesque."[6]

Nietzsche's injunction "Be hard" has nothing whatever to do with politics, and everything to do with taste. When Virginia Woolf praised D. H. Lawrence's "hard" sentences, and wrote that "not a single word had been chosen for its beauty, . . ." she was praising his taste.[7] Yeats taught this apocalyptic fastidiousness of the good taste constituted by the repudiation of "good taste" when he wrote his epitaph in "Under Ben Bulben":

> No marble, no conventional phrase;
> On limestone quarried near the spot.
> By his command these words are cut:
> Cast a cold eye
> On life, on death.
> Horseman, pass by![8]

If avant-garde intellectuality takes shape in the form of the ideologies of Freudianism and Marxism, unmasking, stripping with punitive objectivity,* avant-garde taste in the form of criticism can be equally punishing. This taste is a brutal realism

---

*Cf. John Murray Cuddihy, *The Ordeal of Civility: Freud, Marx, Lévi-Strauss and the Jewish Struggle with Modernity* (New York: Basic Books, 1974; Delta paperback edition, 1976).

against the beaux arts academy. It is the "authenticity" factor in modernity.

I I.

Using the work of the late great German-Jewish humanistic scholar, Erich Auerbach, I maintain that the roots of this mixed realism, the roots of this taste which indicts refinement as "bad taste" and "vulgar spirituality," and celebrates, yes, coarseness as really high taste, are in the Gospel story of the passion and death of Jesus. The roots are not so much directly in primitive Christianity as in the story, the verbal narrative of the Jesus story, as this story collided with the classical theory of styles in late antiquity.

Auerbach's thesis in *Mimesis,* in *Scenes from the Drama of European Literature,* and in his *Dante: Poet of the Secular World* is this: in late antiquity there was a hierarchy of literary genres or styles that matched the hierarchy of social levels of subject that could be written about. "In antique theory, the sublime and elevated style was called *sermo gravis* or *sublimis;* the low style was *sermo remissus* or *humilis;* the two had to be kept strictly separated."[9] This rule of the separation of styles specified that "the realistic depiction of daily life was incompatible with the sublime and had a place only in comedy or, carefully stylized, in idyl. . . ."[10] These differentiated styles can be viewed as censoring the kind of subject matter that enters their precincts: as if a certain genre of novel were to dictate, to all the populace demanding entry, just who were *Romansfähig* or apt for the novel and who not. The hierarchy of literary genres mimed, was in a kind of correspondence with, the hierarchy of social stratification. The former ruled the cultural system as the latter dominated the social system. As social classes did not mix, neither did the style-genres in which they spoke their pieces. The stark realism of the Gospel narrative challenged this rhetorical and social regime. (In the nineteenth century, an analogous revolution occurred once more: French classicism was subverted by the realism of the novels of Stendhal and Balzac.)

But a revolution occurred in late antiquity that broke the

stranglehold of the separation of styles doctrine. "It was the story of Christ," Auerbach writes, "with its ruthless *mixture* of everyday reality and the highest and most sublime tragedy, which had conquered the classical rule of styles."[11] In the story which is the Gospel, the high and the low are merged, fused, especially in the Incarnation and Passion stories, "which realize and combine *sublimitas* and *humilitas* in overwhelming measure."[12] The story of Jesus violates the central rule of antique literary decorum and good taste.

The man from Galilee, the crisis and catastrophe, "the pitiful derision, the scourging and crucifixion of the King of the Jews, . . ." Auerbach writes, "the despairing flight of the disciples, . . . this entire episode, *which was to provoke the greatest of all transformations in the inner and outward history of our civilized world* is astonishing in every respect."[13] Where, exactly, are we to locate this epochal and momentous transformation? "In entering into the consciousness of the European peoples, the story of Christ fundamentally changed their conceptions of man's fate *and how to describe it.*"[14] In diametrical opposition to the ancient feeling, "earthly self-abnegation was no longer regarded as a way from the concrete to the abstract, from the particular to the universal. What presumption to strive for theoretical serenity when Christ himself lived in continuous conflict!"[15] One recalls again those lines of W. B. Yeats, one of the founders of the modernist taste we seek to depict: "Odor of blood when Christ was slain/Made all Platonic tolerance vain/And vain all Doric discipline."[16]

The story of Jesus, then, "transcended the limits of ancient mimetic esthetics. Here [in the Gospel narratives] man had lost his earthly dignity; everything can happen to him, and [thus] the classical division of genres has vanished; the distinction between the sublime and the vulgar style exists no longer."[17] In the gospels as in ancient comedy real persons of all classes put in an appearance, but those of exalted rank do not "act in the style of classical tragedy, nor do the lowly behave as in farce; on the contrary, all social and esthetic limits have been effaced. . . ."[18] A scene like Peter's denial of Christ "fits no antique genre. It is too serious for comedy, too contemporary and everyday for tragedy, politically too insignificant for history. . . ."[19]

But this violation of the "rule of differentiated styles," this fusion and mingling was not, of course, "dictated by an artistic purpose." It was rooted "and graphically and harshly dramatized through [the belief in] God's incarnation in a human being of the humblest social station . . . and through his Passion which, judged by earthly standards, was ignominious."[20] In this fusion of the high and the low, the hieratic and the demotic, the sacred and the secular, God had joined what classical man and ancient Judaism had put asunder.

It is important to note that though the *doctrinal* content of this story was "what first penetrated the minds of men," "the *mimetic* content of the story of Christ required a very long time, more than a thousand years, to enter into the consciousness of the faithful . . . and to reshape their view of destiny."[21] The mimetic and expressive content of the Gospel narrative only gradually shaped the sensibility of Europe. There was a cultural lag. But the powerful literary portrayal of commonplace and inconspicuous figures in the New Testament narrative worked a slow revolution in Western taste. "Unobtrusiveness is the very essence of the 'happening' we call Jesus," writes Father Romano Guardini of Munich. "We have only to compare his outward activity with other biblical or non-biblical happenings to see how the mighty word, bold gesture, powerful deed, fantastic situation and the like are alien to him. Strange as it may seem, the character of the extraordinary is missing even in his miracles . . . [they] seem, one might say, 'natural.' This 'humanity' of which we spoke reappears as unobtrusiveness. . . . His words, too, had this unobtrusive quality about them. If we compare them with the words of Isaiah, or a Paul, they strike us as extremely moderate and brief. Compared with the sayings of a Buddha," Guardini concludes, "they seem brief to the point of bluntness, and almost commonplace."[22]

Jesus loved the commonplace, the ordinary, and the inconspicuous. This reversed the idea of the lovable found in antiquity. "Reverence for inconspicuousness is the final key," writes the late Ernst Bloch, the German-Jewish Marxist, "to this reversal of the motion of love [from *eros* to *agapé*]. . . . This love has no parallel, therefore, in any previous moral faith, not even in the Jewish one, despite the 'Love thy neighbor as thyself' (Lev.

19,18) that was received in Matthew 22, 39. Buddha leaps into
the fire as a rabbit, to give a beggar a meal, but his love does not
lead to the beggar, does not seek divinity in impotence."[23]

But we must return to the Gospel story itself, its verbal tex-
ture: inconspicuous, unostentatious, plain. The way of telling
the story—especially in the Passion narrative—is evocatively expressive of the events it narrates. "The grinding power of the
plain words of the Gospel story," Chesterton writes, "is like the
power of millstones; and those who can read them simply
enough will feel as if rocks had been rolled upon them. Criticism
is only words about words; and of what use are words about such
words as these?"[24]

Well, words about these words *were* spoken and sung and
written: there was liturgy, hymnody, and theology. Each, in its
own way, mimed the scandal and offense which was the Gospel,
its fusion of the highest and the lowest. In the Eucharistic liturgy, vulgar commonplace and ordinary substances of the everyday life of common people, bread and wine (Ignazio Silone
evokes this in his *Bread and Wine*) became the flesh and blood of
God Himself.

In the words of Jesus, too, there was this same offensive fusion
of highest and lowest. In the prayers of Jesus "there is something quite new, absolutely new—the word *abba,*" writes Joachim Jeremias, a convert to Christianity. This humble, Aramaic
term *abba* was the first sound a tiny child would utter to his
father. It is the same as our "Da-Da" (which later evolves into
"Daddy"). "*Abba* was an everyday word, a homely family-word,
. . ." Joachim Jeremias continues. Jesus himself viewed this form
of address for God "as the heart of that revelation which had
been granted him by the Father. In this term *abba* the ultimate
mystery of his mission and his authority is expressed. He, to
whom the Father had granted full knowledge of God, has the
messianic prerogative of addressing him with the familiar address of a son. This term *abba* is an *ipsissima vox* of Jesus and
contains *in nuce* his message and his claim. . . ."

With unspeakable tenderness Jesus addresses the ineffable
Yahweh as "Abba" (Da-Da). "No Jew would have dared address
God in this manner," Joachim Jeremias writes. Most astonishing
of all is the fact that, in teaching his disciples the Lord's Prayer,

Jesus authorizes them to repeat the word *abba* after him. "He gives them a share in his sonship and empowers them, as his disciples, to speak with their heavenly Father in just such a familiar, trusting way as a child would with his father."[25] Since only little children say *Abba,* Jesus' followers must become as little children again or they will not enter the coming Kingdom of Heaven (Matt. 18:3). Christian Eucharistic liturgies ever since have marked this daring turning-point in world-historical religions by prefacing their recitation of the Lord's Prayer: "And now, as our Saviour Christ hath taught us, we are *bold* to say, Our Father [Abba] . . . hallowed be Thy name, . . ."*

Only with a borrowed boldness does one dare enter a relationship of such monumental intimacy. This "style" of address eschews both the easy familiarity of the low style and the distantiating sublimity of the high. This paradoxically "mixed style" is, in origin, Auerbach contends, a uniquely Christian *fusion* of *humilitas* and *sublimitas.* It is an esthetic *mimesis* of the paradox of the Incarnation: Jesus is *both* the sublime God *and* the humiliated man. Its decorum of imperfection comes straight out of the Gospel narrative. The Jesus story is the touchstone of this new taste.

III.

Instead of a triumphal, ostentatious, Messianic entry into Jerusalem, Jesus comes in on the back of an ass. With the entry into Jerusalem on Palm Sunday, a certain correction of taste gets under way. The disciples are scandalized, offended. The Messiahship, as Schweitzer has shown, is inconspicuous; it is a secret. Sublimity in the incognito of humility. The lowliness of the beginning, in a stable, matched by the lowliness of the end, on an ass, on a cross. The humility of the first Advent to be reversed by the return in glory of the second. There is no divinity to point to at the time, no ostensive definition possible. The divinity

---

The Book of Common Prayer (Greenwich, Connecticut: The Seabury Press, 1953), p. 82 (emphasis mine).

must be taken on faith; the glory is but the hope of glory; and, even at the Parousia, the glory will not belong to Jesus; it will be a glory *borrowed* from the father.

All this enters the great hymns. Take "King's Weston":

> Brothers, this Lord Jesus
>   Shall return again,
> With *his Father's* glory
>   O'er the earth to reign;
> For all wreaths of empire
>   Meet upon his brow,
> And our hearts confess him
>   King of glory *now.*[26]

He is King of Glory *now* only for those who confess him. At the Parousia, sight will replace faith.

Charles Wesley's hymn goes thus:

> Lo! he comes, with clouds descending,
>   Once for our salvation slain;
>   . . .
> Every *eye* shall now behold him,
>   Robed in dreadful majesty;
>   . . .
> Saviour, take the power and glory;
>   Claim the kingdom for thine own. . . .[27]

Or, Isaac Watts' hymn:

> Forbid it, Lord, that I should boast,
>   Save in the cross of Christ, my God:
> All the vain things that charm me most,
>   I sacrifice them to his blood.
>
> . . . Did e'er such love and sorrow meet,
>   Or thorns compose so rich a crown?[28]

The fifth and final stanza of H. H. Milman's hymn on the Palm Sunday entry into Jerusalem on an ass goes:

> Ride on! ride on in majesty!
> In *lowly pomp* ride on to die;
> Bow thy meek head to mortal pain,
> Then take, O God, thy power, and reign.[29]

"Lowly pomp" strikes exactly the note of the "mixed" style.

The second stanza of Reginald Heber's famous "Holy, Holy, Holy! Lord God Almighty!" echoes the essential theme:

> Holy! Holy! Holy! though the darkness *hide thee,*
> > Though the eye of sinful man thy glory may not *see,*
> Only thou are holy; there is none beside thee,
> > Perfect in power, in love, and purity.[30]

The famous Advent hymns proclaiming the Incarnation strike the same note of the "mixed style" of the Gospel story: the hush, the *in*eloquence of Divinity, a baby in a manger. *Stille Nacht. Silent night.* Or Philips Brooks's Christmas hymn, "How silently, how silently, the wondrous gift is given." Or the lines of W. C. Dix:

> As with joyful steps they sped
> To that *lowly* manger-bed;
> > . . .
> As they offered gifts most rare
> At that manger *rude and bare;*
> > . . .
> And, when earthly things are past,
> Bring our ransomed souls at last
> Where they need no star to guide,
> Where no clouds thy glory *hide.*[31]

The hymn sung to the tune we know as "Greensleeves" asks:

> Why lies he in such mean estate
> Where ox and ass are feeding?

Now if, as Schweitzer has shown, the ethic of Jesus was an *Interimsethik*—an ethic for the interim—and if, as he writes, the eschatological "secret of the Kingdom of God contains the secret of the whole Christian *Weltanschauung,*"[32] it is my thesis that the story of Jesus—both in the story told and in the manner of its telling—embodies an *Interimsästhetik,* that is, an esthetic for the interim, which puts a ban on all ostentation and triumphalism *for the time being,* before the Parousiatic return, at which time alone triumphalism becomes appropriate and fitting. Implicitly, this esthetic for the interim, this decorum of imperfection, taboos glory *now*. Glory *between* the first and second comings is precisely vainglory—it is vulgar, empty, and in bad theological taste. "Whosoever shall exalt himself shall be abased; and he that shall humble himself *shall be* exalted" (Matt. 23.12), runs one of the eschatological inversions of the Sermon on the Mount. At the time of the great Messianic reversal, when Jesus comes on the clouds of heaven, *then* we will be allowed (perhaps) an *esthetica gloriae*, but for the interim—which of course, still goes on—an *esthetica crucis* is the only fit accompaniment for our *theologia crucis*. The Reformers saw this, as did the New England Puritans, insisting on their plain style* against the Anglo-Catholic divines (as Perry Miller has shown).

The story of Jesus, with its mixed style, the very behavior of Jesus, a self-effacing God with no "side," as the English say, infiltrates the expressive value system of the West, secularizing itself into our consciousness, educating our sensibility and our taste. The story of Jesus has been Europe's "sentimental education." The figure of Jesus in the Gospel story is what Durkheim calls a "collective representation." It hovers over the West.

It is sometimes difficult fully to document the things that are precisely the most pervasively influential. It is only in our own time, for example, that the limitless consequences for our culture of the maleness of the Deity (both Jesus and God the Father) have begun to be noted, for good or ill. Think, analogously, of the teaching power of the Jesus story, in the first place simply as a story, as it has formed Western values and consciousness. It has been sect rather than church, the dissidence of dissent rather than establishmentarianism in either Catholic or Protestant version, it has been the hard-bitten puritan suspiciousness of art, feeding off the Gospel story, that in every generation renews an art that is anti-art, creates a taste that impugns the canons of received beauty, and fashions heroes who are anti-heroic. Modernist taste, modernist "good taste," descends from the "mixed" or Christian style, secularizing it.

---

*"The old faith was something in the mind. Oh, intensely of the mind, the naked ideal hidden in vestments of a life-denying drabness, opposed to display and yet expensive." —Robert Lowell, "Selection: The New England Spirit," *New York Times Book Review*, Oct. 16, 1977, p. 34.

I V.

In his essay *"Sermo Humilis"* (written in 1952) Auerbach shows how Augustine's conversion to Christianity was simultaneously a conversion to "low style," the *sermo humilis* of the New Testamentary style. The word *humilis* was to become the most important adjective characterizing the Incarnation. It picks up the kenotic thrust of Paul's letter to Philemon: "But [he] emptied himself, taking the form of a servant. . . . He humbled himself —*humiliavit semetipsum*—and became obedient unto death, even to the death on the cross" (Phil. 2:7f). In all Christian literature written in Latin, *"humilis"* came to express, Auerbach claims, "the atmosphere and level of Christ's suffering. The word 'level' seems odd in this context, but I know of no other that encompasses *the ethical, social, spiritual, and esthetic aspects of the matter . . . all of these are involved.* It was precisely its wide range of meaning—humble, socially inferior, unlearned, *esthetically crude or even repellent*—that gave [*humilis*] the dominant position . . ."[33] over rival terms to designate the low style (for example: *quotidianus, planus, communis, trivialis* lost out to *"humilis"*).

Most educated pagans, including the young Augustine, regarded the early Christian writings as "ludicrous, confused, and abhorrent, and this applied to the Latin even more than the Greek versions. The content struck them as childish and absurd superstition, and the form as an affront to good taste. They found this literature," Auerbach continues, "gross and vulgar, awkward in syntax and choice of words, and to make matters worse, riddled with Hebraisms. . . . The educated pagan public reacted with ridicule. . . . How could the profoundest of problems, the enlightenment and redemption of mankind, be treated in such barbarous works?"[34] To eliminate this *scandalum*, this stumbling block, this offense, educated Christians *might* well have decided, for apologetic purposes, to assimilate the first translations of Scripture, adapting them to the good literary usage of the classical taste of late antiquity.[35] Thus, "no offense" would have been given.

That this was never done meant that classicist converts of the stature of a St. Augustine had to pass through a theological and an esthetic conversion at the same time. C. N. Cochrane in *Christianity and Classical Culture* shows the dialectic of this *metanoia* on the level of ideas. My interest centers on conversion not as a sacrifice of the intellect but as involving a sacrifice of taste. Before his conversion—I quote Auerbach once more—Augustine "himself had been one of those highly cultivated men [brought up on Cicero's *Hortensius*] who thought they would never be able to overcome their distaste for the style of the Bible."[36]

One of the things Augustine confesses to in his *Confessions*—and this confession is forgotten—is his former cultivated contempt for the Gospel narratives: "They seemed to me unworthy to be compared with the majesty of Cicero," he confesses. "My conceit was repelled by their simplicity. . . ."[37] Conversion for an Augustine meant that the "lowliness" of the New Testament style had to be *reexperienced* as profoundly sublime. St. Augustine is the most important witness to this taste change "because he personally went through [what Auerbach calls] the dialectical reversal it implies."[38] The vast majority of Christians simply received it as a given of their heritage, assimilating it unconsciously. *Sermo humilis:* "It shaped their view of history, their ethical and esthetic conceptions."[39] *Sermo humilis:* "accessible to all, descending to all men in loving-kindness, *secretly sublime,* . . ." concludes Auerbach, thus striking the exact note of this Christian or mixed style.[40]

Augustine's conversion, then, occurs in several dimensions, all interconnected: moral, theological, social, and, not least, esthetic. Since humility—after love *(agapé)*—is the exemplary Christian virtue, pride is the gravest of moral faults and theological sins. But for the convert Augustine, pride is also a *"foeda iactantia,"* an unseemly, vulgar ostentation.[41] Only an esthetic imagination of the sin of pride brings home its unseemliness and vulgarity.

Just as the sin of pride before God is ostentatiousness and vulgarity, so self-regard among men is both sinful and embarrassingly unseemly. Egocentricity and ethnocentricity are violations of taste, as is class-centeredness. Philip Toynbee, for example, reviewing the late Sir Harold Nicolson's *Diaries and Letters* for the London *Observer Review*, takes note of Nicolson's class complacency, and writes: "He hated Negroes and despised Jews; his tragi-comic experiences in the Labour Party confirmed his distaste for his social 'inferiors' . . . But it is, of course, precisely the *communal* part of Nicolson's mind which is making these simplistic, *self-regarding* and deeply *vulgar* judgments."[42]

Under the esthetic regime of an implacably Puritan Christian taste, then, most of the "self-" (or self-hyphen) words have come even to *sound* unseemly and vulgar: self-interested, self-importance, self-seeking, self-congratulatory, self-willed, self-regard, self-opinionated, self-indulgence, self-induced, self-ordained, self-dramatizing, self-involved, self-admiring, self-serving, self-pitying, self-centered—all are stigmatized as lineal descendants of the New Testament "self-righteousness" imputed to the Pharisees. These attitudes are considered by our culture and its critics to be not only moral evils and religious sins, but social and esthetic failings in exceedingly bad taste: "self-regarding and deeply vulgar," in Philip Toynbee's words. Puritan Christianity makes its way into our very perception of vulgarity. Thus even a Lionel Trilling, in his late thirties, wishing to signal his distaste for the social introversion of the bourgeois Jewish community, is compelled to fall back on this "self-" language. "The Jewish social group," he observed, "on its middle and wealthy levels—that is, where there is enough leisure to allow a conscious consideration of social and spiritual problems—is now [1944] one of the most self-indulgent and self-admiring groups it is possible to imagine."[43]

V.

I should like to conclude with an observation on the bearing of this "decorum of imperfection" on the acculturation of immigrant intellectuals. In a sense, the Calvinist WASP core-culture is, socio-culturally, the "carrier" of this mixed style, this "decorum of imperfection." Others learn of it, if they do, frequently from contact with upper-middle-class descendants of this group.

An interesting case in point is the late Christopher Morley's novel *Kitty Foyle*. The book is about the doomed love affair between a lower-class Irish servant girl, Kitty Foyle, and a mainline, well-bred, real nice-guy WASP. What is interesting is how she picks up the very casual well-bred taste of her lover, his decorum of casualness. In fact, she assimilates it to such an extent that, looking over a Jewish suitor named Mark Eisen, on a trip to the wilds of New York, she finds him sartorially too natty, entirely too smart, in a word, vulgar. "A man ought to look like he's put together *by accident,*" she muses to herself, "not added up on purpose. . . ."[44] Kitty may lose her man, but she's far and away into a socio-esthetic conversion.

Self-sacrifice and self-effacement, expectably enough, rank high, both ethically and esthetically. One's rank in the Kingdom of God is determined in part, according to Jesus, Albert Schweitzer tells us, to the extent that "each by his self-humiliation and refusal to rule in the present age has proved his fitness for bearing rule in the future kingdom. . . . To serve, to humble oneself, to incur persecution and death," Schweitzer concludes, "belongs to 'the ethic of the interim' just as much as does penitence."[45] A certain kind of taste, too, belongs to "the esthetic of the interim."

Among literary and artistic critics—literary intellectuals generally—the final proof of acculturation is how profoundly they can use such core words of the culture as "ostentation," "simplicity," "vulgarity." The lexicon of high taste words seals and demonstrates high cultural competence. Ada Louise Huxtable, for example, notes that architect Philip Johnson's houses are palaces of "carefully unostentatious richness."[46] *Times* art critic Hilton Kramer attacks some paintings of James Wyeth's for their "pseudo-aristocratic taste for ostentatiously humble subjects. . . ."[47] Susan Sontag notes that "the discovery of the good taste of bad taste can be very liberating"[48] and also, I would add, the bad taste of good taste. Philip Rieff, for another example, attacks Freud's critics for their "vulgar accusations of vulgarity."[49] Joyce's friend, Italo Svevo, in a note to his wife, requested that his funeral be conducted "without ostentation of any kind, even of simplicity." "How exquisite and deep, witty and serious that remark is!"[50] John Simon remarks ecstatically, as he travels, on

Svevo's words, from the periphery to what Edward Shils calls the "charismatic center" of our culture.

Because of the heritage of what a London *Times Literary Supplement* reviewer of Auerbach calls the "specially Christian mixed style" which resulted from "the crisis of [the Augustinian] *sermo humilis*,"[51] the concept and word "vulgarity" have behaved, linguistically, in a virtually metaphysical way ever since. It is what a Thomist philosopher might call a *"social* transcendental" which, like *ens, bonum,* and *verum,* is, in a way, predicable of everything, including itself. To use words like ostentation, simplicity, and vulgarity in the oxymoronic ways we see Kramer and Rieff doing is deliberately to demonstrate one's cultural competence linguistically—before the WASP reference group which looks on as status audience . . . it is a way of putting vulgarity through its paces. It is a way of flashing one's cultural credentials, the credentials of one's acculturation. With these virtuoso performances, the importunate intellectual is saying: "Look WASP! No hands!"

CONCLUSION:
BOURGEOIS CIVILITY
AS DEFERRED
SOCIALISM, OR THE
POLITY OF
IMPERFECTION

Add to this the structure of the perennial postponement of that which is constituted only through postponement. The two together—"difference" and "deferment"—both senses, present in the French verb "différer," and both properties of the sign under erasure— Derrida calls "différance."
                                          —*Gayatri Chakravorty Spivak*
                                          Translator's Preface to Of Grammatology

In his pathbreaking book on civil religion, *The Broken Covenant,* in the chapter on "The American Taboo on Socialism," Robert Bellah remarks, as I have noted previously, that "the American aversion to socialism goes deeper than rational argument."[1] Indeed it does. American bourgeois liberalism, like socialism, has upheld—as Peter Berger notes in his revealing essay, "The Socialist Myth"—"the threefold promise of the French Revolution—of liberty, equality, and fraternity (although they have very different definitions for these terms). But liberalism has rarely had much to say about fraternity. . . ."[2]

This is because the liberal bourgeois vision accepts "the idea of fraternity in America," as it has been called, not as radical vision proposes it—as a practicable historical possibility—but only as a tragic ideal. The liberal bourgeois vision, unlike socialist Marxism, renounces once and for all the hankering for a pre-modern *Gemeinschaft*-type "community." It renounces it not as ideal, but as blueprint; unlike Marx, it is unwilling to "overturn civilization for the sake of community," as Glenn Tinder writes in "Community: The Tragic Ideal."[3]

Modern, Anglo-American culture proposes, in place of the dense, deep, communal ideal of solidarity—fraternal socialism —what I call a solidarity of the surface and a solidarity for the interim—an *Interimssolidarität*—which the West calls "civility." Western society cannot remedy the ultimately unrequitable longing of *gauchisme* and the "adversary culture"—and the human heart—for what Tinder calls the Marxist "myth of community,"[4] or the dream of what the late Benjamin Nelson called "tribal brotherhood."

In place of the myth of socialism the liberal West substitutes the fiction of civility. Like "legal fictions," civility is a social variant of "bourgeois formalism." It is not the warm, dense closeness of "real" solidarity. It is "formal" solidarity. In a regime of civility, everybody doesn't love everybody. Everybody doesn't even respect everybody. Everybody "shows respect for" everybody. Social equality, like legal equality, is "formal," not "real." In public, everyone is thus equal; yet, one may be private in public, and keep one's "real" feelings to oneself, till one gets home. True, this is not "solidarity forever"; it is solidarity *ad interim,* for the time being. Ultimate community and solidarity are for the "end of days," not for today. The loss of community suffered in the modernization process is historically irrecoverable, irreversible.

Bellah is absolutely right: "the American aversion to socialism goes deeper than rational argument." Early in their history, the canny Puritans fought out the battle of fraternity and liberty, collectivism and individualism. Out of the collision of these two values they constructed their famous compromise, the "half-way covenant": they gave up—for the time being—the familistic and ethnic dream of society as a solidarity of "brothers." They ratified a society of civil and equal citizens. They postponed the dream of a community of "true believers"; they settled for "the artifice of modernity" (to adapt W. B. Yeats), civility—a "polity of imperfection" matching their esthetics with its "decorum of imperfection." They postponed perfect community till the end of time. Civility was the best they could do, and less dangerous than perfection. Rousseau's "general will," like heaven, would have to wait. American Puritan civility, then, was a deferred sociality. "Christianity," Glenn Tinder writes,

at first was not very civil. The earliest Christians stayed apart from political life; later, after gaining recognition and power, they drowned civility in religious intolerance. But there are richer sources of civility in Christianity than this record suggests. What is decisive, perhaps, is that community is affirmed (in the standard of love) but postponed; it becomes the anticipated climax, and end, of history. In leading to such a climax history is meaningful and calls for human participation. Yet, since the conflict between man's essence and condition is historically unresolvable, participants are freed from the demand that strains civility so acutely, the demand for perfect community here and now. Standing on the ground of religious civility, one may look on the present with a resignation outwardly Machiavellian; in looking toward the ultimate future, however, one envisages a far deeper community. . . . Hence resignation is provisional; and fundamentally it is neither Machiavellian nor ethical, for it is subordinated to a limitless hope.[5]

But to put this limitless hope to work in the *political* arena where it would take the form of socialism was, somehow, Americans obscurely felt, a religious and not a political act. In some strange way, it violated the separation of church and state. Because class war was, ultimately, religious war, America set about to pluralize the "class struggle" into multiple "conflicts of interest." By thus institutionalizing conflict, America postponed Armageddon till the end of time.

The Protestant ethic deferred consumption. The Protestant esthetic defers ostentation. The Protestant etiquette—or, bourgeois civility—defers community.

Notes

Epigraphs

Albert Schweitzer, *The Mystery of the Kingdom of God: The Secret of Jesus' Messiahship and Passion*, trans. Walter Lowrie (New York: Macmillan, 1950), p. 72.

J. Milton Yinger, *Sociology Looks at Religion* (New York: Macmillan, 1963), pp. 105–7.

Albert Schweitzer, *The Quest of the Historical Jesus: A Critical Study of Its Progress from Reimarus to Wrede*, trans. W. Montgomery (New York: Macmillan, 1968), p. 360.

Perry Miller, *Errand Into the Wilderness* (Cambridge, Mass.: Harvard University Press-/Belknap Press, 1956; reprint Harper & Row/Harper Torchbook, 1964), p. 13.

Robin M. Williams, Jr., *American Society: A Sociological Interpretation* (New York: Knopf, 1960), p. 440.

Albert Schweitzer, "Paul the Liberator" (sermon delivered at St. Nicolai Church, Strassburg, 1906), in Werner Picht, *The Life and Thought of Albert Schweitzer*, trans. Edward Fitzgerald (New York: Harper & Row, 1964), p. 263.

E. E. Evans-Pritchard, *Witchcraft, Oracles, and Magic among the Azande* (Oxford: Clarendon Press, 1976), p. 69.

Irving Howe, *World of Our Fathers: The Journey of the East European Jews to America and the Life They Found and Made* (New York: Harcourt Brace Jovanovich, 1976), p. 600.

Lionel Trilling, "Two Notes on David Riesman," in *A Gathering of Fugitives* (Boston: Beacon Press, 1956), p. 86.

Introduction: A Nation of Behavers

1. Robert N. Bellah, "Civil Religion in America," in *Beyond Belief: Essays on Religion in a Post-Traditional World* (New York: Harper & Row, 1970), p. 168.

2. Mary L. Schneider, "The American Civil Religion Course: Problems and Perspectives," *Religious Education*, May–June 1976 (vol. 71, no. 3), p. 322.

3. Hymn No. 519, "Ebenezer" ("Once to every man and nation. . . ." James Russell Lowell, 1845), *The Hymnal of the Protestant Episcopal Church in the United States of America* (Greenwich, Conn.: The Seabury Press, 1940).

4. Meg Greenfield, "Carter and the Once Born," *Newsweek*, Aug. 2, 1976, p. 80.

5. Ibid.

6. Harriet Van Horne, "Good Omens," *New York Post*, June 21, 1976, p. 21 (my italics).

7. Jerome Weidman, *I Can Get It For You Wholesale* (New York: Modern Library, 1937), p. 236. The character Harry Bogen is speaking.

8. *Village Voice*, July 26, 1976, p. 90.

9. Philip Rieff, "Fellow Teachers," *Salmagundi*, Summer–Fall 1972, p. 45.

10. Sacvan Bercovitch, *The Puritan Origins of the American Self* (New Haven: Yale University Press, 1975), pp. 143, 148, 151, 234, n.14.

Chapter 1. The Emergence of Denominational Pluralism: "I Happen to Be . . ."

Epigraphs: Talcott Parsons, "Some Comments on the Pattern of Religious Organization in the United States," in *Structure and Process in Modern Society* (Glencoe, Ill.: The Free Press, 1960), p. 311.

Robert T. Handy, Introduction, *Religion in the American Experience: The Pluralistic Style,* ed. Robert T. Handy (New York: Harper & Row, 1972), p. ix.

Irving Howe, letter to the *New York Review of Books,* Dec. 1, 1966 (vol. 7, no. 9), p. 42. Howe's italics: "identification"; my italics: "happen to be."

Irving Howe, *World of Our Fathers* (New York: Harcourt Brace Jovanovich, 1976), p. 294. Howe's italics: "Jewish"; my italics: "happened to be."

1. Charlotte Curtis, "Long Island's South Shore Set Looks Forward to Post-Labor Day Season—September and Early October Form 'Out' Season That's 'In,' " *New York Times,* Sept. 4, 1964, p. 15.

2. Gay Talese, *The Kingdom and the Power* (New York: World Publishing Co., 1969), pp. 111–12.

3. Ibid., p. 112 (my italics).

4. Ibid. (my italics).

5. *Modernization and the Structure of Societies: A Setting for International Affairs* (Princeton: Princeton University Press, 1966; paperback edition 1969), p. 14. My italics.

6. Ibid., p. 128.

7. *Sociology Looks at Religion* (New York: Macmillan, 1963), paperback, p. 90.

8. Robert K. Merton, "The Self-Fulfilling Prophecy," in *Social Theory and Social Structure,* rev. ed. (Glencoe, Ill.: The Free Press, 1956), p. 43.

9. *Conservative Judaism: An American Religious Movement* (Glencoe, Ill.: The Free Press, 1955), pp. 38–39.

10. Ibid., p. 38.

11. Talcott Parsons, "Christianity and Modern Industrial Society," in *Sociological Theory and Modern Society* (New York: The Free Press, 1967), p. 413. His italics.

12. Sklare, *Conservative Judaism,* p. 39.

13. Ibid.

14. Ibid., p. 40.

15. Ibid.

16. Ibid (my italics).

17. Ibid., p. 246.

18. Cf. Edward A. Shils, *The Torment of Secrecy* (Glencoe, Ill.: The Free Press, 1956).

19. Cf. Thomas Luckmann, *The Invisible Religion: The Problem of Religion in Modern Society* (New York: Macmillan, 1967).

20. Gerhard Lenski, *The Religious Factor: A Sociological Study of Religion's Impact on Politics, Economics and Family Life* (Garden City, N.Y.: Doubleday, 1963), p. 54.

21. For this story, see John Murray Cuddihy, *The Ordeal of Civility: Freud, Marx, Lévi-Strauss and the Jewish Struggle with Modernity* (New York: Dell, 1976).

22. Parsons insists that not just moral-value problems are involved, but that "new conceptions of meaning" are needed to ride out the major crisis of our times. Cf. "Christianity and Modern Industrial Society," p. 421.

23. Ibid., p. 418.

24. Ibid., p. 415.

25. Ibid., p. 418.

Chapter 2. Case Studies: Protestant, Catholic and Jew

Epigraphs: Walter Lippmann, "The Logic of Toleration," in *A Preface to Morals* (New York: Macmillan, 1929), pp. 75, 76. My italics.

Talcott Parsons, "Christianity and Modern Industrial Society," in *Sociological Theory and Modern Society* (New York: The Free Press, 1967). pp. 413–14.

1. Peter L. Berger and Thomas L. Luckmann, *The Social Construction of Reality: A Treatise in the Sociology of Knowledge* (Garden City, N.Y.: Doubleday, 1966), p. 125.

2. Ibid.

3. Ibid.

4. Robert N. Bellah, "Response," in Donald R. Cutler, ed., *The Religious Situation: 1968* (Boston: Beacon Press, 1968), p. 389.

5. Ibid., p. 92 (my italics).

Chapter 3. Protestant: The Reinhold Niebuhr–Will Herberg "Treaty"

Epigraph: Talcott Parsons, "Christianity and Modern Industrial Society," *Sociological Theory and Modern Society*, pp. 394–95.

1. June Bingham, *Courage to Change: An Introduction to the Life and Thought of Reinhold Niebuhr* (New York: Scribner's, 1961), p. 363.

2. Ibid., pp. 80, 82n., 83.

3. *Leaves from the Notebook of a Tamed Cynic* (New York: Meridian Books, 1957 [1928]), p. 128. My italics.

4. Ibid.

5. Ibid., p. 131.

6. Ibid., p. 165.

7. Ibid., p. 222.

8. Ibid., pp. 222–23.

9. *Contemporary Jewish Record,* June 1944, p. 239.

10. "Reinhold Niebuhr's Doctrine of Knowledge," in *Reinhold Niebuhr: His Religious, Social and Political Thought,* Charles W. Kegley and Robert W. Bretall, eds. (New York: Macmillan, 1956), pp. 42–3.

11. Bingham, p. 114.

12. Ibid., p. 184.

13. Ibid., p. 27.

14. *New York Times*, May 23, 1951.

15. Bingham, 218.

16. Ibid., p. 219.

17. Ibid., pp. 189, 217–19.

18. Ibid., p. 11.

19. Ibid., p. 12.

20. Ibid., p. 170.

21. Ibid., p. 189.

22. Ibid., p. 190.

23. Ibid.

24. See "From Marxism to Existentialism: Herberg" in John P. Diggins, *Up From Communism: Conservative Odysseys in American Intellectual History* (New York: Harper & Row, 1975), pp. 269–302.

25. Ibid., p. 285.

26. *The Nature and Destiny of Man: A Christian Interpretation,* vol. III, Human Destiny series (New York: Scribner's, 1943), p. 328. n. 24.

27. Ibid., p. 239, n. 25 (my italics).

28. Ibid., p. 243.

29. "Democratic Toleration of the Groups of the Community" in *The Children of Light and the Children of Darkness* (New York: Scribner's, 1944), p. 130. My italics.

30. Ibid.

31. Ibid., pp. 134–35 (my italics).

32. Reprinted in *Pious and Secular America* (New York: Scribner's, 1958).

33. Ibid. (my italics).

34. Ibid. (my italics).

35. Ibid., p. 87 (my italics).

36. Ibid. (my italics).

37. Ibid., p. 88. I shall return to the concept of "provisional tolerance" later.

38. Ibid.

39. Ibid., p. 96.

40. Ibid., p. 106.

41. Ibid.

42. Ibid., p. 108.

43. Ibid.

44. Ibid (my italics).

45. Ibid.

46. See note 29 above.

47. I borrow the phrase from Ronald A. Knox, *Enthusiasm: A Chapter in the History of Religion with Special Reference to the XVII and XVIII Centuries* (New York: Oxford University Press, 1950), pp. 17–18.

48. Arthur Hertzberg, "America Is Different," in Arthur Hertzberg, Martin E. Marty, and Joseph N. Moody, *The Outbursts That Await Us: Three Essays on Religion and Culture in the United States* (New York: Macmillan, 1963), p. 170.

49. "Christians and Jews: A New Rapprochement," *Christian Century,* Mar. 4, 1964 (vol. 81, no. 10), p. 295.

50. Ibid., p. 296 (my italics). Rabbi Rosenberg then concluded with the by now standard Jewish legitimation of "these new Christian teachings" by means of Franz Rosenzweig's "double-covenant" theory.

51. Review of Niebuhr's *Faith and History* in *Commentary,* July 1949 (vol. 8, no. 1), p. 101.

52. Discussion in "Second Round Table Conference" at Tercentenary Conference on American Jewish Sociology, in *Jewish Social Studies,* July 1955 (vol. 17, no. 3), p. 236. My italics.

53. *Reinhold Niebuhr: His Religious, Social and Political Thought,* p. 3. I have taken the liberty of replacing Niebuhr's translation "intellectual despisers" with the more customary "cultured despisers."

54. Cited in Perry Miller, "The Influence of Reinhold Niebuhr," *The Reporter,* May 1, 1958 (vol. 18, no. 9), p. 40.

55. Martin E. Marty, "The Protestant Reinterpretation of Life," in *The Outbursts That Await Us,* p. 5.

56. Marshall Sklare, "The Conversion of the Jews," *Commentary,* Sept. 1973 (vol. 56, no. 3), p. 50.

57. Introduction to Waldo Frank, *The Jew in Our Day* (New York: Duell, Sloan & Pearce, 1944), p. 14.

58. Georg Simmel, *The Sociology of Religion,* trans. Curt Rosenthal (New York: Philosophical Library, 1959), p. 65. Simmel's italics.

59. At the end of the 1950s, domestic religion and politics moved from "cold war" coexistence to respectful détente.

60. Simmel, *Sociology of Religion,* p. 67.

61. "Perry Miller and Our Embarrassment," *The Harvard Review,* Winter–Spring 1964 (vol. 2, no. 2), p. 49.

62. Ibid., p. 50.
63. Lutheran Elmer P. Wentz charged this in a letter, *Christian Century*, Apr. 22, 1964 (vol. 81, no. 17), p. 525.
64. Simmel, *Sociology of Religion*, pp. 67–8.
65. Ibid., p. 69.
66. Philip Rieff, *The Triumph of the Therapeutic: Uses of Faith After Freud* (New York: Harper & Row, 1966), p. 240, n. 6.
67. Simmel, *Sociology of Religion*, p. 68.
68. G. K. Chesterton, *Alarms and Discursions*, quoted in Charles P. Curtis, Jr., and Ferris Greenslet, eds., *The Practical Cogitator or The Thinker's Anthology*, 3rd. ed. (Boston: Houghton Mifflin, 1962), p. 103.
69. Simmel, *Sociology of Religion*, p. 69.

Chapter 4. Catholic: A Tale of Two Jesuits

Epigraph: Jean-Jacques Rousseau, *The Social Contract*, Chapter 8, Book IV.
1. Catherine Goddard Clarke, *The Loyolas and the Cabots: The Story of the Boston Heresy Case* (Boston: The Ravengate Press, 1950). This is the chief sourcebook on the case, written by the Center's president, Mrs. Clarke.
2. Ibid., p. 48. [I attended this school—J.M.C.]
3. Ibid. Twenty-five years later almost to the day, in an interview, "It's Cool Now to Be Catholic at Harvard" (*National Catholic Reporter*, Oct. 29, 1971), the Jesuit chaplain with the Harvard-Radcliffe Catholic Center, Father Richard Griffin, S.J., referred to his predecessor, as the "fiery heresiarch of Harvard Square" who "pushed the Catholic doctrine 'outside the church, no salvation,' so strongly as, by supreme irony, to find himself outside that church," adding: "All this is changed now. The early 60s, the impact of Pope John and Vatican II, along with that of Harvard Catholic John Kennedy, made such narrow polemics passé." But the double Catholic change, a more positive attitude of Catholics toward the secular university and, from the university, "a new respect for the church," had its price. As though in afterthought, Fr. Griffin conceded that "most Catholic students at Harvard are religiously inactive. At least by conventional standards, they have abandoned religious life. Of the estimated 3,000 [Catholic students] the great majority, it appears, seldom if ever go to church" (p. 7).
4. Clarke, *The Loyolas and the Cabots*, p. 49 (my italics).
5. Ibid.
6. Ibid., p. 55.
7. Ibid., p. 51.
8. Ibid., p. 64.
9. Ibid., p. 70.
10. Ibid., pp. 73–5.
11. Ibid., pp. 79, 98.
12. Ibid., pp. 112, 129, 193–99 (my italics).
13. Ibid., p. 177.
14. Ibid., p. 241.
15. Ibid., pp. 243–44.
16. Ibid., p. 287.
17. Erving Goffman, "Remedial Interchanges," *Relations in Public: Microstudies of the Public Order* (New York: Basic Books, 1971), p. 115. My italics.
18. Clarke, *The Loyolas and the Cabots*, pp. 289, 300.
19. Joseph Wershba, "Bobby Kennedy Today" (part five), *New York Post*, Mar. 27, 1964, p. 25.
20. Jack Newfield, *Robert Kennedy: A Memoir* (New York: Bantam Books, 1970), p. 37.
21. Clarke, *The Loyolas and the Cabots*, p. 159 (my italics).
22. Quoted in John H. Fenton, "Cardinal Cushing: Symbol of 'New Boston,' " *New York Times*, Feb. 6, 1964, p. 31.

23. Clarke, *The Loyolas and the Cabots*, p. 243.
24. Ibid., p. 253.
25. Ibid., p. 199.
26. Paul Blanshard, *American Freedom and Catholic Power*, 2nd ed. (Boston: Beacon Press, 1958), p. 44.
27. Ibid., p. 45.
28. Walter Kaufmann, *Cain and Other Poems* (Garden City, N.Y.: Doubleday, 1962), p. 75.
29. Leo Baeck, *Judaism and Christianity: Essays*, trans. Walter Kaufmann (Philadelphia: The Jewish Publication Society of America, 1958), p. 3.
30. Quoted by Martin E. Marty in his "The Religious Situation: An Introduction," in Donald R. Cutler, ed., *The Religious Situation: 1968* (Boston: Beacon Press, 1968), p. xxxviii.
31. "Contributions to the Theory of Reference Group Behavior," in *Social Theory and Social Structure*, rev. ed. (Glencoe, Ill.: The Free Press, 1957), p. 238.
Epigraph: Martin Jarrett-Kerr, "E pur si muove," *Encounter*, Aug. 1966 (vol. 27, no. 2), p. 56.
32. "Governmental Repression of Heresy," *Proceedings of the Third Annual Meeting of the Catholic Theological Society of America* (Chicago: June 1949), III, p. 86.
33. *Social Contract: Essays by Locke, Hume and Rousseau*, with an Introduction by Sir Ernest Barker (New York: Oxford University Press, 1962), p. 307.
34. *Theological Studies*, Sept. 1942 (vol. 3, no. 3), p. 2.
35. Ibid.
36. Ibid. (my italics).
37. Ibid., p. 423. Note the quotes enclosing "ecumenism."
38. Cf. Gabriel L. Almond and Sidney Verba, *The Civic Culture*, and the famous essay by Robert Bellah, "Civil Religion in America."
39. *Theological Studies*, vol. 3, no. 3, p. 431 (my italics).
40. Ibid., pp. 327–28, 330.
41. John LaFarge, S.J., *The Manner Is Ordinary* (New York: Harcourt, Brace, 1954).
42. *Theological Studies*, Dec. 1942 (vol. 3, no. 4), p. 475. My italics. If the articles themselves on "co-operation" with non-Catholics attest to the problem's urgency, the hyphen in "co-operation" surely betrays its delicacy.
43. *Theological Studies*, vol. 4, no. 1, p. 103.
44. Ibid., p. 106.
45. Ibid., p. 107.
46. Ibid (my italics).
47. Ibid.
48. Ibid.
49. Ibid., pp. 107–8 (my italics).
50. Ibid., p. 108, n. 20.
51. Vol. 4, no. 2, p. 182.
52. The phrase is Professor Peter L. Berger's; the use is mine.
53. *Theological Studies*, Sept. 1944 (vol. 5, no. 3), p. 350. My italics.
54. Ibid.
55. "Remarks of Senator John F. Kennedy on Church and State; Delivered to the Greater Houston Ministerial Association, Houston, Texas, September 12, 1960." In Theodore H. White, *The Making of the President* (New York: Atheneum, 1961), pp. 391–92.
56. *Theological Studies*, June 1945 (vol. 6, no. 2).
57. Ibid.
58. Thomas T. Love, *John Courtney Murray: Contemporary Church-State Theory* (Garden City, N.Y.: Doubleday, 1965), p. 48. This is by far the best account of Murray's intellectual-theological itinerary.
59. *America*, Dec. 7, 1946 (vol. 76, no. 10).
60. Ibid., p. 261. These *America* articles run from 1946–1948, viz. Dec. 7, 1946, pp.

261–63; Feb. 7, 1948, pp. 513–16; Mar. 6, 1948, pp. 627–29; and Mar. 20, 1948, pp. 683–86.

61. G. K. Chesterton, *The Victorian Age in Literature* (New York: Henry Holt & Co., 1913), p. 78.

62. A. Norman Jeffares, *W. B. Yeats: Man and Poet* (New Haven: Yale University Press, 1949), p. 237.

63. "Sociology and Social Psychology," in Hoxie N. Fairchild, ed., *Religious Perspectives in College Teaching* (New York: The Ronald Press, 1952), p. 326.

64. "The Problem of 'The Religion of the State' " (vol. 123, no. 9).

65. "The Theory of the 'Lay State,' " *American Ecclesiastical Review*, Dec. 1951 (vol. 125, no. 12), p. 17.

66. *American Ecclesiastical Review*, Jan. 1952 (vol. 126, no. 1), pp. 33, 36, 39, n. 12, 43.

67. Ibid., June 1951 (vol. 124, no. 6), p. 455.

68. Ibid (my italics).

69. Ibid., p. 456.

70. Ibid (my italics).

71. Ibid., p. 458 (my italics).

72. "For the Freedom and Transcendence of the Church," *American Ecclesiastical Review*, Jan. 1952 (vol. 126, no. 1), p. 43.

73. Ibid., p. 47, n. 15. Father Murray insisted he used the term "without prejudice."

74. Ibid., p. 45.

75. Ibid., p. 47.

76. Ibid., p. 46 (my italics).

77. "Separation of Church and State," *America*, Dec. 7, 1946.

78. "For the Freedom and Transcendence of the Church," p. 47.

79. Ibid., p. 48 (my italics).

80. Cited in Kevin Sullivan, *Joyce Among the Jesuits* (New York: Columbia University Press, 1957), p. 226.

81. Ibid., p. 227, n. 49.

82. Peter L. Berger and Thomas Luckmann, "Sociology of Religion and Sociology of Knowledge," *Sociology and Social Research*, July 1963 (vol. 47, no. 4), p. 423. my italics.

83. John Courtney Murray, S.J., *We Hold These Truths: Catholic Reflections on the American Proposition* (New York: Sheed and Ward, 1960).

84. Peter L. Berger, *Invitation to Sociology: A Humanistic Perspective* (Garden City, N.Y.: Doubleday/Anchor, 1963), p. 19.

85. "Texts of Decision on Dr. Oppenheimer as Released by the Atomic Energy Commission," *New York Times*, June 30, 1954, p. 13, col. 1.

86. Lionel Trilling, *The Liberal Imagination: Essays on Literature and Society* (New York: Viking, 1951), p. 260.

87. Cynthia Ozick, "The Unresplendent Dynasties of 'Our Crowd,' " *Congress Bi-weekly*, Dec. 18, 1967, p. 5.

88. Corry, *Golden Clan*, p. 99.

89. Ibid., p. 86.

90. Ibid., p. 12.

91. Ibid., p. 44.

92. Ibid., p. 29.

93. Ibid., pp. 78–9.

94. Ibid., p. 72.

95. Ibid., pp. 79–80.

96. Ibid., p. 76.

97. Ibid., p. 109.

98. Ibid., p. 110.

99. Ibid., p. 111.

100. Ibid., p. 111.

101. Murray, *We Hold These Truths*.

102. Garry Wills, *Bare Ruined Choirs: Doubt, Prophecy and Radical Religion* (New York: Dell, 1972), pp. 82, 86.

103. John Murray Cuddihy, *The Ordeal of Civility: Freud, Marx, Lévi-Strauss and the Jewish Struggle with Modernity* (New York: Dell, 1976), p. 10, n.

104. Garry Wills, *Bare Ruined Choirs*, p. 85.

105. Murray, *We Hold These Truths*, p. 48 (my italics).

106. Ibid., p. 78.

107. Ibid., pp. ix–x.

108. Walter Lippmann, *Essays in the Public Philosophy* (Boston: Little, Brown, 1955).

109. Murray, *We Hold These Truths*, pp. 7–9, 15.

110. Cf. Sir Ernest Barker, *Traditions of Civility* (Oxford: Oxford University Press, 1948).

111. Murray, *We Hold These Truths*, p. 11.

112. Ibid., p. 12.

113. Ibid., pp. 13–14.

114. Ibid., pp. 14, 18–19.

115. Ibid., p. 19.

116. Ibid.

117. Ibid., pp. 19–20.

118. Ibid., pp. 20–22 (my italics).

119. Ibid., p. 22.

120. George Santayana, *The Genteel Tradition at Bay* (New York: Scribner's, 1931).

121. Ibid., p. 40.

122. Ibid., p. 41.

123. New York: Philosophical Library, 1958 (original publication 1957).

124. Murray, *We Hold These Truths*, p. 41.

125. Cf. Clifford Geertz, "The Integrative Revolution: Primordial Sentiments and Civil Politics in the New States," in *Old Societies and New States: The Quest for Modernity in Asia and Africa*, ed. Clifford Geertz (New York: The Free Press of Glencoe/Collier-Macmillan, 1963), pp. 105–57.

126. Introduction to *The Social Teachings of Leo XIII*, ed. Etienne Gilson (Garden City, N.Y.: Image Books, 1954), p. 17.

127. New York: Holt, Rinehart and Winston, 1968; translated by my brother, Michael Cuddihy, and Elizabeth Hughes.

128. Murray, *We Hold These Truths*, p. 204 (my italics).

129. Paulette Martin, "A 'Peasant' Confounds the Intelligentsia," *National Catholic Reporter*, Mar. 8, 1967 (vol. 3, no. 19), p. 9.

130. Martin Jarrett-Kerr, C.R., "E pur si muove," *Encounter*, Aug. 1966 (vol. 27, no. 2), p. 56.

Chapter 5. Jew: Rabbi Arthur Hertzberg and the

Metaphoricality of Jewish Chosenness

Epigraphs: Rabbi Arthur Hertzberg, *The Condition of Jewish Belief: A Symposium Compiled by the Editors of "Commentary" Magazine* (New York: Macmillan, 1966), p. 90.

Devil promising to Adrian Leverkühn in Thomas Mann, *Doctor Faustus*, pp. 243, 307–8 (cited in H. Stuart Hughes, *The Sea Change*, p. 250).

Rabbi Arthur Hertzberg, "Dangers of Vulgarity," Letter to the Editor, *Reconstructionist*, Mar. 10, 1961 (vol. 27, no. 2), p. 29.

Cynthia Ozick, Preface to *Bloodshed and Three Novellas* (New York: Knopf, 1976), p. 9.

Hannah Arendt, Preface to *Antisemitism* (New York: Harcourt, Brace & World, 1968), pp. viii–ix. This is Part One of the 2nd ed. of *The Origins of Totalitarianism*.

Leon Weiseltier, review of Irving Howe's *World of Our Fathers*, in *New York Review of Books*, July 15, 1976 (vol. 23, no. 12), p. 28.

Paul Goodman, letter to *Commentary*, Mar. 1949 (vol. 7, no. 3), p. 293.

Milton Himmelfarb, "Paganism, Religion and Modernity," *Commentary*, Nov. 1968 (vol. 40, no. 5), p. 89.

1. Arthur Hertzberg, "America Is Different," in Arthur Hertzberg, Martin E. Marty, and Joseph N. Moody, *The Outbursts That Await Us: Three Essays on Religion and Culture in the United States* (New York: Macmillan, 1963), p. 137. My italics.

2. Arthur Hertzberg, *The French Enlightenment and the Jews* (New York: Columbia University Press, 1968), p. 277. My italics.

3. Ibid., p. 279.

4. Ibid., p. 282.

5. Léon Poliakov, "Anti-Semitism and Christian Teaching," *Midstream*, Mar. 1966 (vol. 12, no. 3), p. 13.

6. Hertzberg, *The French Enlightenment and the Jews*, p. 282.

7. Ibid., p. 313 (My italics).

8. Ibid., p. 365 (My italics).

9. Ibid., p. 183 (My italics).

10. Arthur Hertzberg, *The Zionist Idea: A Historical Analysis and Reader* (New York: Meridian Books, 1960), p. 23. My italics.

11. G. K. Chesterton, *What I Saw In America* (New York: Dodd, Mead, 1922), p. 10. Speaking as an Englishman, Chesterton wrote: "Because we have a type we do not need to have a test." In my quotation, I have taken the liberty of displacing Chesterton's negative, while preserving his exact meaning.

12. See pp. 121–81 of Arthur Hertzberg, Marty, and Moody, *The Outbursts That Await Us*.

13. Ibid., p. 170.

14. Ibid., p. 170 (My italics).

15. Ibid. (My italics).

16. Ibid. (My italics).

17. Ibid., p. 131 (My italics).

18. Ibid., p. 171.

19. Ibid., p. 133.

20. "An Analysis of Jewish Culture," by "Anonymous" in Isacque Graeber and Steuart Henderson Britt, eds., *Jews in a Gentile World: The Problem of Anti-Semitism* (New York: Macmillan, 1942), p. 253.

21. Isaac Rosenfeld, *Passage From Home* (Cleveland: World Publishing, 1946), p. 118.

22. "Judaism Is a Family Affair," *National Catholic Reporter*, Oct. 11, 1967 (vol. 3, no. 49), p. 8.

23. *The Social System* (Glencoe, Ill: The Free Press, 1951), p. 67.

24. Cf. Mary Matossian, "Ideologies of Delayed Modernization: Some Tensions and Ambiguities," in John H. Kautsky, ed., *Political Change in the Underdeveloped Countries: Nationalism and Communism* (New York: Wiley, 1962), pp. 253–64.

25. The phrase is from Talcott Parsons, *Societies: Evolutionary and Comparative Perspectives* (Englewood Cliffs, N.J.: Prentice-Hall, 1966), p. 20.

26. Ibid., p. 19.

27. Emile Durkheim, *The Division of Labor in Society*, trans. George Simpson (New York: Free Press, 1964), pp. 112–13.

28. A "veneer of consensus" in which participants "conceal" their wants "behind" the shared values they give "lip service" to, writes Erving Goffman in 1959, betraying by his words the "residual" status he accorded the civil behavior he had just "discovered" (*The Presentation of Self in Everyday Life* [Garden City, N.Y.: Doubleday, 1959], p. 9. With the publication of *Behavior in Public Places* (1963), positive redefinition was already under way.

29. "America Is Different," in *The Outbursts That Await Us*, pp. 161, 179 (My italics).

30. Ibid., p. 162 (Hertzberg's italics).

31. Ibid., p. 163.

32. Ibid., p. 162.

33. Rabbi Arthur Hertzberg, "Dangers of Vulgarity," Letter to the Editor, in *The Reconstructionist*, Mar. 10, 1961 (vol. 27, no. 2), p. 29.

34. *The Condition of Jewish Belief: A Symposium Compiled by the Editors of "Commentary" Magazine* (New York: Macmillan, 1966), pp. 118–19. My italics.

35. Cf. "*Commentary* Study Guide" for the Aug. 1966 *Commentary* symposium on "The State of Jewish Belief," *Commentary*, Apr. 1966, comments on Question 2.

36. Erving Goffman, *Behavior in Public Places: Notes on the Social Organization of Gatherings* (New York: The Free Press of Glencoe, 1963), pp. 83–88.

37. "Uniqueness and Universality in Jewish History: A Mid-Century Revaluation," in *The Unique and the Universal: Some Historical Reflections* (New York: George Braziller, 1965), p. 68. My italics.

38. Ibid., p. 69.

39. *The Condition of Jewish Belief*, p. 121.

40. Cf. Thomas Luckmann, *The Invisible Religion: The Problem of Religion in Modern Society* (New York: Macmillan, 1967).

41. "America Is Different," p. 131.

42. "America Is Galut," *Jewish Frontier*, July 1964 (vol. 31, no. 6), p. 8. My italics.

43. Ibid., p. 9.

44. Ibid., p. 8.

45. Ibid.

46. Eliezer Livneh, "An Israeli Looks at American Jews," *Congress Weekly*, Jan. 28, 1952 (vol. 19, no. 4), p. 10. My italics.

47. Marshall Sklare and Mark Vosk, "An Objective Appraisal: A Case Study," *Jewish Heritage*, Winter 1963–1964 (vol. 6, no. 3), p. 37.

48. Lon L. Fuller, *Legal Fictions* (Stanford, Cal.: Stanford University Press, 1967).

49. "Hazards of the Future," *Jewish Heritage*, Winter 1963–1964, p. 17.

50. *Making It* (New York: Random House, 1967), p. 306.

51. Peter L. Berger and Thomas Luckmann, *The Social Construction of Reality: A Treatise in the Sociology of Knowledge* (Garden City, N.Y.: Doubleday/Anchor, 1966), p. 135.

52. Dennis Wrong, "The Psychology of Prejudice and the Future of Anti-Semitism in America," *European Journal of Sociology*, 1965 (vol. 6, no. 2), p. 320. My italics.

53. Ibid., p. 321.

54. "America Is Different," p. 135.

55. "Democratic Toleration and the Groups of the Community" in *The Children of Light and the Children of Darkness* (New York: Scribner's, 1944), p. 126–27. My italics.

56. See chapter XI, "The Self Fulfilling Prophecy," in *Social Theory and Social Structure*, rev. ed. (Glencoe, Ill: Free Press, 1957).

57. Berger and Luckmann, *The Social Construction of Reality*, p. 176.

58. Ibid., p. 179.

59. "The Protestant Reinterpretation of American Life," in *The Outbursts That Await Us*, p. 58.

60. *American Judaism* (Chicago: University of Chicago Press, 1957), p. 8.

61. Ibid., pp. 30–31.

62. Ibid., p. 118.

63. Ibid., p. 147 (my italics).

64. Ibid.

65. Ibid., p. 105.

66. *Jewish Identity on the Suburban Frontier: A Study of Group Survival in the Open Society* [The Lakeville Studies, vol. 1] (New York: Basic Books, 1967).

67. "A Jewish Community," *Commentary*, August 1968 (vol. 46, no. 2), p. 67. My italics.

68. Ibid.

69. Ibid.

70. Ibid., p. 70.

71. Ibid. (my italics).

72. Will Herberg, *Protestant-Catholic-Jew: An Essay in American Religious Sociology*, rev. ed. (Garden City, N.Y.: Doubleday, 1960), p. 240.

73. The controverted thesis implied in Jean-Paul Sartre's *Anti-Semite and Jew*, trans. George J. Becker (New York: Schocken Books, 1948).

74. "A New Dimensions" in *Dimensions*, Fall 1967 (vol. 2, no. 1), p. 5.

75. "War Changes Theology," *Minneapolis Star*, Sept. 2, 1967, p. 9A.

76. Jo-ann Price, "Rabbi Balfour Brickner," *National Catholic Reporter*, Oct. 18, 1967 (vol. 3, no. 50), p. 2.

77. "Politics," in *Esquire*, Nov. 1967, p. 44.

78. Peter L. Berger and Thomas Luckmann, "Secularization and Pluralism," *International Yearbook for the Sociology of Religion*, vol. II, 1966, p. 79.

79. *Conservative Judaism: An American Religious Movement* (Glencoe, Ill.: Free Press, 1955), pp. 39–40. My italics.

80. *Judaism*, Summer 1954 (vol. 3, no. 3), p. 280.

81. Reprinted in *Breakthrough: A Treasury of Contemporary American Jewish Literature* (Philadelphia: Jewish Publication Society of America, 1963), p. 374.

82. Charles S. Liebman, "Reconstructionism in American Jewish Life," *American Jewish Yearbook 1970*, vol. 71 (New York: American Jewish Committee; Philadelphia: Jewish Publication Society of America, 1970), p. 21. My italics.

83. *Goodbye, Columbus* (Boston: Houghton, Mifflin, 1959), p. 141.

84. Cf. Hannah Arendt, "The Jews and Society," in *The Origins of Totalitarianism* (New York: Harcourt, Brace, 1951), pp. 66ff, and Cuddihy, *Ordeal of Civility*, p. 5n. and passim.

85. "Second Dialogue in Israel," panel on The Jewish Intellectual and Jewish Identity, *Congress Bi-weekly*, Sept. 16, 1963 (vol. 30, no. 12), p. 21. My italics.

86. Ibid.

87. Ibid. (my italics).

88. Rabbi Arthur Hertzberg, "Dangers of Vulgarity."

89. The Loeb Classical Library *Confessions*, trans. William Watts (New York: Macmillan, 1912), Book X, Chapter 36, p. 183. Watts translates *foeda iactantia* as a "dishonorable kind of bragging." The translation is the one used by Hofstadter above.

90. "The Seriousness of Moral Philosophy," *Ethics*, July 1956 (vol. 66, no. 4), p. 286. My italics.

91. *The Condition of Jewish Belief*, p. 120.

92. "Dissent and Discovery," *Newsweek*, April 3, 1967, p. 61 (My italics).

93. Introduction, *sidic* (vol. 1, no. 2), p. 2. My italics.

94. Articles in issue of *sidic* cited above.

95. Cf. John Murray Cuddihy, *Ordeal of Civility*, p. 238.

96. "The Jewish World," *The National Catholic Reporter*, July 1964 (vol. 31, no. 6), p. 8.

97. Rabbi Arthur Hertzberg, "America Is Galut," *Jewish Frontier*, July 1964 (vol. 31, no. 6), p. 8.

98. Ibid., p. 8.

99. Ibid., p. 8.

100. Ibid., p. 7.

101. Ibid., pp. 7–8.

102. Ibid., p. 9.

103. Arthur Hertzberg, "Dilemma of the Jewish Secularist," *Congress Monthly*, December 1976 (vol. 43, no. 10), p. 4.

104. Ibid., p. 6 (my italics).

105. Ibid., p. 7.

106. Alvin W. Gouldner, "The Metaphoricality of Marxism and the Context-Freeing Grammar of Socialism," *Theory and Society*, Winter 1974 (vol. I, no. 4), pp. 387–89.

107. Arthur Hertzberg, "Some Reflections on Zionism Today: A Presentation," Opening Session of The 12th American-Israel Dialogue, *Congress Monthly*, Mar./Apr. 1977 (vol. 44, no. 3), p. 3.

108. Cf. Daniel Bell, *The End of Ideology: On the Exhaustion of Political Ideas in the Fifties* (Glencoe, Ill.: Free Press, 1960).

109. Cf. Cuddihy, *The Ordeal of Civility*.

110. Arthur Hertzberg, "Some Reflections on Zionism Today," p. 8.
111. Arthur Hertzberg, "America Is Galut," p. 8.
112. Hertzberg, "Some Reflections on Zionism Today," p. 4 (my italics).
113. Ibid., p. 4 (my italics).
114. Ibid., p. 4.
115. Ibid., p. 27.
116. Ibid., p. 5.
117. Ibid., p. 5.
118. Ibid. (my italics).
119. Ibid. (my italics).
120. Ibid., p. 17 (my italics).
121. Ibid., (my italics).
122. Ibid., p. 18.
123. Lucy S. Dawidowicz, "The Tide of Antisemitism," *Times Literary Supplement,* July 22, 1977, p. 901. My italics. The book reviewed was Prof. Celia S. Heller, *On the Edge of Destruction: Jews of Poland Between the Two World Wars* (New York: Columbia University Press, 1977).
124. Hertzberg, "Some Reflections on Zionism Today," p. 21 (my italics).
125. Ibid., p. 21.
126. Ibid., p. 6.
127. Hertzberg, "America Is Different," p. 162.
128. Ibid. (my italics).
129. Ibid., p. 161.
130. Ibid.
131. Judith Kramer and Seymour Levantman, *Children of the Gilded Ghetto* (New Haven and London: Yale University Press, 1960).
132. *National Review,* August 5, 1977, p. 866.
133. Hertzberg, *The Condition of Jewish Belief,* p. 90.
134. University Seminar on Studies in Religion: Minutes (May 9, 1977), p. 3.

Chapter 6. Postscript to the Case Studies: Littell, Bozell,

Kahane and Menahem Begin

Epigraph: Talcott Parsons, "Christianity and Modern Industrial Society," *Sociological Theory and Modern Society,* pp. 392–93.
1. Franklin H. Littell, *The Crucifixion of the Jews* (New York: Harper & Row, 1975), p. 130.
2. *Triumph,* Sept. 1966 (vol. 1, no. 1), p. 9.
3. Ibid., p. 10.
4. "It's About Time," *Triumph,* Jan. 1969 (vol. 4, no. 1) p. 28.
5. "Liberty II" (editorial), *Triumph,* Apr. 1970 (vol. 5, no. 4) p. 42. Emphasis theirs.
6. *Triumph,* July 1970.
7. "Bare Ruined Lives," *Triumph,* Apr. 1973 (vol. 8, no. 4), p. 10.
8. "Is the JDL Anti-Semitic?" *Triumph,* Feb. 1971 (vol. 6, no. 2), p. 10.
9. Cf. Janet L. Dolgin, *Jewish Identity and the JDL* (Princeton, N.J.: Princeton University Press, 1977).
10. "Begin Near Success in Forming Coalition," *New York Times,* June 10, 1977, p. A11, col. 1.
11. Seymour Krim, "The Begin Image," *New York Times,* July 15, 1977, p. A23.
12. Ibid.
13. Amos Perlmutter, "Israel's DeGaulle," *Newsweek,* Aug. 15, 1977, p. 29 (my italics).
14. *Palestine Studies,* Winter 1977 (vol. 6, no. 2), p. 41.
15. Terence Smith, "The Special Relationship Is Intact But Under Strain," *New York Times,* Aug. 28, 1977, "Review of the Week," Sunday, Section 4, p. 2E.

Chapter 7. American Civil Politics and the "Conversion" of European Class Struggle into Institutional Conflict

Epigraph: Bernard Crick, *In Defense of Politics*, rev. ed. (Baltimore, Penguin Books, 1964), p. 170.

1. Ibid., p. 188.
2. Ibid., p. 31.
3. Ibid., pp. 18, 20.
4. Ibid., pp. 37, 36.
5. Ibid., p. 24.
6. Ibid., p. 54.
7. Ibid., p. 161.
8. Robert N. Bellah, *The Broken Covenant: American Civil Religion in a Time of Trial* (New York: The Seabury Press, 1975), p. 122.
9. Norman Podhoretz, "Faulkner in the 50's," in *Doings and Undoings: The Fifties and After in American Writing* (New York: Farrar, Straus & Company, 1964), p. 15.
10. Ralf Dahrendorf, "Toward a Theory of Social Conflict," *Journal of Conflict Resolution*, vol. 2 (1958), p. 181, n. 19. My italics.
11. Ibid. (my italics).
12. *The Idea of a Party System: The Rise of Legitimate Opposition in the United States, 1780–1840* (Berkeley: University of California Press, 1969), Preface, p. xii. My italics.
13. " 'Voting' and the Equilibrium of the American Political System," in *Sociological Theory and Modern Society* (New York: The Free Press, 1967), pp. 231, 250.
14. *The Stages of Economic Growth. A Non-Communist Manifesto* (Cambridge: Cambridge University Press, 1960), p. 151. The Curtis reference is to his *Commonplace Book* (New York, 1957), pp. 112–13.
15. "Mental Illness and 'Spiritual Malaise,' " in Parsons, *Social Structure and Personality* (New York: The Free Press, 1964), p. 302. Parsons's italics.
16. Ibid. (my italics).
17. "Parsons' Sociological Theory," in Max Black, ed., *The Social Theories of Talcott Parsons: A Critical Examination*, pp. 33–34. My italics.
18. "Urbanism as a Way of Life," in *Reader in Urban Sociology*, ed. Paul K. Hatt and Albert J. Reiss, Jr. (Glencoe, Illinois: The Free Press, 1951), p. 36.
19. Ed. Irving Louis Horowitz (Beverly Hills, California: Sage Publications, 1969). The title was later changed to "Socialism *and* Sociology" (my italics).
20. S. M. Lipset, Preface to *Revolution and Counterrevolution* (Anchor Books edition), p. xix.
21. J. P. Nettl, "Rosa Luxemburg Today," *New Society* Apr. 7, 1966, p. 11.
22. Theodor Geiger, "Law as a Type of Order," in *On Social Order and Mass Society: Selected Papers*, ed. with an Introduction by Renate Mayntz, trans. Robt. E. Peck (Chicago· University of Chicago Press, 1969), p. 72.
23. "The Use of Panels in Social Research," *Proceedings of the American Philosophical Society*, Nov. 1948 (vol. 42, no. 5), p. 405.
24. Cited in R. A. Schermerhorn, *Comparative Ethnic Relations* (New York: Random House, 1970), p. 38.
25. John Galtung, "Rank and Social Integration: A Multidimensional Approach," in *Sociological Theories in Progress*, vol. I, ed. Joseph Berger, Morris Zelditch, Jr., Bo Anderson (Boston: Houghton, Mifflin, 1966), p. 158.
26. Ibid., p. 193.
27. William J. Goode, "A Theory of Role Strain," *American Sociology Review*, vol. 25, p. 485.
28. Ibid., p. 495.
29. *Berkeley Journal of Sociology*, Fall 1959 (vol. 5, no. 1), p. 119.

30. Shils, "Ideology and Civility," *Sewanee Review,* 1958, p. 454.

31. Hannah Arendt, *Rahel Vernhagen: The Life of a Jewess* (London: East and West Library, 1957), p. 103.

32. "A Note on Max Weber's Politics," *Politics,* Feb. 1945 (vol. 2, no. 2), p. 47.

33. Cf. Leo Kaplan's review of *The Coming Crisis in Western Sociology,* in *Critical Anthropology,* Spring 1971 (vol. 2, no. 1), pp. 85–99.

34. Cf. Norman Birnbaum, "Marx in '71: The Heavenly City of the 20th-Century Philosophers," *Worldview,* Jan. 1972 (vol. 15, no. 1), pp. 15–20.

35. *Dissent,* Winter 1963 (vol. 10, no. 1), p. 69.

36. Cf. Philip Rieff, "Socialism and Sociology," *Partisan Review,* Summer 1956 (vol. 23, no. 3), p. 366.

37. Glencoe, Ill.: The Free Press, 1960.

38. *The Coming Crisis of Western Sociology* (New York: Basic Books, 1970), p. 158. Gouldner's title perhaps took its cue from Norman Birnbaum's cognate book of the previous year, *The Crisis of Industrial Society* (New York: Oxford University Press, 1969).

39. "Out of Utopia; Toward a Reorientation of Sociological Analysis," reprinted in Lewis A. Coser and Bernard Rosenberg, eds., *Sociological Theory: A Book of Readings* 3rd ed. (New York: Macmillan, 1969), p. 239, n. 7.

40. "Changes in the Structure of Industrial Societies Since Marx," in Dahrendorf, *Class and Class Conflict in Industrial Society* (Stanford, Cal.: Stanford University Press, 1959), p. 64. (Original German edition, 1957.) My italics.

41. "Some Comments on the Sociology of Karl Marx," in Parsons, *Sociological Theory and Modern Society* (New York: The Free Press, 1967), p. 111.

42. Ibid., pp. 113–14.

43. Ibid., p. 114.

44. Ibid., p. 125.

45. Ibid., p. 128.

46. "Polarization of the World and International Order," in *Sociological Theory and Modern Society,* pp. 132–33.

47. "Some Comments on the Sociology of Karl Marx," pp. 132–33.

48. Philip Roth, *Portnoy's Complaint* (New York: Random House, 1969), p. 75.

49. James S. Coleman, "Social Cleavage and Religious Conflict," *Journal of Social Issues,* 1956 (vol. 12, no. 3), p. 46. My italics.

50. E. A. Ross, *The Principles of Sociology* (New York: The Century Company, 1920), pp. 164–65.

51. New York: Random House, 1970.

52. Oxford: Basil Blackwell, 1955.

53. "Profile: How Does It Come to Be So," *New Yorker,* Jan. 28, 1961 (vol. 36, no. 50), p. 50.

54. Ibid., p. 50.

55. It is interesting that Max Gluckman's *Custom and Conflict in Africa* (1956) begins by citing this very same passage from Eliot's *Notes Towards a Definition of Culture* (pp. 1–2).

56. James S. Coleman, "Social Cleavage and Religious Conflict," p. 47.

57. Ibid. (my italics).

58. Gene Wise, "Implicit Irony in Perry Miller's *New England Mind,*" *Journal of the History of Ideas,* Oct.–Dec. 1968 (vol. 29, no. 4), p. 600.

59. Lewis Coser, *The Function of Social Conflict* (1954), p. 153.

60. "Social Conflict Over Styles of Sociological Work," *International Sociological Association,* 1959, p. 196. My italics.

61. Robert N. Bellah, "Civil Religion in America," in Bellah, *Beyond Belief: Essays on Religion in a Post-Traditional World* (New York: Harper & Row, 1970), p. 182.

62. Ibid., p. 178.

63. Ibid., p. 178. Lowell is quoted by Bellah.

64. Ibid., p. 178.

65. Norman Podhoretz, "Faulkner in the 50's," in his *Doings and Undoings: The Fifties and After in American Writing* (New York: Farrar, Straus & Company, 1964), p. 15.

Chapter 8. Homely Protestant: A Decorum of Imperfection

Epigraph: Wallace Stevens, "The Poems of Our Climate," in *Parts of a World* (New York: Knopf, 1951), p. 9.

Harold Bloom, *Wallace Stevens: Poems of Our Climate* (Ithaca and London: Cornell University Press, 1977), p. 143.

1. Cited in *New York Times Magazine*, Feb. 3, 1974, p. 19, in Martin Kazindort, "Fonda: A Person of Many Parts."

2. Hilton Kramer, "The Worlds of Abstraction and Representation," *New York Times*, Jan. 27, 1974, p. D21.

3. Clive Jones, "Auden's Achievement," *Commentary*, Dec. 1973 (vol. 57, no. 6), p. 56.

4. *New Yorker*, May 12, 1973 (vol. 49, no. 12), p. 45.

5. E. M. Forster, *The Longest Journey* (Norfolk, Connecticut: New Directions, n.d.), p. 238.

6. Grace Glueck, "Artists Find 'In' Place on L.I.," *New York Times*, Sept. 26, 1968, p. 49. My italics.

7. Quoted in Joseph Featherstone, "Mrs. Woolf as Essayist," *The New Republic*, Feb. 10, 1968 (vol. 157, no. 6), p. 22.

8. W. B. Yeats, *The Collected Poems of W. B. Yeats* (New York: The Macmillan Company 1940), pp. 343, 344.

9. *Mimesis: The Representation of Reality in Western Literature*, trans. Willard Trask (Garden City, N.Y.: Doubleday, 1957), pp. 131–32.

10. Ibid., p. 18.

11. Ibid., p. 490 (my italics).

12. Ibid., p. 132.

13. *Dante: Poet of the Secular World* (Chicago, University of Chicago Press, 1961), pp. 11–12. My italics.

14. Ibid., p. 13.

15. Ibid., p. 14.

16. W. B. Yeats, "Two Songs from a Play," from *The Tower*, in Peter Allt and Russell K. Alspach, eds., *The Variorum Edition of the Poems of W. B. Yeats* (New York: Macmillan, 1957), p. 438.

17. *Dante*, p. 14.

18. Ibid.

19. *Mimesis*, p. 40.

20. Ibid., p. 36.

21. *Dante*, p. 15.

22. Romano Guardini, *The Humanity of Christ: Contributions to a Psychology of Jesus*, trans. from the German by Ronald Wells.

23. Ernst Bloch, *Man on His Own: Essays in the Philosophy of Religion*, trans. E. B. Ashton (New York: Herder and Herder, 1971), p. 186.

24. G. K. Chesterton, *The Everlasting Man* (New York: Doubleday/Image), pp. 255–56.

25. Joachim Jeremias, *The Prayers of Jesus*, trans. John Bowden, Christoph Burchard, and John Reumann (Naperville, Ill.: Alec R. Allenson, Inc., 1967), pp. 96–8.

26. C. M. Noel, Hymn 356, *The Hymnal of the Protestant Episcopal Church in the United States of America* (Greenwich, Conn.: The Seabury Press, 1940). My italics.

27. Ibid., Hymn 5 (my italics).

28. Ibid., Hymn 337.

29. Ibid., Hymn 64 (my italics).

30. Ibid., Hymn 266 (my italics).

31. Ibid., Hymn 52 (my italics).

32. Albert Schweitzer, *The Mystery of the Kingdom of God: The Secret of Jesus' Messiahship and Passion*, trans. Walter Lowrie (New York: Macmillan, 1950), p. 72.

33. Erich Auerbach, *"Sermo Humilis,"* in *Literary Language and Its Public in Late Latin Antiquity and in the Middle Ages,* trans. Ralph Manheim (New York: Pantheon Books, 1965), p. 40. My italics.

34. Ibid., p. 45.

35. Ibid.

36. Ibid., p. 48.

37. Quoted in ibid., p. 48.

38. Ibid., p. 48.

39. Ibid., p. 52.

40. Ibid., p. 65 (my italics).

41. *Basic Writings of Saint Augustine,* ed. Whitney J. Oates, vol. I, p. 179.

42. London *Observer Review,* Sept. 1, 1968, p. 23. Review of Nicolson's *Diaries and Letters 1945–1962,* ed. Nigel Nicolson (My italics).

43. Lionel Trilling, "Under Forty: A Symposium on American Literature and the Younger Generation of American Jews," *Contemporary Jewish Record,* Feb. 1944 (vol. 7, no. 1), p. 17.

44. Christopher Morley, *Kitty Foyle,* p. 101.

45. Albert Schweitzer, *The Quest of the Historical Jesus: A Critical Study of Its Progress from Reimarus to Wrede,* trans. W. Montgomery (New York: Macmillan, 1948), p. 366.

46. Ada Louise Huxtable, "He Adds Elegance to Modern Architecture," *New York Times Magazine,* May 24, 1964, p. 18.

47. Hilton Kramer, *New York Times,* Nov. 30, 1966.

48. Susan Sontag, *Against Interpretation and Other Essays* (New York: Farrar, Straus & Giroux, 1966) p. 291.

49. Philip Rieff, Introduction to Sigmund Freud, *Character and Culture* (New York: Collier Books, 1963), p. 9.

50. John Simon, "Split Three Ways," *New York Times Book Review,* April 9, 1967.

51. *Times Literary Supplement,* Nov. 25, 1965.

Conclusion: Bourgeois Civility as Deferred Socialism, or The

Polity of Imperfection

Epigraph: Gayatri Chakravorty Spivak, Translator's Preface to Jacques Derrida, *Of Grammatology* (Baltimore: Johns Hopkins University Press, 1976), p. xliii.

1. Robert N. Bellah, *The Broken Covenant: American Civil Religion in Time of Trial* (New York: The Seabury Press, 1975), p. 122.

2. Peter L. Berger, "The Socialist Myth," *Public Interest,* Summer 1976 (no. 44), p. 7.

3. Glenn Tinder, "Community: The Tragic Ideal," *Yale Review,* Summer 1976 (vol. 65, no. 4), p. 551.

4. Ibid.

5. Ibid., p. 563.

Index